Family
Violence
and
Religion

Family Violence and Religion

AN INTERFAITH RESOURCE GUIDE

Compiled by the staff of Volcano Press

Foreword by the Rev. Dr. Brian Ogawa

VOLCANO
· PRESS ·

Volcano, CA

Library of Congress Cataloging-in-Publication Data

Family violence and religion : an interfaith resource guide when praying isn't enough / compiled by the staff of Volcano Press ; foreword by Brian Ogawa.
    p.   cm.
    Includes bibliographical references.
    ISBN 1-884244-10-6
    1. Wife abuse—United States. 2. Wife abuse—Religious aspects—Christianity. 3. Family violence—United States. 4. Family violence—Religious aspects—Christianity. 5. Church work with abused women—United States.
HV6626.2.F35 1995
362.82'92075'0973—dc20
                                            95-19940
                                                CIP

Volcano Press participates in the Cataloging in Publication program of the Library of Congress. However, in our opinion, the data provided above by CIP for this book does not adequately nor accurately reflect the book's scope and content. Therefore, we are offering our librarian and bookstore users the choice between CIP's treatment and an Alternative CIP prepared by Sanford Berman, Head Cataloger at Hennepin County Library, Edina, Minnesota.

Alternative Cataloging-in-Publication Data

Volcano Press.
    Family violence and religion: an interfaith resource guide. Compiled by the staff of Volcano Press. Foreword by Brian Ogawa. Volcano, CA: Volcano Press, copyright © 1995.
    PARTIAL CONTENTS: Practical helps for clergy counseling abused women. –Myths and facts about domestic violence. –Assessing whether batterers will kill. –Building self-esteem: overcoming barriers to recovery. –Asian-American patriarchies. –Battered women: an African-American perspective. –Christian abused women. –Spousal abuse in rabbinic and contemporary Judaism. –Hispanic-American battered women. –Battered women of age: the experiences of WEAVE. –Elder abuse. –Ministry in response to violence in the family: pastoral and prophetic. –Transformation of suffering: a Biblical and theological perspective.
    1. Woman battering. 2. Woman battering—Religious aspects. 3. Battered women—Pastoral counseling. 4. Elder abuse. 5. Family violence. 6. Family violence—Religious aspects. 7. Afro-American battered women. 8. Battered Latinas. 9. Jewish-American battered women. 10. Asian-American battered women. 10. Christian battered women. 11. WEAVE. 12. Battered senior women. I. Ogawa, Brian. II. Title. III. Title: Religion and family violence.
362.882

Jacket and Text designed by David Charlsen
Page composition by Jeff Brandenburg/ImageComp
Permissions by Joanna McKenna

Edited by Zoe Brown and David Charlsen

See order form at the end of this book for additional titles on the subject of domestic violence from Volcano Press.

Printed in the United States of America
1 2 3 4 5 6 7 — 98 97 96 95

CONTENTS

FOREWORD

What could be more menacing than living in danger of violent and abusive behavior within one's own home? Yet, every 15 seconds, a woman in the United States experiences that terror and humiliation because she is battered by a spouse or partner. Two to four million women are assaulted each year by their husbands or boyfriends. Family life is meant to be the haven for personal safety, affectionate relationships, and shared trust. Instead, abused women discover a trap of restraint, injury, and even death.

As clergy, we must teach that violence is not the inevitable result of conflict. We are present as symbol, officiant, or enabler at almost every significant occurrence in the lives of people, and thus can fill an unparalleled role in offering healing and hope to abused women. Such help must include nurturing of the spirit and faith, nonjudgmental and compassionate caring, and practical and forthright guidance.

For 20 years I have been a pastor and university campus minister; abusive relationships were both hidden and evident among those I served. For the past 13 years I have directed a victim assistance program for a prosecutor's office. A significant number of those we counsel are victims of domestic violence. From the experience gained in both professions, I attest to the importance of having clergy realize and enact their responsibility for addressing violence within our homes. Such violence is criminal and profane. It is not merely private and confessional, but a violation of societal norms and personal rights.

This book provides an exceptional resource for clergy to understand family violence and respond appropriately. It acknowledges both secular awareness and religious concerns. It identifies how the issues of diverse theology, ethnicity, age and community particularize the prevailing characteristics of family violence. Armed with this information, clergy may more fully realize the commitment to resist evil, protect the harmed, and affirm the purpose and strength of families.

The Rev. Dr. Brian Ogawa
United Church of Christ

Director, Victim/Witness Assistance Division
Department of the Prosecuting Attorney
County of Maui, Hawaii

Practical Helps for Clergy Counseling Abused Women

Carol Findon Bingham

- **Listen empathetically with active listening skills.** Speak to reflect back to her the information which she has given you. Your primary role is to be her confessor; therefore, listen. Silently pray that God's grace is present as the healing process toward wholeness begins.
- **Affirm her courageous act, that of coming to you.** You may in fact be the first person whom she has approached. Healing begins when the victim speaks of the violence and names it as such.
- **Counsel the battered woman without physically touching her.** Give comfort without putting your arm around her shoulder or holding her hand. If she has been sexually or physically abused, any touch may recall painful memories.
- **Acknowledge your limits.** It is wise to know how well you are prepared to deal with domestic

violence. Unless you are clinically trained on the issues of domestic violence, refer her to someone who can be a healing resource leading her toward recovery.

- **Be aware of your own emotional shields of protection.** As you hear her painful story, your feelings and emotions will come to the surface. Therefore, try not to block the reception of her story in an attempt to protect your own feelings and to prevent your emotions from surfacing.
- **Believe everything she says; do not doubt her; and do not question her accuracy.** She needs a trusting pastor and a compassionate shepherd. Remember that she is probably minimizing the violence. What you hear may only be the tip of the iceberg. In time she may share more with you.
- **Tell her that it is not her fault.** No one deserves to be abused. It is not God's intention that she should suffer and be violated. All blame rests with the abuser. She did not in any way cause this abuse.
- **Tell her that she is not alone.** It is important and empowering for a battered woman to realize that millions of women suffer abuse at the hands of their partners.
- **Affirm her faith no matter where she stands theologically.** At this time of crisis her present faith stance may be the *only* thing she has to hold on to. It may not be "theologically correct" in your mind, but at the moment of crisis, this is all she has. Respond with positive statements about God ("God loves you and is with you in your suffering"). Respond with "I" statements ("I believe, however, that God does not want you to suffer or to be a victim of violence").

- **Offer her options in her search for wholeness.** Give her choices within her faith stance as she searches for a faithful understanding of what is happening to her. Also, remember that there is no right way and, concerning one's theological stance, no one person has all the right answers.
- **Quote Scripture passages which are liberating and which offer hope in times of suffering.** Quoting Scripture which is oppressive and which calls her to be submissive only encourages her to endure more violence at home.
- **Encourage her to contact the domestic violence program in your area.** There she will connect with counselors and support groups, receive legal advice and begin to bond with other victims and other women offering support and nurturance.
- **Encourage her to find a safe place.** Separation from the abuser prevents further violence. The church historically has offered sanctuary. Today the church can offer a safe home or a referral to a shelter for the victims of domestic violence.
- **Help her find economic assistance.** Because of the economic instability of society, it is difficult for a woman in crisis to find sufficient income to meet the needs of herself and her children. This is one of the reasons a woman may choose to stay in the violent home. Try to find a victim advocate in the parish who can help her secure public aid and/or other forms of economic assistance, if she is not in contact with a domestic violence program.
- **Be with her in her suffering and in her healing.** Do not stand withdrawn from her.

Acknowledge your fears and pain as you hear
her stories. But also praise her as she moves
toward wholeness.

- **Confidentiality is of utmost importance.** She
  has come to you because she needs your help
  and trusts that you will be willing to help. That
  which she shares with you must be kept confidential. Unless you have her specific consent,
  you are ethically bound to tell no one.
- **The decision to pursue therapy is hers to
  make.** Not all battered women will wish to or
  need to seek therapy. Remember that it is your
  role to empower her, not to control her choices.
- **Assure her that all her statements to you are
  strictly confidential,** and that you will not
  speak to anyone else about her situation except
  to a helping agency when she has given you
  express permission to do so.

Carol Findon Bingham (Ed.) (1986) *Doorway to Response: The Role of Clergy in Ministry with Battered Women.* Reprinted with the permission of the Illinois Conference of Churches, Ministry on Church Response to Family Violence, 615 South Fifth Street, Springfield, Illinois 62703.

A Letter from a Battered Wife

I am in my thirties and so is my husband. I have a high school diploma and am presently attending a local college, trying to obtain the additional education I need. My husband is a college graduate and a professional in his field. We are both attractive and, for the most part, respected and well liked. We have four children and live in a middle-class home with all the comforts we could possibly want.

I have everything, except life without fear.

For most of my married life I have been periodically beaten by my husband. What do I mean by "beaten"? I mean that parts of my body have been hit violently and repeatedly, and that painful bruises, swelling, bleeding wounds, unconsciousness, and combinations of these things have resulted.

Beating should be distinguished from all other kinds of physical abuse — including being hit and shoved around. When I say my husband threatens me with abuse I do not mean he warns me that he may lose control. I mean that he shakes a fist against my face or nose, makes punching-bag jabs at my shoulder, or makes similar gestures which may quickly turn into a full-fledged beating.

I have had glasses thrown at me. I have been kicked in the abdomen when I was visibly pregnant. I have been kicked off the bed and hit while lying on the floor — again, while I was pregnant. I have been whipped, kicked and thrown, picked up again

5

and thrown down again. I have been punched and kicked in the head, chest, face, and abdomen more times than I can count.

I have been slapped for saying something about politics, for having a different view about religion, for swearing, for crying, for wanting to have intercourse.

I have been threatened when I wouldn't do something he told me to do. I have been threatened when he's had a bad day and when he's had a good day.

I have been threatened, slapped, and beaten after stating bitterly that I didn't like what he was doing with another woman.

After each beating my husband had left the house and remained away for days.

Few people have ever seen my black-and-blue face or swollen lips because I have always stayed indoors afterwards, feeling ashamed. I was never able to drive following one of these beatings, so I could not get myself to a hospital for care. I could never have left my young children alone, even if I could have driven a car.

Hysteria inevitably sets in after a beating. This hysteria — the shaking and crying and mumbling — is not accepted by anyone, so there has never been anyone to call.

My husband on a few occasions did phone a day or so later so we could agree on the excuse I would use for returning to work, the grocery store, the dentist appointment, and so on. I used the excuses — a car accident, oral surgery, things like that.

Now, the first response to this story, which I myself think of, will be "Why didn't you seek help?"

I did. Early in our marriage I went to a clergyman who, after a few visits, told me that my husband meant no real harm, that he was just confused and felt insecure. I was encouraged to be more tolerant and understanding. Most important, I was told to forgive him the beatings just as Christ had forgiven me from the cross. I did that, too.

Things continued. Next time I turned to a doctor. I was given little pills to relax me and told to take things a little easier. I was just too nervous.

I turned to a friend, and when her husband found out, he accused me of either making things up or exaggerating the situation. She was told to stay away from me. She didn't, but she could no longer really help me. Just by believing me she was made to feel disloyal.

I turned to a professional family guidance agency. I was told there that my husband needed help and that I should find a way to control the incidents. I couldn't control the beatings — that was the whole point of my seeking help. At the agency I found I had to defend myself against the suspicion that I wanted to be hit, that I invited the beatings. Good God! Did the Jews invite themselves to be slaughtered in Germany?

I did go to two more doctors. One asked me what I had done to provoke my husband. The other asked if we had made up yet.

I called the police one time. They not only did not respond to the call, they called several hours later to ask if things had "settled down." I could have been dead by then!

I have nowhere to go if it happens again. No one wants to take in a woman with four children. Even if there were someone kind enough to care, no one wants to become involved in what is commonly referred to as a "domestic situation."

Everyone I have gone to for help has somehow wanted to blame me and vindicate my husband. I can see it lying there between their words and at the end of their sentences. The clergyman, the doctor, the counselor, my friend's husband, the police — all of them have found a way to vindicate my husband.

No one has to "provoke" a wife-beater. He will strike out when he's ready and for whatever reason he has at the moment.

I may be his excuse, but I have never been the reason.

I know that I do not want to be hit. I know, too, that I will be beaten again unless I can find a way out for myself and my children. I am terrified for them also.

As a married woman I have no recourse but to remain in the situation which is causing me to be painfully abused. I have suffered physical and emotional battering and spiritual rape because the social structure of my world says I cannot do anything about a man who wants to beat me. . . . But staying with my husband means that my children must be subjected to the emotional battering caused when they see their mother's beaten face or hear her screams in the middle of the night.

I know that I have to get out. But when you have nowhere to go, you know that you must go on your own and expect no support. I have to be ready for that. I have to be ready to support myself and the children completely, and still provide a decent environment for them. I pray that I can do that before I am murdered in my own home.

I have learned that no one believes me and that I cannot depend upon any outside help. All I have left is the hope that I can get away before it is too late.

I have also learned that the doctors, the police, the clergy, and my friends will excuse my husband for distorting my face, but won't forgive me for looking bruised and broken. The greatest tragedy is that I am still praying, and there is not a human person to listen.

Being beaten is a terrible thing; it is most terrible of all if you are not equipped to fight back. I recall an occasion when I tried to defend myself and actually tore my husband's shirt. Later, he showed it to a relative as proof that I had done something terribly wrong. The fact that at the moment I had several raised spots on my head hidden by my hair, a swollen lip that was bleeding, and a severely damaged cheek with a blood clot that caused a permanent dimple didn't matter to him. What mattered was that I tore his shirt! That I tore it in self-defense didn't mean anything to him.

My situation is so untenable I would guess that anyone who has not experienced one like it would find it incomprehensible. I find it difficult to believe myself.

It must be pointed out that while a husband can beat, slap, or threaten his wife, there are "good days." These days tend to wear away the effects of the beating. They tend to cause the wife to put aside the traumas and look to the good — first, because there is nothing else to do; second, because there is nowhere and no one to turn to; and third, because the defeat is the beating and the hope is that it will not happen again. When it does, she simply hopes again, until it becomes obvious after a third beating that there is no hope. That is when she turns outward for help to find an answer. When that help is denied, she either resigns herself to the situation she is in or pulls herself together and starts making plans for a future life that includes only herself and her children.

For many the third beating may be too late. Several of the times I have been abused I have been amazed that I have remained alive. Imagine that I have been thrown to a very hard slate floor several times, kicked in the abdomen, the head, and the chest, and still remained alive!

What determines who is lucky and who isn't? I could have been dead a long time ago had I been hit the wrong way. My baby could have been killed or deformed had I been kicked the wrong way. What saved me?

I don't know. I only know that it has happened and that each night I dread the final blow that will kill me and leave my children motherless. I hope I can hang on until I complete my education, get a good job, and become self-sufficient enough to care for my children on my own.

Excerpted from *Battered Wives,* © 1976, 1981 by Del Martin. All rights reserved. To order, contact Volcano Press, Inc., P.O. Box 270 FVR, Volcano CA 95689. (209) 296-3445.

What Is Domestic Violence?

DEFINITION

Domestic violence is the mistreatment of one family member by another. Most often perpetrators of abuse and battering are: a spouse, ex-spouse, boyfriend, ex-boyfriend or lover. Most often victims of abuse are women and children. The abuse can be physical, sexual, verbal, emotional and psychological.

Types of Abuse

Physical abuse

pushed	kicked	raped
dragged through the house	poked	held down
threatened with a weapon	slapped	hair pulled
restrained	arm twisted	squeezed
locked in the house	choked	pinched
thrown down stairs	punched	spitting
bent fingers backwards	cut	grabbed
threw objects at me	tripped	kidnapped
pushed out of the car	bumped into	suffocated
banged my head in wall	burned	

Sexual abuse

raped
said my body disgusted him
friends wanted sex after abuse
distasteful sex acts forced on me
brought other women home
told me I was fat and ugly
made constant sexual demands
withheld sex from me

accused me of affairs
told I was inadequate in bed
forced pregnancy
beaten if I refused sex
criticized my appearance
bragged about his infidelity
didn't care about my pleasures
forced cohabitation

Financial abuse

took my money
all bills are in my name
no money of my own
sold my furniture
destroyed belongings worked for
never given enough money for bills
his wants came before family needs
made to work
forced to commit robberies

he controlled the checkbook
didn't know about our assets
I had inadequate clothing
had to account for every dime
quit his job
forced to write bad checks
not allowed to go to school or work
spent money on drugs and alcohol

Verbal abuse

yelled at
nagged at
put-down of women in general
always called stupid
talked to as a child
put down my appearance
threatened to take kids
told I was crazy/stupid/ugly/dumb

called names
called racial slurs
cussed at
told no one else would want me
threatened to kill
belittled important things I did
constant phone calls
told I was an alcoholic/drug user

Emotional abuse

embarrassed me in front of others
created crises so I had to pay attention to him
living with his alcoholism/drug abuse
constant demands on my time
only allowed to see his friends, never mine
had to do everything, even when sick
always worried [about] his next step
threats to hurt or kill me or the kids
threats to hurt or kill himself
his suicide attempts
couldn't have any privacy
couldn't tell when he'd be nice or mad
made me lie about how injuries occurred
threatened to hurt family/friends
threatened or actually hurt the pets
not allowed to use the phone
told me others didn't like me
destroyed belongings important to me
physically withdrew from me
didn't talk to me — the silent treatment

Excerpt used with permission from The Center for the Prevention of Domestic Violence, 23875 Commerce Park Rd., Beachwood, Ohio 44122.

Physical Violence / Nonviolence Wheels

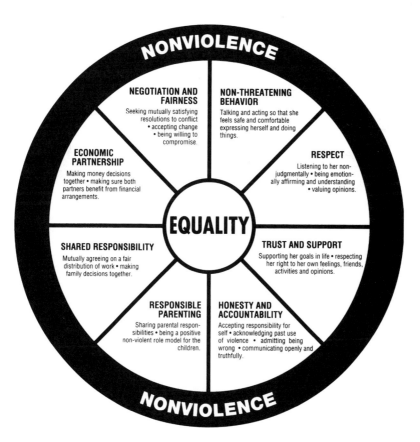

NONVIOLENCE

NEGOTIATION AND FAIRNESS
Seeking mutually satisfying resolutions to conflict • accepting change • being willing to compromise.

NON-THREATENING BEHAVIOR
Talking and acting so that she feels safe and comfortable expressing herself and doing things.

ECONOMIC PARTNERSHIP
Making money decisions together • making sure both partners benefit from financial arrangements.

RESPECT
Listening to her non-judgmentally • being emotionally affirming and understanding • valuing opinions.

EQUALITY

SHARED RESPONSIBILITY
Mutually agreeing on a fair distribution of work • making family decisions together.

TRUST AND SUPPORT
Supporting her goals in life • respecting her right to her own feelings, friends, activities and opinions.

RESPONSIBLE PARENTING
Sharing parental responsibilities • being a positive non-violent role model for the children.

HONESTY AND ACCOUNTABILITY
Accepting responsibility for self • acknowledging past use of violence • admitting being wrong • communicating openly and truthfully.

NONVIOLENCE

Myths and Facts About Domestic Violence

Adapted from the Domestic Violence Project, Inc.
Ann Arbor, Michigan

Myth # 1
Battering is rare.

FACT: Domestic violence is extremely common. The F.B.I. estimates that a woman is battered every fifteen seconds in the United States.

Myth #2
Domestic violence occurs only in poor, poorly educated, minority or "dysfunctional" families. It could never happen to anyone I know.

FACT: There are doctors, ministers, psychologists, and professionals who beat their wives. Battering happens in rich, white, educated and respectable families. About half of the couples in this country experience violence at some time in their relationship.

17

Myth #3
Battering is about couples getting into a brawl on Saturday night, beating each other up, and totally disrupting the neighborhood.

FACT: In domestic assaults, one partner is beating, intimidating, and terrorizing the other. It's not "mutual combat" or two people in a fist fight. It's one person dominating and controlling the other.

Myth #4
The problem is not really woman abuse. It is spouse abuse. Women are just as violent as men.

FACT: In over 95% of domestic assaults, the man is the perpetrator. This fact makes many of us uncomfortable, but is no less true because of that discomfort. To end domestic violence, we must scrutinize why it is usually men who are violent in partnerships. We must examine the historic and legal permission that men have been given to be violent in general, and to be violent towards their wives and children specifically. There are rare cases where a woman batters a man. Battering does occur in lesbian and gay male relationships. Survivors of abuse in such relationships should hear that because their situation is rare — or because they are in a societally unacceptable relationship — that does not make it less valid or serious. The National Domestic Violence Hotline believes that violence is unacceptable in intimate relationships and provides services to any person who has been victimized.

Myth #5
When there is violence in the family, all members of the family are participating in the dynamic, and therefore all must change for the violence to stop.

FACT: Only the perpetrator has the ability to stop the violence. Many women who are battered make numerous attempts to change their behavior in the hope that this will stop the abuse. This does not work. Changes in family members' behavior will not cause or influence the batterer to be nonviolent.

Myth #6
Batterers are crazy.

FACT: An extremely small percentage of batterers are mentally ill. The vast majority seem totally normal, and are often charming, persuasive, and rational. The major difference between them and others is that they use force and intimidation to control their partners. *Battering is a behavioral choice.*

Myth #7
Domestic violence is usually a one-time event, an isolated incident.

FACT: Battering is a pattern, a reign of force and terror. Once violence begins in a relationship, it gets worse and more frequent over a period of time. Battering is not just one physical attack. It is a number of tactics (intimidation, threats, economic deprivation, psychological and sexual abuse) used repeatedly. Physical violence is one of those tactics. Experts have compared methods used by batterers to those used by terrorists to brainwash hostages.

Myth #8
Battered women always stay in violent relationships.

FACT: Many battered women leave their abusers permanently, and despite many obstacles, succeed in building a life free of violence. Almost all battered women leave at least once. The perpetrator dramatically escalates his violence when a woman leaves (or tries to), because it is necessary for him to reassert control and ownership. Battered women are often very active (and far from helpless) on their own behalf. Their efforts often fail because the batterer continues to assault, and institutions fail to offer protection.

Myth #9
The community places responsibility for violence where it belongs — on the criminal.

FACT: Most people blame the victim of battering for the crime, some without realizing it. They expect the woman to stop the violence, and repeatedly analyze her motivations for not leaving, rather than scrutinizing why the batterer keeps beating her, and why the community allows it.

Myth #10
Drinking causes battering.

FACT: Assailants use drinking as one of many excuses for violence, and as a way of putting responsibility for their violence elsewhere. There is a 50% or higher correlation between substance abuse and domestic violence, but no causal relationship. Stopping the assailant's drinking will not end his violence. Both problems must be addressed.

Myth #11
Stress causes domestic assault.

FACT: Many people who are under extreme stress do not assault their partners. Assailants who are stressed at work do not attack their co-workers or bosses.

Myth #12
Men who batter do so because they cannot control themselves or because they have "poor impulse control."

FACT: Men who batter are usually not violent towards anyone but their wives/partners or their children. They can control themselves sufficiently to pick a safe target. Men often beat women in parts of their bodies where bruises will not show. Sixty percent of battered women are beaten while they are pregnant, often in the stomach. Many assaults last for hours. Many are planned.

Myth #13
Rapists are strangers.

FACT: One out of every seven married women is raped by her husband. At least 60%, and possibly all, physically battered women are sexually abused by their partners. This abuse includes, but is not limited to: forced sex in front of children, forced sex with animals or in groups and prostitution.

Myth #14
If a battered woman wanted to leave, she could just call the police.

FACT: Police have traditionally been reluctant to respond to domestic assaults, or to intervene in what they think of as a private matter. Police have usually temporarily separated the couple, leaving the woman vulnerable to further violence.

Myth #15
If a battered woman really wanted to leave, she could easily get help from her religious leader.

FACT: Some priests, clergy, and rabbis have been extremely supportive of battered women. Others ignore the abuse, are unsupportive, or actively support the assailant's control of his partner.

Myth #16
Men who batter are often good fathers, and should have joint custody of their children.

FACT: At least 70% of men who batter their wives, sexually or physically, abuse their children. All children suffer from witnessing their father assault their mother.

Myth #17
If a battered woman really wanted to leave, she could just pack up and go somewhere else.

FACT: Battered women considering leaving their assailants are faced with the very real possibility of severe physical damage or even death. Assailants deliberately isolate their partners, and deprive them of jobs, of opportunities for acquiring education and job skills. This, combined with unequal opportunities for women in general and lack of affordable child care, make it excruciatingly difficult for women to leave.

Reprinted with permission. The Domestic Violence Project, Inc., SAFE HOUSE (Shelter Available for Emergency), P.O. Box 7052, Ann Arbor, Michigan 48107.

Assessing whether Batterers Will Kill

Some batterers are life-endangering. While it is true that all batterers are dangerous, some are more likely to kill than others and some are more likely to kill at specific times. Regardless of whether there is a protection order in effect, police officers, prosecutors, probation counselors and advocates should evaluate whether an assailant is likely to kill his* partner, other family members and/or criminal justice system personnel and take appropriate action.

It is important that responding officers conduct an assessment at every call, no matter how many times an officer has responded to the same household. The dispatcher and responding officer can utilize the indicators described below in making an assessment of the batterer's potential to kill. Prosecutors,

---

* We have assumed that the victim is a woman and the abuser is a man. It may be that the victim is a man and the abuser a woman or that the abuser and the victim are of the same sex. Assessment is basically the same despite these gender differences. The only additional indicator to be assessed in a lesbian or gay relationship is whether the abuser has been firmly closeted and is now risking exposure as a lesbian or gay person in order to facilitate their severe, life-threatening attacks. When a person has been desperately closeted, losing the protection of invisibility in order to abuse potentially suggests great desperation and should be included in the assessment.

probation counselors and advocates should, likewise, make an assessment during each interview with a battered woman.

Assessment is tricky and never fool-proof. Considering these factors may or may not reveal actual potential for homicidal assault. But, the likelihood of a homicide is greater when these factors are present. The greater the number of indicators that the batterer demonstrates or the greater the intensity of indicators, the greater the likelihood of a life-threatening attack.

The evaluation should use all information available about the batterer. Reliable information cannot be obtained from an interview conducted with the victim and perpetrator together. Furthermore, information obtained from the victim is significantly more reliable than from the batterer.

1. Threats of homicide or suicide. The batterer who has threatened to kill himself, his partner, the children or her relatives must be considered extremely dangerous.

2. Fantasies of homicide or suicide. The more the batterer has developed a fantasy about who, how, when, and/or where to kill, the more dangerous he may be. The batterer who has previously acted out part of a homicide or suicide fantasy may be invested in killing as a viable "solution" to his problems. As in suicide assessment, the more detailed the plan and the more available the method, the greater the risk.

3. Weapons. Where a batterer possesses weapons and has used them or has threatened to use them in the past in his assault on the battered woman, the children or himself, his access to those weapons increases his potential for lethal assault. The use of guns is a strong predictor of homicide. If a batterer has a history of arson or the threat of arson, fire should be considered a weapon.

4. "Ownership" of the battered partner. The batterer who says "Death before Divorce!" or "You belong to me and will never belong to another!" may be stating his fundamental belief that the woman has no right to life separate from him. A batterer who believes he is absolutely entitled to his female partner, her services, her obedience and her loyalty, no matter what, is likely to be life-endangering.

5. Centrality of the partner. A man who idolizes his female partner, or who depends heavily on her to organize and sustain his life; or who has isolated himself from all other community, may retaliate against a partner who decides to end the relationship. He rationalizes that her "betrayal" justified his lethal retaliation.

6. Separation violence. When a batterer believes that he is about to lose his partner, if he can't envision life without her or if the separation causes him great despair or rage, he may choose to kill.

7. Escalation of batterer risk. A less obvious indicator of increasing danger may be the sharp escalation of personal risk undertaken by a batterer; when a batterer begins to act without regard to the legal or social consequences that previously constrained his violence, chances of lethal assault increase significantly.

8. Hostage-taking. A hostage-taker is at high risk of inflicting homicide. Between 75% and 90% of all hostage-takings in the US are related to domestic violence situations.

9. Depression. Where a batterer has been acutely depressed and sees little hope for moving beyond the depression, he may be a candidate for homicide and suicide. Research shows that many men who are hospitalized for depression have homicidal fantasies directed at family members.

10. Repeated outreach to law enforcement. Partner or spousal homicide almost always occurs in a context of historical violence. Prior calls to the police indicate elevated risk of life-threatening conduct.

11. Access to the battered woman and/or to family members. If the batterer cannot find her, he cannot kill her. If he does not have access to the children, he cannot use them as a means of access to the battered woman. Careful safety planning and police assistance are required for those times when contact is required, e.g., court appearances and custody exchanges.

If a criminal justice system professional concludes that a batterer is likely to kill or commit life-endangering violence, extraordinary measures should be taken to protect the victim and her children. This may include providing transportation and conducting meticulous follow-up. The victim should be advised that the presence of these indicators may mean that the batterer is contemplating homicide and that she should immediately take action to protect herself and should contact the local battered woman's program to further assess lethality and develop safety plans.

Assessment by Battered Women. It is important that advocates and criminal justice system personnel help each battered woman assess the threat that her batterer poses to her life and safety. Often a professional's confirmation of a battered woman's suspicions impels her to implement her most careful safety plan, and she may go into hiding or flee.

Assessment of a batterer should be made at the time of the crisis call, during intake, in preparation for legal proceedings and on a continuing basis until the batterer is no longer a part of the battered woman's life. Ongoing assessment is critical since batterers may have periods when they present no danger to battered women and others when they are acutely dangerous. Therefore, it is important that advocates and criminal justice personnel encourage battered women to frequently assess the lethality of their assailants.

Assessment by Batterers' Counselors. Batterers' counselors should also carefully assess lethality. Invariably, batterers deny threats of homicide or suicide. The counselor may want to obtain information from third parties in order to complete an assessment of the batterer. Caution should always be taken to preserve confidentiality when a counselor seeks information from a battered woman. If a batterer hears that a battered woman has spoken with his counselor, it may trigger a felonious assault. Similarly, should the batterer hear that a counselor has sought information from someone else, he may very well blame the battered woman for this intrusion on his privacy, precipitating a life-imperiling assault. Thus, lethality assessment should be conducted discreetly and information obtained from persons other than the batterer must not be shared with him.

One danger in asking batterers' counselors to undertake lethality assessment is that they may reach different conclusions than the battered woman and because of a counselor's professional status and apparent expertise, she may defer to his or her assessment and fail to act or plan in accord with her own conclusions about the batterer's lethality.

Counselors should be careful to encourage the battered woman to believe in her own assessment, especially if she concludes that the batterer may be highly dangerous.

Cautionary Note: Intuition, rather than the factors set forth in this section, may be the best guide to gauging lethality. Intervention with battered women must always include concrete safety planning which covers strategies for responding to lethal assaults even if the battered woman concludes that her assailant does not currently represent a lethal threat.

NAME: _____

DATE: _____

REVIEW DATES: _____

PERSONALIZED SAFETY PLAN

The following steps represent my plan for increasing my safety and preparing in advance for the possibility for further violence. Although I do not have control over my partner's violence, I do have a choice about how to respond to him/her and how to best get myself and my children to safety.

Step 1: <u>Safety during a violent incident</u>. Women cannot always avoid violent incidents. In order to increase safety, battered women may employ a variety of strategies.

I can use some or all of the following strategies:

A. If I decide to leave, I will _____. (Practice how to get out safely. What doors, windows, elevators, stairwells or fire escapes would you use?)

B. I can keep my purse and car keys ready and put them _____ (place) in order to leave quickly.

C. I can tell _____ about the violence and request they call the police if they hear suspicious noises coming from my house.

D. I can teach my children how to use the telephone to contact the police and the fire department.

E. I will use _____ as my code word with my children or my friends so they can call for help.

F. If I have to leave my home, I will go _____. (Decide this even if you don't think there will be a next time.)

G. I can also teach some of these strategies to some/all of my children.

H. When I expect we are going to have an argument, I will try to move to a space that is lowest risk, such as _____ _____. (Try to avoid arguments in the bathroom, garage, kitchens, near weapons or in rooms without access to an outside door.)

I. I will use my judgment and intuition. If the situation is very serious, I can give my partner what he/she wants to calm him/her down. I have to protect myself until I/we are out of danger.

Step 2: <u>Safety when preparing to leave</u>. Battered women frequently leave the residence they share with the battering partner. Leaving must be done strategically in order to increase safety. Batterers often strike back when they believe that a battered woman is leaving a relationship.

I can use some or all of the following safety strategies:

A. I will leave money and an extra set of keys with _____ _____ so I can leave quickly.

B. I will keep copies of important documents or keys at _____ _____.

C. I will open a savings account by _____ to increase my independence. [Keep in mind, monthly bank statements may be sent out to my home address.]

D. Other things I can do to increase my independence include:

_____

_____

_____

E. The hotline number for the domestic violence program in my area is _____. I can seek shelter by calling this hotline.

F. I can keep change for phone calls on me at all times. I understand that if I use my telephone credit card, the following month the telephone bill will tell my batterer those numbers that I called after I left. To keep my telephone communications confidential, I must either use coins or I might get a friend to permit me to use their telephone credit card for a limited time when I first leave.

G. I will check with _____ and _____ to see who would be able to let me stay with them or lend me some money.

H. I can leave extra clothes with _____.

I. I will sit down and review my safety plan every _____ in order to plan the safest way to leave the residence. _____ (domestic violence advocate or friend) has agreed to help me review this plan.

J. I will rehearse my escape plan and, as appropriate, practice it with my children.

Step 3. Safety in my own residence. There are many things that a woman can do to increase her safety in her own residence. It may be impossible to do everything at once, but safety measures can be added step by step.

Safety measures I can use include:

A. I can change the locks on my doors and windows as soon as possible.

B. I can replace the wooden doors with steel/metal doors.

C. I can install security systems including additional locks, window bars, poles to wedge against doors, an electronic system, etc.

D. I can purchase rope ladders to be used for escape from second-floor windows.

E. I can install smoke detectors and purchase fire extinguishers for each floor in my house/apartment.

F. I can install an outside lighting system that lights up when a person is coming close to my house.

G. I will teach my children how to use the telephone to make a collect call to me and to _____ (friend/ minister/other) in the event that my partner abducts the children.

H. I will tell people who take care of my children which people have permission to pick up my children and that my partner is not permitted to do so. The people I will inform about pick-up permission include:

_____ (school)
_____ (teacher/principal)
_____ (day care staff)
_____ (babysitter)
_____ (Sunday school teacher)
_____ (others)
_____ (others)

I. I can inform . . .

_____ (neighbor)
_____ (pastor)

that my partner no longer resides with me and they should call the police if he is observed near my residence.

Step 4: <u>Safety with a protection order</u>. Many batterers obey protection orders, but one can never be sure which violent partner will obey and which will violate protection orders. I recognize that I may need to ask the police and the courts to enforce my protection order.

The following are some steps that I can take to help the enforcement of my protection order:

A. I will keep my protection order _____ (location).

B. I will give my protection order to police departments in the community where I work, in those communities where I usually visit family or friends, and the community where I live.

C. There should be a county registry of protection orders that all police departments can call to confirm the validity of a protection order. I can check to make sure that my order is in the registry. The telephone number for the county registry of protection orders is _____.

D. For further safety, if I often visit other counties in _____ (state) I might file my protection order with the court in those counties. I will register my protection order in the following counties: _____ and _____.

E. I can call the local domestic violence program if I am not sure about B, C or D above, or if I have some problem with my protection order.

F. I will inform my employer, my minister, my closest friend, [school, etc.] _____ that I have a protection order in effect.

G. If my partner destroys my protection order, I can get another copy from the courthouse by going to _____ _____ located at _____.

H. If my partner violates the protection order, I can call the police and report a violation, contact my attorney, call my advocate, and/or advise the court of the violation.

I. If the police do not help, I can contact my advocate or attorney and will file a complaint with the chief of the police department.

J. I can also file a private criminal complaint with the district justice in the jurisdiction where the violation occurred or with the district attorney. I can charge my battering partner with a violation of the protection order and all the crimes that he commits in violating the order. I can call the domestic violence advocate to help me with this.

Step 5: <u>Safety on the job and in public</u>. **Each battered woman must decide if and when she will tell others that her partner has battered her and that she may be at continued risk. Friends, family and co-workers can help to protect women. Each woman should consider carefully which people to invite to help her safety.**

I might do any or all of the following:

A. I can inform my boss, the security supervisor and _____ at work of my situation.

B. I can ask _____ to help screen my telephone calls at work.

C. When leaving work, I can _____ _____.

D. When driving home, if problems occur, I can _____
_____.

E. If I use public transit, I can _____
_____.

F. I can use different grocery stores and shopping malls to conduct my business and shop at hours that are different than those when residing with my battering partner.

G. I can also _____.

Step 6: <u>Safety and drug or alcohol consumption</u>. Most people in this culture consume alcohol. Many consume mood-altering drugs. Much of this consumption is legal and some is not. The legal outcomes of using illegal drugs can be very hard on a battered woman, may hurt her relationship with her children and put her at a disadvantage in other legal actions with her battering partner. Therefore, women should carefully consider the potential cost of the use of illegal drugs. But beyond this, the use of any alcohol or other drugs can reduce a woman's awareness and use of alcohol or other drugs by the batterer may give him/her an excuse to use violence. Therefore, in the context of drug or alcohol consumption, a woman needs to make specific plans.

If drug or alcohol consumption has occurred in my relationship with the battering partner, I can enhance my safety by some or all of the following:

A. If I am going to consume, I can do so in a safe place and with people who understand the risk of violence and are committed to my safety.

B. I can also _____.

C. If my partner is consuming, I can _____
   _____.

D. I might also _____.

E. To safeguard my children, I might _____
   and _____.

Step 7. <u>Safety and my emotional health</u>. The experience of being battered and verbally degraded by partners is usually exhausting and emotionally draining. The process of building a new life for myself takes much courage and incredible energy.

To conserve my emotional energy and resources, and to avoid hard emotional times, I can do some of the following:

A. If I feel down and ready to return to a potentially abusive situation, I can _____.

B. When I have to communicate with my partner in person or by telephone, I can _____.

C. I can try to use "I can . . ." statements with myself and be assertive with others.

D. I can tell myself "_____,"
   whenever I feel others are trying to control or abuse me.

E. I can read _____ to help
   me feel stronger.

F. I can call _____ and _____
   _____ as other resources
   to be of support to me.

G. Other things I can do to help me feel stronger are _____

_____ and _____

_____.

H. I can attend workshops and support groups at the domestic violence program or _____,

_____ or _____

to gain support and strengthen my relationships with other people.

Step 8. <u>Items to take when leaving</u>. When women leave partners, it is important to take certain items with them. Beyond this, women sometimes give an extra copy of papers and an extra set of clothing to a friend just in case they have to leave quickly.

Items with asterisks (*) on the following list are the most important to take. If there is time, the other items might be taken, or stored outside the home.

These items might best be placed in one location, so that if we have to leave in a hurry, I can grab them quickly.

When I leave, I should take:

* Identification for myself
* Children's birth certificates
* My birth certificate
* Social Security cards
* School and vaccination records
* Money
* Checkbook, ATM card
* Credit cards
* Keys to house, car, office
* Driver's license and registration
* Medications

Welfare identification
Work permits
Green card
Passport(s)
Divorce papers
Medical records — for all family members
Lease/rental agreement, house deed, mortgage payment book
Bank books
Insurance papers
Small salable objects
Address book
Pictures
Jewelry
Children's favorite toys and/or blankets
Items of special sentimental value

Telephone numbers I need to know:

Police dept. (home) _____
Police dept. (school) _____
Police dept. (work) _____
Battered women's program _____
County registry of protection orders _____
Work number _____
Supervisor's home number _____
Minister _____
Other _____

NAME: _____
DATE: _____
REVIEW DATES: _____

PERSONALIZED SAFETY PLAN
FOR STALKING VICTIMS

The following steps represent my plan for increasing my safety and preparing in advance for the possibility of violence. Although I do not have control over another person, I do have a choice about how to respond to him/her and how to best get myself and/or my children to safety.

Step 1: <u>Safety during a violent incident</u>. You cannot always avoid violent incidents. In order to increase safety, you may employ a variety of strategies.

I can use some or all of the following strategies:

A. If I have to get away, I will _____.
    (Practice how to get out safely. What doors, windows, elevators, stairwells or fire escapes would you use?)

B. I can keep my purse/wallet and car keys ready and put them _____ (place) in order to leave quickly.

C. I can tell _____ about the stalking/harassment and request they call the police if they hear suspicious noises coming from my house/workplace/parking area.

D. I can teach my children how to use the telephone to contact the police and the fire department.

E. I will _____ as my code word with my children or my friends so they can call for help.

F. I will frequently change the route I use to get to or from work/home/family/friends and be aware not to always leave or come home at the same time every day.

G. I will check to be sure that no automobile is following me on the road or any individual is following me on the street.

H. If I decide to get away, I will go to _____. (Decide this even if you don't think there will be a next time.)

I. I can also teach some of these strategies to some/all of my children.

J. If I think there might be a confrontation, I will try to move to a space that is lowest risk, such as _____ _____. (Try to avoid arguments in the bathroom, garage, kitchens, near weapons or in rooms without access to an outside door.)

K. I will use my judgment and intuition. If the situation is very serious, I can give the offender what he/she wants to calm him/her down. I have to protect myself until I/we are out of danger.

Step 2: Safety when preparing to leave work, home, social event. Leaving must be done strategically in order to increase safety.

I can use some or all of the following safety strategies:

A. I will leave money and an extra set of keys with _____ _____ so I can leave quickly.

B. I will keep copies of important documents or keys at _____ _____.

C. I will walk with someone.

D. I will assess where are safe places to go if I feel I am being followed.

E. Important numbers I need:
Police _____
Mini Police Station _____
Auxiliary Police _____

F. Other things I can do to increase my safety include:

_____

_____

_____

G. I can keep change for phone calls on me at all times.

H. I will check with _____ and _____ to see who would be able to let me stay with them or lend me some money.

I. I can leave extra clothes with _____.

J. I will sit down and review my safety plan every _____ in order to plan the safest way to escape. _____ (domestic violence advocate or friend) has agreed to help me review this plan.

K. I will rehearse my escape plan and, as appropriate, practice it with my children.

Step 3. <u>Safety in my own residence</u>. There are many things you can do to increase your safety in your own residence. It may be impossible to do everything at once, but safety measures can be added step by step.

Safety measures I can use include:

A. I can change the locks on my doors and windows as soon as possible.

B. I can replace the wooden doors with steel/metal doors.

C. I can install security systems including additional locks, window bars, poles to wedge against doors, an electronic system, etc.

D. I can purchase rope ladders to be used for escape from second-floor windows.

E. I can install smoke detectors and purchase fire extinguishers for each floor in my house/apartment.

F. I can install an outside lighting system that lights up when a person is coming close to my house.

G. I will teach my children how to use the telephone to make a collect call to me and to _____ (friend/minister/other) in the event that there is an emergency.

H. I will tell people who take care of my children which people have permission to pick up my children and that my partner is not permitted to do so. The people I will inform about pick-up permission include:

School _____

Day Care Staff _____

Babysitter _____

Sunday school teacher: _____

Supervisor/co-worker: _____

I. I can inform . . .

Neighbor _____

Pastor _____

Friend _____

Supervisor/co-worker _____

that they should call the police if the offender is observed near my residence/business.

Step 4: <u>Safety with a protection order</u>. Many people will obey protection orders, but one can never be sure who will obey and who will violate protection orders. I recognize that I may need to ask the police and the courts to enforce my protection order.

The following are some steps that I can take to help the enforcement of my protection order:

A. I will keep my protection order _____ (location). (Always keep it on or near your person.)

B. I will give my protection order to police departments in the community where I work, in those communities where I usually visit family or friends, and the community where I live.

C. There should be a registry of protection orders that all police departments can call to confirm the validity of a protection order. I can check to make sure that my protection order is in the registry. The telephone number for the registry of protection orders is _____.

D. For further safety, I often visit other counties in _____ _____ (state). I might file my protection order with the court in those counties. I will register my protection order in the following counties: _____ _____ and _____.

E. I can call the local prosecutor's office or witness/victim center if I am not sure about B, C or D above, or if I have some problem with my protection order.

F. I will inform my employer, my minister, my closest friend, school and _____ and _____ that I have a protection order in effect.

G. If my protection order is lost or destroyed, I can get another copy from the courthouse by going to the _____ _____ located at _____.

H. If the offender violates the protection order, I can call the police and report a violation, go to the prosecutor's office, call my advocate, and/or advise the court of the violation.

I. If the police do not help, I can contact my advocate or attorney and will file a complaint with the chief of the police department.

J. I can also file a private criminal complaint with the jurisdiction where the violation occurred at the city prosecutor's office. I can charge the offender with a violation of the protection order and all the crimes that he/she commits in violating the order. I can call the victim advocate to help me with this.

Step 5: <u>Safety on the job and in public</u>. **You must decide if and when you will tell others that you may be at continued risk. Friends, family and co-workers can help to protect you. You should consider carefully which people to invite to help secure your safety.**

I might do any or all of the following:

A. I can inform my boss, the security supervisor and _____ at work of my situation.

B. I can ask _____ to help screen my telephone calls at work.

C. When leaving work, I can _____ _____.

D. When driving home, if problems occur, I can _____ _____.

E. If I use public transit, I can _____ _____.

F. I can use different grocery stores and shopping malls to conduct my business and shop at hours that are different from those I have used.

G. I can request the phone company to put a tap on my line. I can use a tape recorder or answering machine if I have one.

H. I can also _____.

Step 6: <u>Safety and drug or alcohol consumption</u>. Most people in this culture consume alcohol. Many consume mood-altering drugs. Much of this consumption is legal and some is not. The legal outcomes of using illegal drugs can be very hard on you and may hurt your relationship with your children and put you at a disadvantage in other legal actions. Therefore, you should carefully consider the potential cost of the use of illegal drugs. But beyond this, the use of any alcohol or other drugs can reduce your awareness and ability to act quickly to protect yourself from the offender. Furthermore, the use of alcohol or other drugs by the offender may give him/her an excuse to use violence. Therefore, in the context of drug or alcohol consumption, you need to make specific plans.

I can enhance my safety by some or all of the following:

A. If I am going to consume, I can do so in a safe place and with people who understand the risk of violence and are committed to my safety.

B. I can also _____.

C. I might also _____.

D. I might also _____.

E. To safeguard my children, I might _____
    and _____.

Step 7. <u>Safety and emotional health</u>. The experience of being stalked or harassed is usually exhausting and emotionally draining. The process of building a new life for myself takes much courage and incredible energy.

To conserve my emotional energy and resources, and to avoid hard emotional times, I can do some of the following:

A. If I feel down and ready to return to a potentially abusive situation, I can _____.

B. If the offender communicates with me in person or by telephone, I can _____.

C. I can try to use "I can . . ." statements with myself and be assertive with others.

D. I can tell myself "_____," whenever I feel others are trying to control or abuse me.

E. I can read _____ to help me feel stronger.

F. I can call _____ and _____ _____ as other resources to be of support to me.

G. Other things I can do to help me feel stronger are _____ _____ and _____.

Step 8. Items to take when leaving. When people have to escape, it is important to take certain items with them. Beyond this, people sometimes give an extra copy of papers and an extra set of clothing to a friend just in case they have to leave quickly.

Items with asterisks (*) on the following list are the most important to take. If there is time, the other items might be taken, or stored outside the home.

These items might best be placed in one location, so that if we have to leave in a hurry, I can grab them quickly.

When I leave, I should take:

* Identification for myself
* Children's birth certificates
* My birth certificate
* Social Security cards
* School and vaccination records
* Money
* Checkbook, ATM card
* Credit cards
* Keys to house, car, office
* Driver's license and registration
* Medications
Welfare identification
Work permits
Green card
Passport(s)
Divorce papers
Medical records — for all family members
Lease/rental agreement, house deed, mortgage payment book
Bank books
Insurance papers
Small salable objects
Address book
Pictures
Jewelry
Children's favorite toys and/or blankets
Items of special sentimental value

Telephone numbers I need to know:

Witness/victim center _____

Prosecutor's office _____

Police dept. (school) _____

Police dept. (work) _____

County registry of protection orders _____

Work number _____

Supervisor's home number _____

Minister _____

Other _____

Documentation is very important. Record all events, list any witnesses, police reports, complaints filed at prosecutors' offices, any prior court cases, current court cases, phone contacts by stalker, etc.

It is best to do in the order that the things have happened.

_____

Adapted from "Personalized Safety Plan," Office of the City Attorney, City of San Diego, California, April 1990.

Used with permission from Barbara Hart and Jane Stuehling (1992). Pennsylvania Coalition Against Domestic Violence, 524 McKnight Street, Reading, Pennsylvania 19601.

Violence against Women by Male Partners: Prevalence, Outcomes, and Policy Implications

Angela Browne

Violence against women has only recently been addressed in national policy and legislation. Responses by most societal institutions to women assaulted by male partners are still based primarily on a lack of knowledge about the prevalence, severity, and outcomes of violence perpetrated by men against female intimates. Although well suited to make a vital contribution, psychologists still rarely involve themselves in proactive interventions with women victims. This article reviews empirical literature on the physical and sexual assault of women by their male intimates and discusses potential physical and psychological outcomes, with a focus on linking what is known about abused women's reactions with the rich literature on survivors' responses to trauma. Implications for research, treatment interventions, and policy are discussed.

Early writings on violence in marital or dating relationships focused primarily on abused women who had sought special services (Kleckner, 1978; Schultz, 1960; Shainess, 1977; Snell, Rosenwald, & Robey, 1964). Interpreted without regard to the general pervasiveness of male violence toward women, information about the alleged characteristics of women assaulted by male partners quickly became biased toward that small proportion of victims who sought psychological or other help. Although pioneering work in the late 1970s and early 1980s explicated the broader context of male violence against female intimates (e.g., Martin, 1976; Russell, 1982; Walker, 1979), psychologists continue to risk pathologizing women victims and failing to identify potential danger by not integrating what is known about assaults by relational partners with the rich literature on human responses to trauma. Given the high base rates of violence by men against their female intimates, an overemphasis on characteristics of abused women as the cause of their victimization risks limiting our understanding of the phenomenon, thus increasing the possibility of ineffective or inappropriate interventions and erroneous diagnoses.

INCIDENCE AND PREVALENCE OF MALE VIOLENCE AGAINST FEMALE INTIMATES

Abuse in couple relationships may include intense criticisms and put-downs, verbal harassment, sexual coercion and assault, physical attacks and intimidation, restraint of normal activities and freedoms, and denial of access to resources (e.g., Pagelow, 1984; Walker, 1979). Although all of these dimensions have significant impacts on women victims, this discussion focuses primarily on acts of physical aggression. The term *violence* is used more narrowly in this article to connote physical assaults with the potential to cause physical harm, sexual aggression, forcible restraint, and threats to kill or harm.

Physical Assault

Historically, society's concept of violent victimization has focused on assaults occurring between acquaintances and strangers. Yet women's greatest risk of assault is from their intimates. Women victims of violence by male partners are more likely to be repeatedly attacked, raped, injured, or killed than are women assaulted by other types of assailants (Browne & Williams, 1989, 1993; Finkelhor & Yllo, 1985; Langan & Innes, 1986; Lentzner & DeBerry, 1980; Russell, 1982). This repetition and severity of aggression is facilitated by the fact that intimates are readily available, the amount of time at risk is high, and assaults can be carried out in private when the target is completely off guard. Estimates based on probability samples suggest that a minimum of from 2 to 3 million women are assaulted by male partners each year in the United States (Straus & Gelles, 1990; Straus, Gelles, & Steinmetz, 1980) and that between 21% and 34% of all women will be physically assaulted by an intimate male during adulthood (Frieze, Knoble, Washburn, & Zomnir, 1980; Russell, 1982). In a nationally representative survey of couples in 1985, nearly one-eighth of the husbands had carried out one or more acts of physical aggression against their wives just during the 12 months preceding the survey (Straus & Gelles, 1990). More than three out of every 100 — or 1.8 million — women were *severely* assaulted (i.e., they were punched, kicked, choked, beaten, threatened with a knife or gun, or had a knife or a gun used on them).

It should be noted that figures based on such surveys represent marked underestimates of the problem. National estimates are derived from self-reports obtained through telephone or in-person interviews. Such surveys typically do not include the very poor; those who do not speak English fluently; those whose lives are especially chaotic; military families living on base; and individuals who are hospitalized, homeless, institutionalized, or incarcerated at the time the survey is conducted. Furthermore, estimates are based only on those respondents who are home when the interviewers knock or call, who are willing to report, even anonymously, acts of violence they have experienced or perpetrated in their relationship. On the basis of the last 17 years' empirical findings, experts now suggest that a more accurate national estimate may be as high as *4 million women severely assaulted by male partners in an average 12-month period* (Straus & Gelles, 1990; Straus et al., 1980).

For some women, assaults in couple relationships are perpetrated by female intimates (Kahuna, 1990; Levy, 1991; Lobel, 1986; Renzetti, 1992). Much less is known about the frequency or severity of this type of violence, although recent estimates indicate that physical aggression occurs in up to 40% of lesbian relationships (Bologna, Waterman, & Dawson, 1987). Theorists disagree as to whether the occurrence of partner violence in same-sex relationships negates theories linking male violence toward female partners together with gender and societal roles. Saakvitne and Pearlman (1993) have contended that lesbians are subjected not only to cultural misogyny but also to cultural homophobia and that, when they internalize this misogyny, they may project their self-hatred or frustration and discontent onto their partners. Feelings of stigma and the sense that no one will understand are especially severe for women victimized in lesbian relationships, contributing to an additional silence shrouding their abuse (Levy, 1991; Lobel, 1986; Renzetti, 1992).

Sexual Assault

Like physical assault, most sexual assault of women is perpetrated by male intimates. Empirical studies during the past 15 years document the incidence of sexual aggression toward women by intimate partners versus acquaintances or strangers (Finkelhor & Yllo, 1985; Kilpatrick, Edmunds, & Seymour, 1992; Russell, 1982). For example, using a conservative definition of rape, in a rigorous random sample study of 930 women, 14% of ever-married women reported being raped by a husband or ex-husband — more than twice as many as were assaulted by strangers (Russell, 1982). Rape by male partners seems to occur most frequently in relationships in which other forms of physical aggression are ongoing. In empirical studies using detailed questions and face-to-face interviews with women interviewers, sexual assault has been reported by from 34% to 59% of women who have been nonsexually assaulted by male partners (Frieze, 1983; Shields & Hanneke, 1983; Walker, 1984). Violent episodes often include sexual as well as physical attack, with men who are both physically and sexually aggressive perpetrating more severe levels of nonsexual aggression than that perpetrated by other abusers (Bowker, 1983; Shields & Hanneke, 1983; Walker, 1984).

Mutuality of Assault

A predominant debate in the literature on spouse abuse has been the question of the mutuality of aggression between adult relational partners. Both men and women can be verbally or physically aggressive. However, in terms of the definition of violence used in this discussion (physical aggression with the potential to cause physical harm, sexual aggression, forcible restraint, and threats to kill or to harm), men are the primary perpetrators of violence in intimate relationships.

Contentions of evidence for an equality of violence between partners have been based primarily on men and women's responses to the Conflict Tactics Scales (CTS; Straus 1990a). Such conclusions are drawn solely from participation rates; that is, in national surveys, approximately as many women as men report that they have perpetrated at least one of the behaviors listed on a scale (push, shove, slap, kick, hit, beat up, etc.) at least one time during their relationship. On the basis of these data, some researchers concluded that women are approximately "as violent as men" in couple relationships (e.g., Stets & Straus, 1990, pp. 157-163; Straus, 1990b, p. 11).

Several oversights led to error in these conclusions. First, although definitions of violence are sometimes clearly stated by researchers (e.g., intent to cause harm: Straus et al., 1980), parameters of those definitions are not measured by the CTS (e.g., intent), nor are outcomes indicating harm specifically assessed (e.g., injuries resulting from assaultive incidents). Second, these conclusions were based on only one respondent per couple, not a clean test of mutuality. Third, even with the limited measures, offending rates (types of aggressive actions and frequency of these actions) for men are much higher than for women (Fagan & Browne, 1993). The same national surveys used to assert that women and men are equally violent in couple relationships find that (a) men perpetrate *more* aggressive actions against their female partners than women do against their male partners; (b) men perpetrate more severe actions, at least by the name of the action (e.g., punch, kick, choke, beat up, threaten with or use a knife or gun) than do women; (c) men are more likely to perpetrate multiple aggressive actions during a single incident than are women; and (d) women are much more likely to be injured during attacks by male partners than men are during attacks by female partners (Stets & Straus, 1990; Straus et al., 1980).

Gender-blind analyses also ignore the role that perceptions of risk play on responses of victims and processes such as decision-making and choice. The potential for severe bodily harm of being kicked, punched with a fist, "beat up," or raped by a typical unarmed man versus a typical unarmed woman cannot be simply equated. It is unlikely that many unarmed women, simply by physical menace, would put their mates in fear of severe bodily harm or death. Yet physical menace is a powerful dynamic in assaultive male-to-female interactions. A recognition of the potential for severe bodily harm deeply affects women's, but usually not men's, responses to actual or threatened physical assaults by an opposite-sex partner. Finally, assertions that men and women are equally violent in partner relationships fail to incorporate the prevalence or impact of forcible sexual assaults in intimate relationships, virtually all of which are perpetrated by men.

PHYSICAL OUTCOMES OF PARTNER VIOLENCE FOR WOMEN

Aggressive acts reported by women in epidemiologic studies range from being slapped, punched, kicked, or thrown to being scalded, cut, choked, smothered, or bitten. In relationships with ongoing violence, assaultive episodes often involve a combination of assaultive acts, verbal abuse, sexual aggression, and threats (Browne, 1987; Frieze, 1983; Walker, 1984). Typical injuries range from bruises, cuts, black eyes, concussions, broken bones, and miscarriages to permanent injuries, such as damage to joints; partial loss of hearing or vision; scars from burns, bites, or knife wounds; or even death. Women attacked by male partners may also have evidence of old injuries, such as fractures, strained or torn ligaments, and bruises in various stages of healing.

Although questions about violence at home are not usually included in medical history-taking, studies in medical settings give some idea of how serious partner violence is for women. On the basis of a medical records review of 3,676 randomly selected patients seen at an urban area emergency room during a one-year period, Stark, Flitcraft, Zuckerman, Grey, Robison, and Frazier (1981) estimated that 21% of all women using emergency surgical services were there for sequelae of partner violence, that one-half of all injuries presented by women were the result of a partner's aggression, and that more than one-half of all rapes to women over the age of 30 were partner rapes (see also Randall, 1990). Women assaulted by male partners were 13 times more likely to sustain injury to the breasts, chest, or abdomen than were accident victims and were more likely to sustain multiple injuries. In a recent face-to-face study conducted in a large, community-based family practice clinic (N = 351), Hamberger, Saunders, and Hovey (1992) found a lifetime prevalence for assaults by a male partner of 39% and a lifetime injury rate of 25%. Considering only those women at risk during the year preceding the study (living with a partner, recently separated, or divorced), the incidence rate for physical assault by a male partner was 25%, with an injury rate of 15%.

Women who are pregnant and involved with a violent partner face the risk of especially severe outcomes (Saltzman, 1990). In the 1985 National Family Violence Survey of a representative sample, 154 of every 1,000 pregnant women were assaulted by their partners during the first four months of pregnancy, and 170 per 1,000 were assaulted during the fifth through the ninth month (Gelles, 1988). Advanced stages of pregnancy leave a woman less able to maneuver to avoid blows or escape attacks and more at risk for secondary injuries to herself and the fetus (Helton, McFarlane, & Anderson, 1987a, 1987b; McFarlane, Parker, Soeken, & Bullock, 1992). Assaults involving blows or kicks directed toward the back or abdomen can result in placental separation; antepartum hemorrhage; fetal fractures; rupture of the uterus, liver, or spleen; and preterm labor (Goodman, Koss, & Russo, 1993; Saltzman, 1990).

Lethal Outcomes

Homicide figures for the United States further demonstrate the potential severity of partner violence for women. Analyzing all criminally negligent homicides from 1976 through 1987, Browne and Williams (1993) found that the deaths of approximately 38,648 individuals aged 16 and above during this period involved one partner killing another (including married, common-law, ex-married, or dating partners). Of these deaths, 61% were women killed by male partners, and 39% were men killed by female partners. For White couples, the difference was more marked: Seventy percent of the victims were women. Women are more likely to be killed by their male partners than by all other categories of persons combined. More than half of all women murdered in the United States during the first half of the 1980s (52%) were victims of partner homicide (Browne & Williams, 1989). Of course, Supplementary Homicide Report figures do not provide information about the previous history of specific couples; thus, no estimates are available on the numbers of partner homicides that involve a history of physical assault and threat prior to the lethal incident. However, city and county studies of criminal homicide have demonstrated that, in addition to the fact that women commit fewer homicides than men do, a significant proportion of partner homicides by women occur in response to the partners' aggression and threat (see Wilbanks, 1983; Wolfgang, 1967).

PSYCHOLOGICAL OUTCOMES OF PARTNER VIOLENCE FOR WOMEN

Although studies from some special populations of battered women stress symptomatology, these characteristics appear to be sequelae of partner assaults, rather than antecedents (Hotaling & Sugarman, 1986; Margolin, 1988; Romero, 1985). Empirically, characteristics of the man with whom the woman is involved are better predictors of a woman's risk of becoming a victim than are characteristics of the woman herself (Hotaling & Sugarman, 1986).

Survivors' Responses to Trauma

Several theories specific to victimized women have been developed in an effort to explain their reactions to physical and sexual attack by intimates. In 1979, Alexandra Symonds proposed the "psychology of catastrophic events" as a useful model with which to view the emotional and behavioral responses of women to violence directed against them (see also Browne, 1987; M. Symonds, 1978). Although little subsequent work has been done to integrate the literature on the psychological reactions of victims across traumas as it relates to battered women (see Dutton, 1992a, and Herman, 1992, for recent exceptions), abused women's reactions to violence from male partners closely parallel general reactions of survivors across a variety of traumatic events.

As with other types of victims, during assaults women victims' primary focus is usually on self-protection and survival (Kerouac & Lescop, 1986). Reactions of shock, denial, withdrawal, confusion, psychological numbing, and fear are common (Browne, 1987; Dutton, 1992b; A. Symonds, 1979; Walker, 1979). During — and even after — an assault, a victim may offer little or no resistance in an attempt to minimize the threat of injury or renewed aggression. Survivors of physical assaults by male partners evidence high levels of depression, suicide ideation, and suicide attempts (Hilberman & Munson, 1977-78; McGrath, Keita, Strickland, & Russo, 1990; Stark & Flitcraft, 1988). Some women also respond by abusing substances following the onset of severe or chronic assault (Jones & Schechter, 1992; Walker, 1984). Chronic fatigue and tension, intense startle reactions, disturbed sleeping and eating patterns, and nightmares also occur in women survivors (Goodman, Koss, & Russo, 1993; Herman, 1992).

Assaulted women, post attack, may become dependent and suggestible and may find it difficult to carry out long-range planning or to make decisions alone (see Bard & Sangrey, 1986). In an attempt to avoid becoming psychologically overwhelmed, they may voice unrealistic expectations about recovery and convince themselves that they can rebuild and that everything will be all right (see Mileti, Drabek, & Haas, 1975). The impact on a woman of even a single incident of physical violence in an intimate relationship should not be underestimated. Although women who are assaulted "only once" are rarely labeled as battered and still less often studied, any use of violence in a relationship can dramatically alter the balance of power, destroying a sense of openness and trust and resulting in a permanent sense of inequality, threat, and loss.

Ongoing experiences of victimization may produce long-term manifestations of emotional numbing, extreme passivity, and helplessness (Dutton, 1992b; Frieze, Hymer, & Greenberg, 1987; Herman, 1992; Walker, 1979, 1984). As levels of threat and violence escalate, women's perceptions of alternatives become increasingly restricted, and taking action on any of those alternatives may seem too dangerous to pursue (Browne, 1987). With all types of trauma, the fear is of a force that has been out of control. Like other victims of interpersonal violence, women assaulted by male intimates learn to weigh all alternatives against their perception of the assailant's ability to control or to harm (see Arnold, 1967; Lazarus, 1967). For women whose assailant is their husband or other intimate partner, predictable effects of attack are further compounded by the fact that the assailant is someone they may love, someone they are supposed to be able to trust, and someone on whom they may depend for shelter and other components of survival (Browne, 1991). Given the severity of threats against leaving made by many abusers and the possibility of severe or even lethal reprisals, women victims often choose the known danger and hope for improvement.

Cumulative Effects of Trauma

Although even one assault can have permanent negative effects, the severity and repetition of violence clearly affects resulting psychological adjustment (Follingstad, Brennan, Hause, Polik, & Rutledge, 1991). In a nationally representative sample of 366 women who had been assaulted by male partners and 2,622 women who reported no violence by their intimate partners, multivariate analyses revealed that the more violence experienced by a woman, the more she suffered from various forms of psychological distress (Gelles & Harrop, 1989). Exposed to repeated attack and threat, survivors often live with increasing levels of isolation and anticipatory terror. Women who are assaulted frequently, sustain physical injuries, are sexually assaulted, or experience death threats are much more likely to manifest extreme sequelae — including an overwhelming sense of danger, intrusive memories or flashbacks, and thoughts of suicide (Browne, 1987; Dutton, 1992a, 1992b; Herman, 1992; Hilberman, 1980). Studies of survivors also suggest a risk of more severe psychological sequelae for women who are victims of both physical and sexual aggression in a marital relationship (Browne, 1987; Frieze, 1983; Frieze et al., 1980; Pagelow, 1984; Walker, 1984). For example, in a study comparing women whose partners' aggression included sexual violence, women who were physically but not sexually assaulted, and nonvictimized women, those respondents who experienced *both* physical and sexual aggression exhibited the most severe sequelae, including lower levels of self-esteem and greater risk of alcohol use in response to depression (Shields & Hanneke, 1983).

Realistic Appraisals of Threat and Danger

In addition to psychological and physical responses to violence, women victims' perception of danger and the risks attendant in various alternatives are often based in and reinforced by external realities. With the removal of the psychological responses of denial or unrealistic hopes for improvement, women at risk from their male partners may become even more frightened by the lack of viable alternatives for safety and well-being. Especially for women who are married to their assailants, decisions about their relationships are complicated by legal and financial ties, overlapping family and support networks, and issues related to the care and custody of children.

Behaviors that outside observers may interpret as helplessness — such as staying with the abuser or refraining from initiating legal actions against him — may simply be accurate evaluations of the assailant's potential for violent responses and others' inability to intervene in time to guarantee safety. Forcing a violent individual to stop aggressive behavior is virtually impossible, short of extreme medical or criminal justice measures. Orders restraining the assailant from the home or from proximity to the victim work only if the assailant respects those orders or at least does no harm during times of violation. Living in hiding is incompatible with maintaining gainful employment, raising and educating children, and other components of normal life. Economic circumstances also play a major role in the choices facing a woman who is experiencing violence at home. If, in leaving a violent mate, she lacks adequate financial resources and must live in an unsafe dwelling in a crime-ridden community, a survivor may have changed only the type of danger to be braved and may have added the risk of assaults by strangers to the risk of her partner's reprisals.

In evaluations of the post-trauma responses in women victims of partner violence, the impact of both psychological responses to trauma and the realities of danger must be considered. For example, psychological responses to trauma, postassault, may cloud a woman's perceptions and impede her ability to make decisions or take effective action to improve her situation. At the same time, for a woman who is reasoning clearly, social realities may in themselves engender a sense of entrapment and helplessness.

CURRENT CONCEPTUALIZATIONS: THE APPLICABILITY OF POST-TRAUMATIC STRESS DISORDER

One way of systematizing some of the psychological responses evidenced by women victims of partner assault is the diagnostic construct of post-traumatic stress disorder (PTSD; Burge, 1989; Dutton, 1992a; Kemp, Rawlings, & Green, 1991). This construct has been used to understand a range of psychological responses to traumatic experiences, from natural disaster or military combat to rape and other forms of criminal attack (Davidson & Foa, 1993; Figley, 1985; Herman, 1992, van der Kolk, 1987). On the basis of clinical and empirical inquiries, a growing number of clinicians now suggest that PTSD may also be the most accurate diagnosis for many survivors of interpersonal and family violence (Browne, 1992; Bryer, Nelson, Miller, & Krol, 1987; Burge, 1989; Davidson & Foa, 1991; Dutton, 1992a; Gelinas, 1983; Gondolf, 1990; Herman, 1986, 1992; Kemp et al., 1991; Koss, 1990; Koss & Harvey, 1991; van der Kolk, 1987; Walker, 1991, 1992).

Although the concept was initially constructed to explain re-action patterns in survivors of natural disasters and combatants in war, it is not surprising to find a high prevalence of PTSD among survivors of family violence. The most common traumata sug-gested for PTSD in the *Diagnostic and Statistical Manual of Mental Disorders* (3rd ed., rev., [*DSM-III-R*]; American Psychi-atric Association, 1987) is "a serious threat to one's life or physi-cal integrity; [or] a serious threat or harm to one's children . . ." (p. 247), experiences known to characterize the lives of women in relationships with violent mates. Factors most often associated with the development of PTSD include perception of life threat, threat of physical violence, physical injury, extreme fear or ter-ror, and a sense of helplessness at the time of the incident (Davidson & Foa, 1993; Herman, 1992; March, 1990). Human-made violence seems particularly likely to lead to extreme sequelae (Davidson & Baum, 1990). The presence of ongoing physical or sexual abuse is listed under the Extreme Stressors category (Num-ber 5) on Axis IV classifications of severity of stressors. The only category more severe (Number 6) is reserved for catastrophic events and includes captivity as a hostage or in concentration camps. Moreover, some researchers suggest that PTSD is most likely to develop when traumatic events occur in an environment previously deemed safe (Foa, Steketee, & Rothbaum, 1989), an-other dimension clearly applicable to violence occurring in the home.

Many of the psychological after-effects of violence against women can be understood as elements of a PTSD diagnosis. Women survivors of severe violence by partners respond over the long term with fear and terror, flashbacks during which past abusive incidents are reexperienced, marked expression of de-nial and avoidance, loss of memory for parts of traumatic epi-sodes, constricted affect, psychic numbing, chronic anxiety and hypervigilance, difficulty sleeping, nightmares, and marked physi-ological reactivity (Dutton, 1992b). Providers may be particu-larly confused when periods of denial — an integral part of survival for most individuals faced with ongoing aggression —

are interspersed with expressions of extreme fear or desperation at the dangers being faced. Recognizing the potential for at least some post-traumatic stress responses to be present in any individual exposed to physical attack, threat, or rape gives clinicians and researchers a basis from which to evaluate these seemingly contradictory or inconsistent responses.

The PTSD construct has the advantage of providing a framework for recognizing the severe impact of events external to the individual, thus validating the presence of even dramatic responses to these events (Herman, 1992; van der Kolk, 1987). However, *for reactions to be seen as expectable responses to severe stressors, the trauma must be known.* Unfortunately, in most mental health settings, routine screening for a history of family violence is almost never done; thus, serious or chronic psychological and physical conditions are treated without knowledge of the core trauma that may underlie presenting symptomatology. Failure to identify the presence of PTSD can have tragic consequences. For example, drug treatments alone have shown little utility in alleviating the effects of PTSD, with some improvement in intrusive symptomatology but little effect on avoidance and numbing (Fairbanks & Nicholson, 1987; Solomon, Gerrity, & Muff, 1992). Current empirical and clinical results indicate that, for individuals suffering from PTSD, the trauma must be dealt with directly in order for interventions to be effective (Dutton, 1992a; Foa, Rothbaum, Riggs, & Murdock, 1991; Herman, 1992).

Finally, it is vitally important for PTSD sufferers to become aware of the potential links between the symptoms that plague them and the exposure to an extreme stressor external to themselves. Clinical researchers consistently note how abused women internalize the derogatory attributions and justifications of the violence against them (Browne, 1987; Pagelow, 1984; Walker, 1979, 1984). An enhanced understanding of the range of responses manifested by all types of persons who are faced with physical or sexual danger or attack expands the interpretation of symptoms beyond internal or gender explanations and empowers both survivors and providers to proceed with focused goals of safety, symptom mastery, reintegration, and healing (Herman, 1992; Leibowitz, Harvey, & Herman, in press).

INTERVENTIONS WITH PARTNER VIOLENCE

A variety of critical services currently exists for women victims of a partner's violence, most of them engendered by grass-roots or advocacy movements — including safe houses for women victims and their children, crisis lines, support groups, and legal advocacy (e.g., Schechter, 1982). Most of these endeavors are seriously underfunded and hard-pressed to deal with the numbers of women and children needing assistance, however, and most require that a woman first identify herself as abused.

Although ideally suited to make a vital contribution, the psychological community still rarely involves itself in proactive interventions with women abused by male partners. The same attitudes that produced decades of resistance to recognition of the prevalence and severity of violence by men against their female partners — and that lead medical doctors to simply itemize injuries and not inquire as to the context, perpetrator, or ongoing risk to the patient — are evident in the psychological community's failure to incorporate current knowledge on intimate violence into routinized psychological practice (Koss et al., 1993). As Koss (1990) noted, "Standard procedures of psychological history-taking, evaluation of suicide risk, assessment of psychopathology and personality, and measurements of life events all routinely fail to include questions about victimization by violence" (p. 376; see also Gondolf, 1990). Even when partner violence is addressed, the reality of risk to a woman victim and the potential psychological outcomes are frequently not understood, sometimes leading to inappropriate victim blaming and attributions of disorder or to ill-timed couples intervention that minimize the threat posed by an active assailant and increase the risk for coercion and retaliation outside of the therapy setting.

Standardized gender-neutral or male-based assessments typically do not capture predominant patterns of trauma for women (Koss et al., 1993). For example, the *DSM-III-R* description of traumatic events as "outside the range of usual human experience" — now a candidate for revision (Davidson & Foa, 1993) — restricted the assessment of post-traumatic responses in women and children for whom physical or sexual trauma may be a weekly reality. Similarly, introductory paragraphs to current PTSD assessment protocols, with their emphasis on primarily male experiences such as war and heavy combat, cause many professionals to overlook the potential for similar responses in survivors of experiences more typical of the lives of women and girls. (See Dutton, 1992a; Herman, 1992; Kilpatrick et al., 1992; and Walker, 1991, for exceptions.)

RECOMMENDATIONS AND IMPLICATIONS

Research Implications

Space precludes a comprehensive discussion of implications. However, some critical areas in need of further empirical assessment include the following:

1. *The lifetime prevalence of violence by relational partners for single adult women, poor women, incarcerated women, and women from ethnically diverse backgrounds.* As noted, these groups are typically underrepresented or completely missing from the past 15 years of survey research. Definitions of what is abusive; perceived and actual alternatives to abuse; and meanings attached to violence, connectedness, and safety differ sharply across cultural and other groupings (see Koss et al., 1993). These variations are lost in studies that primarily reflect the experiences of women in the majority culture. For these assessments, methodologies such as those used by Russell (1982) to assess experiences of violence across relationships would be most

appropriate for women who may have experienced a variety of abusive interactions over time.

2. *The post-trauma effects on women of physical and sexual assaults in adult intimate relationships.* Although national studies have documented the incidence and prevalence of assaults against majority women by male partners, no nationally representative studies exist on the psychological aftereffects of these assaults. Such studies are critical to inform clinical understanding of survivors' presentations and behaviors and to develop therapeutic supports. Systematic criteria are now being developed to assess the effects of physical and sexual assaults on victims that might then guide clinical efforts to facilitate recovery (Dutton, 1992a, 1992b; Herman, 1992; Leibowitz et al., in press). Future endeavors should seek to replicate and refine these assessments and to integrate this understanding with diagnostic schemata not sensitive to etiology.

3. *Contributing factors to the perpetration and maintenance of male violence against relational partners.* Within psychology, our intense focus on why some women stay in abusive relationships has distracted us from advancing our understanding of the precursors and persistence of male violence against wives or girlfriends (Dutton, 1988a, 1988b; Saunders, 1992; Sonkin, 1988; Sonkin, Martin, & Walker, 1985). Even after a decade, we know relatively little about what leads some men to use physical aggression as a relational tool, the maintenance of aggression once abusive interactions have occurred, or the likelihood that aggression will escalate given separation or the threat of separation from the target (Sonkin & Dutton, 1988). Prospective research on patterns of perpetration and desistance is vital — both as a basis for comprehensive evaluations of existing intervention strategies and for the design of more effective mechanisms for creating and maintaining change in men who direct violence against their adult intimates.

4. *Patterns of reassault and threat for victims who leave their abusers or take other steps to end the aggression.* Although as a society we have fairly clear ideas of what a woman "should" do if

faced with violence in her relationship, we have relatively little knowledge about the *outcomes* for women victims who follow these societal prescriptions. Research is needed on the risks of reassault (and lethal assault) for women who leave violent partners or who pursue legal alternatives, as well as on which alternatives or choices most effectively mitigate against further harm (Browne & Dutton, 1990).

5. *Protective factors to the perpetration of partner violence by men and mechanisms for enhancing those factors in the lives of children and adolescents.* Although the prevalence and severity of family violence have been recognized for nearly two decades, almost no research has been conducted focusing on primary prevention. Prospective research is urgently needed to identify protective factors at various stages of development and to inform strategies for reaching an optimal number of at-risk children and adolescents.

Treatment Implications

The importance of knowledge of a history of traumatic victimization and potential post-trauma responses in designing effective supports and interventions must not be underestimated. For example, a treatment plan structured around only the *manifestations* of trauma cannot succeed if assaults are ongoing and post-traumatic responses continually recur or if the effects of past assaults maintain current behaviors and distress (Browne, 1992). Intervention goals for women victims of violence include the attainment of physical health, psychological health, and safety. In order to attain these goals, mental health interventions should involve:

1. *Routine screening for histories of victimization.* Such screenings should take into account issues of privacy, confidentiality, and safety for women in making disclosures (e.g., victims should not be asked questions about physical or sexual violence in the presence or within the hearing of a potential assailant; disclosures of violence should not be carelessly revealed to

assailants). Settings and practitioners conducting screenings should have previously established links with resources for protection, shelter, legal aid, and other services that may be needed by victims or other family members.

2. *Validation of the experience.* An explanation that many women experience physical and sexual assault from intimates, that such assaults may lead to a range of physical and psychological sequelae, that such assaults are illegal and inappropriate, and that a variety of resources exist for individuals who have experienced these assaults should accompany assessments for victimization, even if disclosures are not forthcoming. For many victims, such statements by a professional are a first step toward reframing abusive experiences and seeking intervention or counsel.

3. *Consideration of responses to trauma in diagnoses and treatment planning.* Knowledge that a woman has experienced traumatic events with the potential to cause a variety of post-trauma responses should be taken into account in evaluations for diagnoses and in treatment planning. For example, it is often helpful to evaluate for PTSD soon after a history of trauma becomes known, so that interventions can be structured in part to address and alleviate identified PTSD symptomatology.

4. *Safety planning with victims and survivors.* Women who are separated from abusive partners and women who are still with violent mates can benefit from assessments of their personal safety and feelings of safety. Even when the abuser is no longer present, survivors of partner violence may be at risk of reassault or recontact by that assailant. Survivors may also be experiencing difficulty in assessing current relationships for safety or danger. Assessments of current safety and ways to enhance personal safety are vital components of interventions with a survivor of any type of physical or sexual assault.

Safety planning should also be discussed with women making disclosures of violent aggression by a current partner, whether or not their immediate decision is to separate from or remain with the abuser. Basic safety issues to be addressed include such questions as these: Does the woman need immediate police protection, legal intervention, or safe shelter, and is she aware of resources available in her community to address these needs? Does she have a safety plan if the danger escalates or she makes a decision to terminate with her abuser or take legal action? What are her plans if a child is threatened with danger? Knowledge of societal resources for protection and aid — regardless of whether she makes a decision to take advantage of them — may expand a woman's perception of alternatives and mitigate against the sense of isolation and entrapment reported by so many abused women (Browne & Williams, 1989).

5. *Record-keeping.* Documentation of assault histories and observed sequelae is an essential component of both short- and long-term mental health interventions (Browne, 1992; Dutton, 1992b). For women currently at risk from a violent or threatening partner, it is particularly important to include indications of trauma history; specific detailing of types of assaults, threats made, and changes in patterns of assault and threat over time; a description of symptomatology potentially linked to the victimization; and descriptions of assaults or threats made in response to victim attempts to obtain help or terminate the relationship.

6. *Expanded interventions for men who physically or sexually assault female partners.* Dealing with the victims and survivors of violence by male partners is a first priority. However, enhanced interventions for abusive men must be developed if the tide of victims and traumatized children is to be stemmed. Priorities include the development of mechanisms for early identification of abusive men when they are seen in mental health settings, improved interventions for creating and maintaining change in violent behavior, and — potentially the most difficult — strategies for engaging a wider population of abusive men in interventions for abusers.

7. *Expanded interventions for children and adolescents who have witnessed violence between adult caretakers.* Witnessing physical and sexual violence between adult caretakers in the home has profound and pervasive effects on children and adolescents' development and well-being (Davis & Carlson, 1987; Jaffe, Wolfe,

& Wilson, 1990; Jaffe, Wolfe, Wilson, & Zak, 1986; Silvern & Kaersvang, 1989). Preventive interventions — too often exclusively focused on issues of physical custody — should prioritize ongoing and supportive responses for children who have been exposed to assaults against their mothers or other female caretakers. Such interventions should address cognitive, emotional, and behavioral effects of witnessing adult violence (Jaffe et al., 1990).

Some child and adolescent witnesses are also at increased risk for involvement in abusive relationships as adults. Although the majority of child witnesses do not go on to become involved in abusive relationships (Widom, 1989), national and other studies indicate that (a) boys are at greatly increased risk to use physical aggression against female partners in adult relationships if they witnessed violence between parental figures; (b) girls are at somewhat increased risk to experience violence from a male partner in adulthood if they witnessed violence between parental figures (Hotaling & Sugarman, 1986; Kalmuss, 1984; Straus et al., 1980).

Preventive interventions would include generalized education for children and adolescents, early identification of children and adolescents at increased risk of later involvement in violent dating or marital relationships, and interventions geared to offset negative exposure and strengthen protective factors and attitudes. Group models based on interventions with the children of battered women provide examples of postidentification approaches that may deter later adverse outcomes of exposure to violence against women and the attitudes that accompany it (e.g., Jaffe et al., 1986). Group or one-on-one interactions that involve children with nonviolent men are especially important for those who have been exposed to male aggression in family members or other intimates, to establish the viability of other ways of relating without the use of intimidation.

Policy Implications

The past two decades have witnessed sweeping policy changes and legal innovations to address violence by men against their female intimates (Browne & Williams, 1989; Koss et al., 1993). However, in the aggregate, women are not much safer, at least from severe and lethal violence (e.g., see findings on increases in male-perpetrated homicides in nonmarital intimate relationships; Browne & Williams, 1993). In part, this persistence of violence by male partners is due to a dearth of preventive and interventive efforts with children, adolescents, and abusive men. The existence of policies or legal statutes does not tell much about the ways in which those policies are applied in specific cases or jurisdictions. Until further attention is given to evaluating the application of these policies, it will be impossible to evaluate whether existing statutes are sufficient to offer adequate protections to women.

Some regional applications of present policy are quite controversial and may actually work against deterrence of male violence toward women and the empowerment of women living with danger. For example, mandatory arrest of male abusers given evidence that an assault has occurred removes a woman's choice of whether to press charges once the immediate danger is passed, and ramifications of arrest may deter women from calling for immediate protection or transportation to safety when an assault is in progress. Policies of arresting both the man and woman when an alleged abuser insists that she also was aggressive act as a deterrent to legitimate reporting and encourage assailants to report their victims as a shield for their own aggression. Mandatory mediation for couples involved in divorce hearings in which physical aggression is a factor and the extension of child protection statutes to children in homes in which the mother is the target of violence are other examples of policies at the state or local level that may act to empower an aggressive mate and constrain women victims from seeking legal remedies.

Except for mandatory arrest policies for misdemeanor assaults against wives (which have not shown a consistent deterrent effect across empirical trials), little empirical evaluation exists to track the impact of these policies on victims' safety or to justify present applications. Such evaluations should be a top priority. In areas on which there is more consensus, further efforts are also needed to:

1. *Make legal protections and options available to all women.* This would include equal enforcement of orders of protection and other statutes, regardless of ethnicity, economic status, or locale of the complainant; uniform attention to waiting periods when a woman is in danger; attention to transportation issues involved in making appearances and filing petitions and to the affordability of filing fees, representation, and other costs; provisions for obtaining emergency orders by telephone; attention to language or reading barriers in preparation for legal proceedings, understanding orders and other court documents, and appearing before the court; and provisions for safety from intimidation or potential harm in arriving at courthouses and during waiting times before and during court proceedings. Special policies are needed for women without ready access to state-based provisions, such as Native American women on reservations and women without permanent residency status or citizenship.

2. *Provide for economic and other necessities related to the adequate care of children.* Orders that contain economic resources such as property possession (e.g., house, car, and household items), child support, and assistance with medical or other necessary expenses can make the difference between a woman's remaining separated from an abusive partner and returning to him to avoid impoverishing her family. Such orders need to be accompanied by mechanisms for enforcing child support and other economic payments.

3. *Coordinate legal proceedings related to assault and threat with proceedings related to child custody and other matters.* Frequently, women with children find themselves attempting to obtain protection and shelter from a violent or threatening mate,

while at the same time complying with required appearances, visitation procedures, or mandatory mediations that put them in frequent proximity to their assailants. Disputes related to children are an effective and long-term way for an abuser to maintain regular contact with his former victim, keep track of her whereabouts and activities, and hold an emotional threat over her related to the loss of her children. Court procedures need to be developed that account for the physical risk to the victim without compromising the integrity of a particular court's jurisdiction.

4. *Enhance the knowledge of judges, court masters, attorneys, and other legal professionals regarding the prevalence, severity, and persistence of male violence against female intimates.*

SUMMARY

Violence against women by male partners has only recently been addressed on the level of national policy and legislation (see Goodman, Koss, Fitzgerald, Russo, & Keita, 1993; Biden, 1993). For example, although so-called women's issues such as abortion rights are supposedly critical factors in political processes, the issue of male violence against women has yet to become part of an election-year platform or a presidential initiative. Only in the past two years have entities concerned with physical and psychological trauma, such as the American Medical Association and the American Psychological Association, prepared reviews and policy statements on the topic. Responses to women assaulted by male partners by most societal institutions are still based primarily on a lack of knowledge about the potential for a current or past history of victimization in women's lives, the risks faced by women who experience threat or assault from male partners, the persistence of this risk whether the woman is with or separated from the abuser, or the resources available for safety and other interventions.

An enhanced understanding of the prevalence, severity, and tenacity of men's violence against female intimates would lead to

(a) different bases for initial and long-term responses by mental health and legal practitioners and other professionals, (b) a different understanding of the legitimacy of women's reactions to trauma and life threat, (c) expansions in society's remedies of choice. There is a desperate need for the development of long-term resources for the stabilization of women and children apart from violent mates, (d) new emphasis on proactive remedies for male violence against women given the resilience of this violence in the face of current levels of awareness, interventions, and sanctions; and (e) new emphasis on preventive strategies for children and adolescents to offset the damage of witnessing violence by adult caretakers and to avoid the regeneration of violence in adult intimate relationships.

REFERENCES

American Psychiatric Association (1987). *Diagnostic and statistical manual of mental disorders* (3rd ed., rev.). Washington, DC: Author.

Arnold, M. B. (1967). Stress and emotion. In M. H. Appley & R. Trumbull (Eds.), *Psychological stress*. New York: Appleton-Century-Crofts.

Bard, M., & Sangrey, D. (1986). *The crime victim's book* (2nd ed.). New York: Brunner/Mazel.

Biden, J. R., Jr. (1993). Violence against women: The congressional response. *American Psychologist, 48,* 1058-1060.

Bologna, M. J., Waterman, C. K., & Dawson, L. J. (1987, July). Violence in gay male and lesbian relationships: Implications for practitioners and policymakers. Paper presented at the Third National Conference for Family Violence Researchers, Durham, NH.

Bowker, L. (1983). *Beating wife-beating.* Lexington, MA: Heath.

Browne, A. (1987). *When battered women kill.* New York: Macmillan/Free Press.

Browne, A. (1991). The victim's experience: Pathways to disclosure. *Psychotherapy, 28,* 150-156.

Browne, A. (1992). Violence against women: Relevance for medical practitioners (Report of the Council on Scientific Affairs, American Medical Association). *Journal of the American Medical Association, 267*(23), 3184-3189.

Browne, A., & Dutton, D. (1990). Escape from violence: Risks and alternatives for abused women — What do we currently know? In R. Roesch, D. G. Dutton, & V. F. Sacco (Eds.), *Family violence: Perspectives on treatment, research, and policy* (pp. 67-91). Burnaby, BC Canada: British Columbia Institute on Family Violence.

Browne, A., & Williams, K. R. (1989). Exploring the effect of resource availability and the likelihood of female-perpetrated homicides. *Law & Society Review, 23,* 75-94.

Browne, A., & Williams, K. R. (1993). Gender, intimacy, and lethal violence: Trends from 1976-1987. *Gender & Society, 7,* 78-98.

Bryer, J. B., Nelson, B. A., Miller, J. B., & Krol, P. A. (1987). Childhood sexual and physical abuse as factors in adult psychiatric illness. *American Journal of Psychiatry, 144,* 1426-1430.

Burge, S. K. (1989, September-October). Violence against women as a health care issue. *Family Medicine,* pp. 368-373.

Davidson, J. R., & Foa, E. B. (1991). Diagnostic issues in post-traumatic stress disorder. Considerations for the DSM-IV. *Journal of Abnormal Psychology, 100,* 346-355.

Davidson, J. R., & Foa, E. B. (1993). *Posttraumatic stress disorder: DSM-IV and beyond.* Washington, DC: American Psychiatric Press.

Davidson, L. M., & Baum, A. (1990). Post traumatic stress in children following natural and human-made trauma. In L. M. Davidson & A. Baum (Eds.), *Handbook of developmental psychopathology.* New York: Plenum Press.

Davis, L. V., & Carlson, B. (1987). Observation of spouse abuse: What happens to children? *Journal of Interpersonal Violence, 3,* 278-291.

Dutton, D. G. (1988a). The domestic assault of women: Psychological and criminal justice perspectives. Boston, MA: Allyn & Bacon.

Dutton, D. G. (1988b). Profiling of wife assaulters: Preliminary evidence for a trimodal analysis. *Violence and Victims, 3,* 5-29.

Dutton, M. A. (1992a). Assessment and treatment of PTSD among battered women. In D. Foy (Ed.), *Treating PTSD: Procedure for combat veterans, battered women, adult and child sexual assaults.* New York: Guilford Press.

Dutton, M. A. (1992b). *Empowering and healing the battered woman: A model for assessment and intervention.* New York: Springer.

Fagan, J., & Browne, A. (1993). Violence between spouses and intimates: Physical aggression between women and men in intimate relationships. In A. Reiss, Jr., & J. Roth (Eds.), *Understanding and preventing violence: Vol. 3. Social and psychological perspectives of violence.* Washington, DC: National Academy Press.

Fairbanks, J. A., & Nicholson, R. A. (1987). Theoretical and empirical issues in the treatment of post-traumatic stress disorder. *Journal of Clinical Psychology, 43,* 44-45.

Figley, C. R. (Ed.) (1985). *Trauma and its wake: The study and treatment of post-traumatic stress disorder.* New York: Brunner/ Mazel.

Finkelhor, D., & Yllo, K. (1985). *License to rape: Sexual abuse of wives.* New York: Holt, Rinehart & Winston.

Foa, E. B., Rothbaum, B. O., Riggs, D. S., & Murdock, T. B. (1991). Treatment of post-traumatic stress disorder in rape victims: A comparison between cognitive behavioral procedures and counseling. *Journal of Consulting and Clinical Psychology, 59,* 715-723.

Foa, E. B., Steketee, G., & Rothbaum, B. (1989). Behavioral/ cognitive conceptualization of post-traumatic stress disorder. *Behavior Therapy, 20,* 155-176.

Follingstad, D. R., Brennan, A. F., Hause, E. S., Polik, D. S., & Rutledge, L. L. (1991). Factors moderating physical and psychological symptoms of battered women. *Journal of Family Violence, 6*(1), 81-95.

Frieze, I. H. (1983). Investigating the causes and consequences of marital rape. *Signs, 8,* 532-552.

Frieze, I. H., Hymer, S., & Greenberg, M. S. (1987). Describing the crime victim: Psychological reactions to victimization. *Professional Psychology, 18,* 299-315.

Frieze, I. H., Knoble, J., Washburn, C., & Zomnir, G. (1980, Marvh). *Types of battered women.* Paper presented at the meeting of the Annual Research Conference of the Association for Women in Psychology. Santa Monica, CA.

Gelinas, D. (1983). The persisting negative effects of incest. *Psychiatry, 46,* 312-332.

Gelles, R. J. (1988, August). Violence and pregnancy: Are pregnant women at greater risk of abuse? *Journal of Marriage and the Family,* pp. 841-847.

Gelles, R. J., & Harrop, J. W. (1989). Violence, battering, and psychological distress among women. *Journal of Interpersonal Violence, 4,* 400-420.

Gondolf, E. W. (1990). *Psychiatric responses to family violence: Identifying and confronting neglected danger.* Lexington, MA: Lexington Books.

Goodman, L. A., Koss, M. P., Fitzgerald, L. F., Russo, N. F., & Keita, G. P. (1993). Male violence against women: Current research and future directions. *American Psychologist, 48,* 1053-1057.

Goodman, L. A., Koss, M. P., & Russo, N. F. (1993). Violence against women: Physical and mental health effects. *Applied and Preventive Psychology, 2,* 79-89.

Hamberger, L. K., Saunders, D. G., & Hovey, M. (1992). The prevalence of domestic violence in community practice and rate of physician inquiry. *Family Medicine, 24*(4), 283-287.

Helton, A., McFarlane, J., & Anderson, E. (1987a). Battered and pregnant: A prevalence study. *American Journal of Public Health, 77,* 1337-1339.

Helton, A., McFarlane, J., & Anderson, E. (1987b). Prevention of battering during pregnancy: Focus on behavioral change. *Public Health Nursing, 4,* 166-174.

Herman, J. L. (1986). Histories of violence in an outpatient population: An exploratory study. *American Journal of Orthopsychiatry, 56,* 137-141.

Herman, J. L. (1992). *Trauma and recovery.* New York: Basic Books.

Hilberman, E. (1980). Overview: The "wife-beater's wife" reconsidered. *American Journal of Psychiatry, 137,* 1336-1347.

Hilberman, E., & Munson, K. (1977-1978). Sixty battered women. *Victimology: An International Journal, 2*(3-4), 460-470.

Hotaling, G. T., & Sugarman, D. B. (1986). An analysis of risk markers in husband to wife violence: The current state of knowledge. *Violence and Victims, 1,* 101-124.

Jaffe, P., Wolfe, D., & Wilson, S. (1990). *Children of battered women: Issues in child development and intervention planning.* Newbury Park, CA: Sage.

Jaffe, P., Wolfe, D., Wilson, S., & Zak, L. (1986). Similarities in behavioral and social maladjustment among child victims and witnesses to family violence. *American Journal of Orthopsychiatry, 56,* 142-146.

Jones, A., & Schechter, S. (1992). *When love goes wrong: What to do when you can't do anything right.* New York: Harper Collins.

Kahuna, V. (1990). Compounding the triple jeopardy: Battering in lesbian of color relationships. *Women and Therapy, 9,* 169-184.

Kalmuss, D. (1984). The intergenerational transmission of marital aggression. *Journal of Marriage and the Family, 46,* 11-19.

Kemp, A., Rawlings, E. I., & Green, B. L. (1991). Post-traumatic stress disorder (PTSD) in battered women: A shelter example. *Journal of Traumatic Stress Studies, 4,* 137-148.

Kerouac, S., & Lescop, J. (1986). Dimensions of health in violent families. *Health Care for Women International, 7,* 413-426.

Kilpatrick, D. G., Edmunds, C. S., & Seymour, A. K. (1992). *Rape in America: A report to the nation.* Arlington, VA: National Victims Center and Medical University of South Carolina.

Kleckner, J. H. (1978). Wife beaters and beaten wives: Co-conspirators in crimes and violence. *Psychology, 15*(1), 54-56.

Koss, M. P. (1990). The women's mental health research agenda: Violence against women. *American Psychologist, 45,* 374-380.

Koss, M. P., Goodman, L. A., Browne, A., Fitzgerald, L. F., Keita, G. P., & Russo, N. F. (1993). *No safe haven: Violence against women, at home, at work, and in the community* (Final report of the American Psychological Association Women's Programs Office Task Force on Violence Against Women). Manuscript in preparation.

Koss, M. P., & Harvey, M. (1991). *The rape victim: Clinical and community interventions.* Newbury Park, CA: Sage.

Langan, P. A., & Innes, C. A. (1986). *Preventing domestic violence against women.* Washington, DC: U.S. Department of Justice, Bureau of Justice Statistics.

Lazarus, R. S. (1967). Cognitive and personality factors underlying threat and coping. In M. H. Appley & R. Trubull (Eds.), *Psychological stress.* New York: Appleton-Century-Crofts.

Leibowitz, L., Harvey, M. R., & Herman, J. (in press). A stage by dimension model of recovery from sexual trauma. *Journal of Interpersonal Violence.*

Lentzner, H. R., & DeBerry, M. M. (1980). *Intimate victims: A study of violence among friends and relatives.* Washington, DC: U.S. Department of Justice, Bureau of Justice Statistics.

Levy, B. (1991). *Dating violence: Young women in danger.* Seattle, WA: Seal Press.

Lobel, K. (Ed.) (1986). *Naming the violence: Speaking out about lesbian battering.* Seattle, WA: Seal Press.

March, J. S. (1990). The nosology of post-traumatic stress disorder. *Journal of Anxiety Disorders, 4,* 61-82.

Margolin, G. (1988). Interpersonal and intrapersonal factors associated with marital violence. In G. T. Hotaling, D. Finkelhor, J. T. Kirkpatrick, & M. A. Straus (Eds.), *Family abuse and its consequences: New directions for research* (203-217). Newbury Park, CA: Sage.

Martin, D. (1976). *Battered wives.* San Francisco: Glide.

McFarlane, J., Parker, B., Soeken, K., & Bullock, L. (1992). Assessing for abuse during pregnancy: Severity and frequency of injuries associated with entry into prenatal care. *JAMA, 267*(23), 3176-3178.

McGrath, E., Keita, G. P., Strickland, B. R., & Russo, N. F. (Eds.) (1990). *Women and depression: Risk factors and treatment issues.* Washington DC: American Psychological Association.

Mileti, D. S., Drabek, T. E., & Haas, J. E. (1975). *Human systems in extreme environments.* Boulder: Institute of Behavioral Science, University of Colorado.

Pagelow, M. D. (1984). *Family violence.* New York: Praeger.

Randall, T. (1990). Domestic violence intervention calls for more than treating injuries. *Journal of the American Medical Association, 264*(8), 939-944.

Renzetti, C. (1992). *Violent betrayal: Partner abuse in lesbian relationships.* Newbury Park, CA: Sage.

Romero, Mary (1985). A comparison between strategies used on prisoners of war and battered wives. *Sex Roles, 13,* 537-547.

Russell, D. E. H. (1982). *Rape in marriage.* New York: Macmillan.

Saakvitne, K. W., & Pearlman, L. A. (1993). The impact of internalized misogyny and violence against women on feminine identity. In E. P. Cook (Ed.), *Women, relationships, and power* (pp. 247-274). Alexandria, VA: American Counseling Association.

Saltzman, L. E. (1990). Battering during pregnancy: A role for physicians. *Atlanta Medicine, 64,* 45-48.

Saunders, D. G. (1992). A typology of men who batter: Three types derived from cluster analysis. *American Journal of Orthopsychiatry, 62,* 264-275.

Schechter, S. (1982). *Women and male violence.* New York: Macmillan.

Schultz, L. G. (1960). The wife assaulter. *Journal of Social Therapy, 6,* 103-112.

Shainess, N. (1977). Psychological aspects of wife-battering. In M. Roy (Ed.), *Battered women* (pp. 111-119). New York: Van Nostrand Reinhold.

Shields, N., & Hanneke, C. R. (1983). Battered wives' reactions to marital rape. In D. Finkelhor, R. J. Gelles, G. T. Hotaling, & M. A. Straus (Eds.), *The dark side of families* (132-148). Beverly Hills, CA: Sage.

Silvern, L., & Kaersvang, L. (1989). The traumatized children of violent marriages. *Child Welfare, 68,* 421-436.

Snell, J., Rosenwald, R., & Robey, A. (1964). The wife beater's wife: A study of family interaction. *Archives of General Psychiatry, 11,* 107-113.

Solomon, S. D., Gerrity, E. T., & Muff, A. M. (1992). Efficacy of treatments for post-traumatic stress disorder: An empirical review. *Journal of the American Medical Association, 268*(5), 633-638.

Sonkin, D. J. (1988). The male batterer: Clinical and research issues. *Violence and Victims, 3*(1), 65-79.

Sonkin, D. J., & Dutton, D. G. (Eds.) (1988). Special issue on wife assaulters. *Violence and Victims, 3*(1), 65-79.

Sonkin, D. J., Martin, D., & Walker, L. E. A. (Eds.) (1985). *The male batterer: A treatment approach.* New York: Springer.

Stark, E., & Flitcraft, A. (1988). Violence among intimates: An epidemiological review. In V. B. Van Hasselt, R. L. Morrison, A. S. Bellack, & M. Hersen (Eds.), *Handbook of family violence* (pp. 293-317). New York: Plenum Press.

Stark, E., Flitcraft, A., Zuckerman, D., Grey, A., Robison, J., & Frazier, W. (1981). *Wife abuse in the medical setting: An introduction for health personnel* (Monograph No. 7). Washington, DC: Office of Domestic Violence.

Stets, J. E., & Straus, M. A. (1990). Gender differences in reporting of marital violence and its medical and psychological consequences. In M. A. Straus & R. J. Gelles (Eds.), *Physical violence in American families: Risk factors and adaption to violence in 8,145 families* (pp. 151-165). New Brunswick, NJ: Transaction.

Straus, M. A. (1990a). The Conflict Tactics Scales and its critics: An evaluation and new data on validity and reliability. In M. A. Straus & R. J. Gelles (Eds.), *Physical violence in American families: Risk factors and adaption to violence in 8,145 families* (pp. 49-73). New Brunswick, NJ: Transaction.

Straus, M. A. (1990b). The national family violence surveys. In M. A. Straus & R. J. Gelles (Eds.), *Physical violence in American families: Risk factors and adaption to violence in 8,145 families* (pp. 3-16). New Brunswick, NJ: Transaction.

Straus, M. A., & Gelles, R. J. (1990). *Physical violence in American families: Risk factors and adaption to violence in 8,145 families.* New Brunswick, NJ: Transaction.

Straus, M. A., Gelles, R. J., & Steinmetz, S. (1980). *Behind closed doors: Violence in the American family.* Garden City, NJ: Anchor Press.

Symonds, A. (1979). Violence against women: The myth of masochism. *American Journal of Psychotherapy, 33*(2), 161-173.

Symonds, M. (1978). The psychodynamics of violence-prone marriages. *American Journal of Psychoanalysis, 38*(3), 213-222.

van der Kolk, B. A. (1987). *Psychological trauma.* Washington, DC: American Psychiatric Press.

Walker, L. E. (1979). *The battered woman.* New York: Harper & Row.

Walker, L. E. (1984). *The battered woman syndrome.* New York: Springer.

Walker, L. E. (1991). Post-traumatic stress disorder in women: Diagnosis and treatment of battered woman syndrome. *Psychotherapy, 28*(1), 21-29.

Walker, L. E. (1992). Battered women syndrome and self-defense. *Notre Dame Journal of Law, Ethics, & Public Policy, 6*(2), 321-334.

Widom, C. S. (1989). Does violence beget violence? A critical examination of the literature. *Psychological Bulletin, 106,* 3-28.

Wilbanks, W. (1983). The female homicide offender in Dade County, Florida. *Criminal Justice Review, 8.*

Wolfgang, M. E. (1967). A sociological analysis of criminal homicide. In M. E. Wolfgang (Ed.), *Studies in homicide.* New York: Harper & Row.

Domestic Violence Update

This is the first issue of Domestic Violence Update
by The Center for the Prevention of Domestic
Violence (CPDV). The purpose of this periodic
publication is to inform the community of the
many ways in which we strive to eliminate the
societal pattern of physical and emotional abuse
and violence in relationships.

The Center provides a broad range of services
including two shelters for battered women and their
children, the 24-Hour Battered Women's Hotline,
transitional housing and support groups for women,
and a counseling program for both victims/survi-
vors and batterers. The Center also has an established Speakers Bureau and a volunteer program.
If you have any questions about a particular
service, call The Center at 216/831-5440.

IDENTIFYING HIGH-RISK BATTERERS

by Dr. Jim Schuerger, Clinical Supervisor, CPDV Counseling Program, and Professor of Psychology, CSU

One of the findings of 20 years of research into domestic violence is that batterers are not the same. That is, there are various types of batterers rather than a batterer type.

Recent studies have identified a proportion of batterers who differ from others in that their violence is more dangerous and likely to end up in death or significant injury to the victim. The incidence of this segment of the batterer population ranges from 7 percent to 29 percent.

The following summary is based on a study geared toward identifying high-risk batterers in the form of a Risk Scale. The results of the study include a list of specific questions that have emerged as useful in identifying high-risk batterers.

The study cites the following behaviors — provided as answers to a list of questions used in the study — as effective predictors of high-risk batterers.

1. The batterer has a record of at least two severely violent incidents (beating up, choking, using a weapon, etc.) outside the home in the past five years.

2. The batterer has threatened family members with weapons (guns, knives, axes, clubs, etc.) or has used weapons against members of the family.

3. The batterer is an active user of drugs and/or alcohol and is either a heavy daily user or uses cocaine, crack, speed, angel dust or another drug with a known tendency to provoke violence.

4. The batterer has repeatedly threatened death or physical harm to his partner.

5. When speaking of his partner, the batterer usually claims ownership and denies partner her right to free choice.

6. At least sometimes the batterer speaks of the details of killing or harming his partner.

The research indicates that a *yes* response to any two of the questions puts the batterer in the high-risk group.

The results of this study summarily support using the Risk Scale as part of an assessment procedure in a context of family violence. Shelter advocates, therapists working with victims and batterers and legal specialists all report that on a trial basis they found the Risk Scale useful.

If you or someone you know would like to learn more about the Risk Scale or the research study, call The Center at 216/831-5440.

Reprinted with permission by author and CPDV. Domestic Violence Update. September 1993. Issue #1.

Guidelines for Talking to Abusive Husbands

1. ASK SPECIFIC, CONCRETE QUESTIONS.

Usually, battering husbands minimize their violence and refer to it only in vague, nonspecific ways. For instance, they may talk about "fighting," "getting angry," or "losing my temper." These kinds of terms must be pursued with questions like, "And what happens when you lose your temper?" and "Did you become violent?"

2. DEFINE VIOLENCE.

Remember, he may not think of many of the things he does as violent. Therefore, you must prompt him with specific questions such as "What about grabbing or shaking?" "Have you hit her?" "When you hit her, was it a slap or a punch?" Besides prompting him with specific questions, it is important for you to define violence as any action (physical or otherwise) that either forces her to do something she doesn't want to do or makes her afraid. This would include things like verbal threats, taking her car keys away, throwing things in her presence, damaging her property, or punching walls.

3. FIND OUT WHEN THE VIOLENCE HAS OCCURRED AND WHO IT HAS BEEN DIRECTED AT.

Ask detailed questions about the last incident. It is also good to ask about the first incident, the most serious incident (in terms of injuries) and other incidents. Use questions like "Have there been other times that you slapped her?" "How many times have you threatened her?" "Who else have you been violent towards?" "How about toward the kids?" "How do you discipline or punish them?" "How about friends or co-workers?"

4. BE DIRECT AND CANDID.

Often caseworkers and therapists transmit their own hesitancy or uncomfortableness about an issue onto their clients. The more hesitant and vague you are about inquiring into the violence, the more hesitant he is likely to be. Being direct in asking about the man's violence helps him in two ways. First, it establishes that he can talk about something that he has avoided. It also helps him to see that there is a pattern to his violence; they are not just isolated incidents. Second, talking about *his violence* instead of "the fighting between us" helps him to begin taking responsibility for his own behavior. Usually, abusive men are so focused on their wives' actions that they don't look at their own behavior. It is up to you to shift the focus.

5. BECOME FAMILIAR WITH MEN'S EXCUSES FOR THEIR BEHAVIOR.

These include the following:

minimizing:	"It's only happened once or twice," "I only pushed her," "She bruises easily," "She's exaggerating."
citing good intentions:	"I just wanted her to listen to me," "I didn't mean to hurt her," "She was hysterical, so I slapped her to calm her down."
alcohol or drugs:	"I don't know what happened, I was really wrecked last night," "It only happens when I drink," "I just blacked out," "I'm not myself when I'm drinking."
claiming loss of control:	"I just lost it," "Something snapped inside of me," "A man can only take so much," "I was so angry I didn't know what I was doing."
blaming her:	"She drove me to it," "She really knows how to push my buttons," "If she hadn't provoked me . . ."
blaming someone or something else:	"I'm under a lot of pressure at work," "It's my upbringing," "I've been out of work."

6. DON'T BE MANIPULATED OR MISLED BY THE MAN'S EXCUSES.

The important thing to emphasize is that violence is never justified and that it always makes matters worse. Violence is an attempt to control the other person. For instance, it is a way of having the last word in an argument or of getting the other person to shut up. Also, many men are afraid of losing their wives. Their physical and psychological abuse not only makes her afraid to leave but also causes her to feel doubtful about her ability to make it on her own.

Though many abusive men claim loss of control, it is important to establish that this loss of control tends to be *selective*. For instance, he may punch her but not pick up a knife and stab her. Other men slap their wives but never punch them. A man may get just as angry at his boss but somehow manage to maintain control over this emotion. Therefore, it is not really true that men "lose control." Men decide how they want to hurt their wives and how they *don't want* to hurt them — even in the heat of the moment. Claiming loss of control becomes a convenient way of denying responsibility for one's actions.

Abusive men, like alcoholics, are usually good at shifting attention away from themselves and blaming others. When convenient, they can also be quite good at getting others to feel sympathy for them, even as they continue to abuse their wives. The best general approach to use is supportive confrontation. By confrontation, we mean identifying the violence as a problem and challenging the ways the man minimizes or denies responsibility for it. Such confrontation and education can be done in a supportive manner. For instance, you can point out that the violence is not a sickness, but a learned behavior that can be unlearned. Also, by helping the man to see how *self-defeating* his violence is, he becomes more able to recognize the need for change.

Reprinted with permission from EMERGE: A Men's Counseling Service on Domestic Violence, 2380 Massachusetts Ave., Cambridge, MA 02140.

Am I in a Battering Relationship?

YES, you may be a BATTERED WOMAN if you:

- are frightened of your partner's temper
- are often compliant because you are afraid of your partner's feelings or are afraid of your partner's anger
- have the urge to "rescue" your partner when your partner is troubled
- find yourself apologizing to yourself or to others for your partner's behavior when you are treated badly
- have been hit, kicked, shoved or had things thrown at you by your partner when he or she was jealous or angry
- make decisions about activities and friends according to what your partner wants or how your partner will react
- drink heavily or use drugs
- (for some people) have been abused as a child or seen your mother abused

YES, you may be a BATTERER if you:

- are very jealous
- sulk silently when upset
- have an explosive temper
- criticize and put down your partner a lot
- have difficulty expressing feelings
- drink heavily or use drugs
- believe that it is the male role to be in charge, or have contempt for women
- are protective of your partner to the point of controlling
- control your partner's behavior, money, and decisions
- have broken things, thrown things at your partner, hit, shoved, or kicked your partner when angry
- (for some people) were physically or emotionally abused by a parent
- (for some people) have a father who abuses (or abused) his wife

---

Are You in an Abusive and Potentially Violent Relationship?

Answering the following questions will help the person already in a relationship in determining if it is an abusive one or becoming abusive.

DOES YOUR PARTNER . . .

___ embarrass you in front of people?

___ belittle your accomplishments?

___ make you feel unworthy?

___ constantly contradict himself to confuse you?

___ do things for which you are constantly making excuses to others or yourself?

___ isolate you from many of the people you care most about?

__ make you feel ashamed a lot of the time?

__ make you believe he/she is smarter than you and, therefore, more able to make decisions?

__ make you feel that it is you who is crazy?

__ make you perform acts that are demeaning to you?

__ use intimidation to make you do what he/she wants?

__ prevent you from going or doing commonplace activities such as shopping, visiting friends and family, talking to the opposite sex?

__ control the financial aspects of your life?

__ use money as a way of controlling you?

__ make you believe you cannot exist without him/her?

__ make you feel that there is no way out and that "you made your bed and must lie in it"?

__ make you find ways of compromising your feelings for the sake of peace?

__ treat you roughly — grabbing, pinching, pushing or shoving you?

__ threaten you — verbally or with a weapon?

__ hold you to keep you from leaving after an argument?

__ lose control when he/she is drunk or using drugs?

___ get extremely angry, frequently without an apparent cause?

___ escalate his/her anger into violence — slapping, kicking, etc.?

___ not believe that he/she hurt you nor feels sorry for what he/she has done?

___ physically force you to do what you do not want to do?

DO YOU . . .

___ believe that you can help your partner change the abusive behavior if you were only to change yourself in some way, if you only did something differently, if you really loved him/her?

___ find that not making him/her angry has become a major part of your life?

___ do what he/she wants you to do rather than what you want to do out of fear?

___ stay with him/her only because you're afraid he/she might hurt you if you tell?

If you said yes to many of the above questions, you have identified an abusive relationship and need to seek help and advice. Call one of your area domestic violence shelters.

Used with permission from Templum House, P.O. Box 5466, Cleveland, Ohio 44101.

Study Asks Why
Battered Women Return

Associated Press
Cincinnati

A University of Cincinnati graduate student hopes her doctoral thesis, being lauded by experts, will help people understand the plight of battered women.

Gail Allen, a former prosecutor studying clinical psychology, examined why women repeatedly return to abusive mates. She questioned 247 women at more than 24 shelters and found that 95% of them had left their abusers more than once.

Allen said her research showed that a battered woman goes through four stages of psychological and emotional "unbonding" from her abuser.

First, the woman loses her sense of self and becomes "immersed" in her abuser, she said. Second, the woman begins to realize she has lost her sense of self. Third, she still feels some attachment but wonders how she can love someone who beats her. Finally, the woman reclaims her sense of self and begins repairing her self-esteem.

A woman must complete all four steps before making a clean break from an abusive relationship, Allen found.

97

Experts said her theory could teach victims' advocates why the same women appear at shelters time after time. It also may help police better understand why they are called regularly to the same house for domestic disturbances.

And it could lead to more help for the estimated 3 million to 4 million women beaten every year in the United States, experts said.

"There's still the attitude that our society holds that it should be simple, that, gee, this woman is being beaten, and she should just leave," said Teresa Milholland, director of the YWCA's Protection From Abuse program.

"But it's not that simple. And I don't know when people are going to learn that. I really wish they would."

Allen's work already prompted the Women's Transitional Living Center in Orange County, Calif., to change a policy that limited how often a woman may seek shelter.

Her theory is based on the Stockholm Syndrome, a psychological phenomenon in which hostages identify with their captors and try to please them.

Allen's faculty adviser, UC psychologist Dee Graham, first linked the syndrome to domestic violence. Battered women feel captive in their abusive relationships and therefore are affected the same as hostages who experience the Stockholm Syndrome, Graham theorized.

"When hostages develop Stockholm, we recognize it as a survival strategy and we applaud them for doing that," Graham said. "But we label the same behavior as masochistic in battered women, and we think it's pathetic. That's what has to change."

Battered women stay with their abusers in order to survive, Allen said. "I really hope my research will make people understand that and have more empathy," she said.

This article appeared in *The Plain Dealer* on July 19, 1993.
Reprinted with permission, the Associated Press, 50 Rockefeller Plaza, New York, NY 10020.

Building Self-esteem: Overcoming Barriers to Recovery

Ginny NiCarthy

Battering is a pattern of control and coercion by means of physical and emotional abuse. Physical and emotional abuse negatively affects many women's sense of worth and their beliefs in their capacity to reorganize and control their lives. For many women this is a problem of short duration, but for others severe damage to self-esteem takes months or years to repair. There are many specific areas of self-esteem that you or the victim may see as important. This chapter will discuss relationships, negative self-talk, self-care, emotional control, and moral stature and describe how a formerly abused woman can be helped in each of these areas.

THE RECOVERY OF SELF-ESTEEM

Research has presented no solid information about the situations or personalities that produce differential responses. The following are the most useful operating assumptions you can make about abused women's recovery of self-esteem:

99

1. The battered woman does not fall neatly into a certain psychological category or personality profile.

2. Her complex view of herself may not be immediately evident and may include many contradictions. For instance, she may work as a business executive from nine to five, yet be socially shy or afraid to dine alone in a restaurant.

3. She may see herself as generally competent, but emotionally or interpersonally out of control, or as a moral failure.

4. She may believe she is weak and impaired now, but see her "possible self" as successful and strong, or she may interpret her present inadequacies as evidence she will never achieve the standards she or others set for her "possible self." [1]

You can best discover the condition of the woman's self-esteem by sensitive listening. If she does not spontaneously provide information about her self-esteem, you can ask her what she likes and admires about herself now; how she contrasts that with the past and with her hopes, fears, and expectations for the future; how she thinks others see her; and how their standards compare with her own.

EFFECTS OF PHYSICAL AND EMOTIONAL ABUSE

Physical abuse gives a person a feeling of physical helplessness. Bruises and scars destroy her feeling of attractiveness. The knowledge that she continues to endure assault without leaving the partner may make her feel demeaned. Being assaulted by the person who claimed to love her most may have been especially humiliating, and may have contributed to her belief that no one else will ever love her or treat her with respect.

There are countless ways to emotionally abuse a partner, some of which are difficult to recognize and name. A woman may be prohibited from seeing or talking to other people, so that she is robbed of their appreciation of her valued qualities. Her partner may have found many ways to humiliate and degrade her, to enforce performance of menial tasks, to demonstrate power over her, and to insist that she focus all her attention away from herself and onto the threatening partner.

A major method of emotional abuse is to insult and verbally degrade, which over time causes the abused woman to doubt her competence and her judgment. An abusive partner may use many techniques to make the woman feel "crazy" or "invisible." [2] Emotional abuse may have been much more damaging to a woman's self-concept than physical abuse. Together they are powerful ways to control another person, and that control is the fundamental drive of the abusive person.

THE ROLE OF RELATIONSHIPS IN RECOVERING SELF-ESTEEM

As the formerly battered woman's spiritual advisor, you can play an important role in her recovery. *Recovery* is used to connote not a sickness, but a condition more analogous to that experienced by a war veteran. You may be the first person the woman has spoken to openly since she left the "battle zone," and her sense of worth may begin to revive through her interactions with you. She will begin to appreciate herself as she realizes that you are sharing a bit of her pain, anxiety, and sadness and that you can occasionally laugh with her even in the midst of her grief. Because laughter and tears are genuine, it will be hard for her to persuade herself that you are just doing a job.

If you keep a professional distance, avoiding an honest display of your feelings, you will contribute to the woman's sense of emotional isolation and the belief that no one can really care for her. So being emotionally open is important. If you are a man, you will need to exercise caution that she does not misunderstand your concern and feeling. Avoiding the formality of professional distance does not imply a lack of boundaries, and those should be made clear.

REBUILDING RELATIONSHIPS

Isolation is a major aspect of abuse for many women. Often, partners have forbidden them to see other people. A woman may also have been too ashamed of her bruises to socialize with others, or so intent on keeping her secret that she limited the depth of her relationships, even with her friends. She will benefit from making new acquaintances and contacting old friends, and you can be important in helping her get started.

Whatever the woman's lifestyle or orientation, once you have established a rapport and a sense of trust, you can encourage her to branch out to other people, step by step. If you can locate a community group, shelter, or safe home system that has groups or individual advocacy for battered women, as well as safe space, that may be the first place the woman is willing to go, and such a place is likely to be the most helpful. A group will help her understand her situation through the mirror of others who have had similar experiences. Other social contacts can be made through the relatively nonthreatening structure of classes, or with invitations to co-workers. These might begin with a carefully planned overture by her to share a cup of coffee with a classmate or co-worker.

Make it clear that you have faith that she can manage these contacts and can gradually learn to trust herself enough to know the extent to which she can trust others. At the same time let the woman know that you appreciate the impact of the abuse and her relative isolation during the abusive relationship — and that she has good reason to follow her own timetable, regardless of how it may appear to an outsider.

ABUSER CONTROL

If the woman behaves as if she is still involved with and restricted by the partner, you need to find out whether that is the situation or whether her fears may indicate she has not yet adapted to her new situation. It is important to make careful inquiries about how much contact she and the ex-partner still have as a result of custody arrangements, mutual work sites, or common family, friends, and entertainment spots. The abuser may be harassing her by telephone or in person. The harassment may be very subtle, yet she may have good reason to fear that she is in danger if the ex-partner sees her with friends or perceives her to be enjoying her expanded activities.

The abuser may control the woman by threats to withdraw child support or other monetary assistance, and she may continue to feel helpless and trapped. You can help her evaluate the reality of the current threat, weigh it against maintaining the relationship, and consider the likelihood of its diminishing as the ex-partner adapts to the new situation. It may take months or even years, during which the woman must be very self-protective, to determine whether the ex-partner will give up the harassment. Meanwhile, she must be certain she is not providing reinforcement in the form of unnecessary contact or emotional involvement.

In some instances, it will require a major move, or even a new identity, for the woman to free herself of the abusive person. While she is evaluating her options, you can play a crucial role in helping her realize that she is going through a process of gaining control, beginning with the way she respects herself, makes decisions, handles her feelings, and relates to you. It is not your job to assess the danger, but rather to help her evaluate it in a realistic manner. She is the one who will suffer the consequences — and it is she who must make the decision.

Trust — of others and herself — may be a major issue for the formerly battered woman, and for good reason. She placed her trust in someone who betrayed it, and she may now conclude (depending on who beat her) that all men, all white men, all charmers, or all lesbians, are not to be trusted. She might also fear that because her judgment was bad once, it can never be relied on again.

You can help her explore the reasons she chose her partner or allowed herself to be chosen and how she would make such a choice now. She can be encouraged to consider the qualities she will look for in friends, lovers, or acquaintances in order to maximize her safety.[3] You can help her see that she can slowly develop trust in herself by making tentative judgments, checking them out, and taking very small risks one at a time. You can reassure her that if she changes her feelings or her opinion of another person, she can shift the relationship from intimacy to a more casual basis. She *can* say "No"; she can be the one to end a relationship. You can help her view potential partners and friends as people whom she probably will not completely trust or distrust, but on whom she can rely in certain ways — ways that take time to discover and test. As she gains confidence, she will not need to place people in categories because she will be able to trust herself.

CHANGING SELF-TALK

An abused woman may have absorbed her former partner's stated view of her and developed a habit of verbal self-abuse. After she has severed the relationship, she may still lash at herself with verbal insults, aloud or silently. You can heighten the woman's awareness of the derogatory remarks she makes about herself, and you can suggest that to speak in such an abusive way is colluding with the abusive partner, even after the relationship is ended. You can help the woman see that her statements about herself make a major contribution to her feelings of low self-esteem and fears about her future.

In an effort to reverse this negative self-talk, ask her to write a list each day of the self-criticisms she says aloud or silently, and talk with her about the dysfunction and indefensibility of broad criticisms such as "stupid" and "disgusting." Then ask her to substitute more factual, specific criticisms or a neutral comment. "I'm so stupid!" can become "I'm slower than I'd like to be at learning the word processor," and "I'm a horrible mother" can be changed to "I yelled at Mary twice today." [4]

Once the comments are specific, you can work with her on a specific plan. For instance, she can gradually speed the learning process or reduce the number of times she raises her voice when speaking to the children. Rather than becoming mired in the hopelessness to total failure, the woman is encouraged to recognize her specific shortcomings, put them in perspective, and work on slow but steady changes. An important role for you is to help her focus on the achievements she has made, choose reasonable goals, and appreciate each small change.

It is also important to be aware of social messages that may underlie feelings of low self-esteem. For instance, if the woman is part of an ethnic or racial minority, considers herself too old to try new activities, is physically disabled, belongs to a socially disdained religion, or is a lesbian, some of her self-criticisms may take the form of society's most demeaning slurs. If this occurs, you may want to discuss the idea of collusion again, and to find out if the partner has used those social stigmas to demean the woman. Even if the partner is also black, disabled, or a lesbian, he or she may still use the woman's identification with the same group to humiliate her. It will be useful to help her find others who have been battered and survived, who are part of the same group, or who share the same lifestyle or orientation.[5]

Along with messages of self-criticism, the woman may be beset by an inner monologue of helplessness and hopelessness statements: "I'm never going to change" or "It's too late for me to get an education." These ideas too can be modified by the woman's

becoming aware of them, restating them in precise factual, be-
lievable statements, then beginning to test them. For instance,
"I'm never going to change" might become "I don't know how
much I'll change now that I'm fifty-two, but maybe I can learn to
be more assertive on the job." Then the program of practicing
assertiveness can begin. Each time some small accomplishment is
recognized, it builds esteem so that another can be tried.

SELF-CARE AND
PHYSICAL ACTIVITY

Self-care, exercise, and sports programs are all ways of saying to
oneself "I am worth bothering with. I can take charge of my body."
Most women who have been abused are far from ready to join a
volleyball team, but they can be persuaded to take a walk a few
times a week, even if just around the block. If even this is difficult to get started, you can get up from your chair and simply say
"Let's walk around the neighborhood while we talk." When you
return, ask the woman how she feels, compared with before she
walked with you. She will probably be surprised that she feels
better, even if she is a bit tired. This will be a good time to ask her
to exercise on her own at specific times during the week. Ask her
to name the day and the hour right there, rather than accepting a
vague agreement to exercise "a few times."

CONTROL OF FEELINGS

During the abusive relationship the woman may have felt that
her feelings were out of control, even though her fear, sadness,
anger, or despair were appropriate reactions to her situation. Now
that she is out of the relationship, she may feel ashamed that she
is still out of control, when she thinks she should feel wonderful.
Reassure the woman that her feelings are to be expected and that

she is the one to decide whether to work at changing them and to decide when and how to express them. Knowing she can do so when she gets ready will give her a sense of control and bolster her esteem.

Fear

Fear may be a dominant feeling right after the woman separates from her partner, and sometimes it lasts for months or years. She may try to persuade herself she is exaggerating the danger, or she may take it as an indication she cannot endure the separation. Let her know it makes sense to be more afraid when she does not know her partner's whereabouts than when they lived together. At least then she had some knowledge of the partner's mood and intentions, and might have been able to prepare for the next assault.

It is important to help the woman recognize her fear as a potential protective device that must not be dismissed or denied. When she feels afraid in the house, she might double-check the locks on the doors and windows, see that the phone is working, and perhaps practice (with the receiver down) dialing 911 and saying "I'm at 622 Cedar Street and a man has just broken in." Or her fear may be a clue to purchase more effective locks or iron grates for the windows, or to make plans to move to a secret or safer residence.

Encourage the woman to remind herself of the precautions she has taken and that she has learned to protect and care for herself (and perhaps her children): "I've checked the locks, changed my telephone number, arranged for my neighbor to call the police if there are any strange noises. I'm taking care of myself. I'm using my fear to protect myself." This kind of message has a remarkable effect in reducing fear while validating the need for protection. The woman may also be encouraged to keep a daily log in which she notes the degree of her fear. If she finds that it is diminishing each day or week, she can hope that it will, in time, recede to a tolerable level.

Depression

The woman may be surprised, and even ashamed, to find that she is depressed, just at the time she has finally succeeded in rearranging her life. A letdown is commonly experienced after a whirlwind of moving, filing for divorce, changing the children's schools, finding a new job, or arranging to get public assistance, and perhaps going into and out of a shelter. You can let her know that she may experience a low period after the crisis, that she can weather it, and that you will be there to support her. If a woman does not allow for this period, she may believe her feeling of emptiness, depression, or hopelessness will always be with her. She might feel she has made a big mistake in separating and return to her former partner.

Stress

Discomfort in facing a stress-free existence does not mean the woman wants or likes stress; there are a number of possible reasons for it. It may indicate she is used to a certain level of stress or trauma and needs some time to get used to a new, relaxed pace. If she has not mourned the loss of her partner, she may be prolonging the crisis in order to deny the sadness. She may be embarrassed about feeling sad at the end of a relationship in which she has been brutalized, but she should remember that it is hard to give up the hope that the good times in the relationship might come again. That dream, which she must let go of, may be the most painful of her losses. During the relationship, there was always some shred of hope for change. When the partnership ends, the dream must die, and it is important for the woman to respect her feelings of sadness.

Sadness

If the woman fears her sadness will overwhelm her, she can choose a special time each day to indulge her feelings. She can play sentimental music or look through her photo album and cry. Then at the end of the time she has set — usually a half hour or an hour — she puts those feelings away until the next designated period. When she feels sad at other times, she reminds herself "I don't have to feel sad or cry now. I can do that at eight tonight." If she fears that once she lets herself cry she will never stop, this little gimmick helps her gain a sense of control. It works equally well for the woman who is overwhelmed by grief and "can't stop" crying, though her mourning times may need to be somewhat longer and more frequent.

Anger

As you learn about what has been done to the woman, you may be so angry yourself that any amount of rage seems justified. Justification does not, however, necessarily indicate that the feeling is useful for the person who experiences it. A high degree of rage that persists long after the separation and interferes with a woman's desire to "get on with her life" may indicate that most of the feeling is displaced rage at herself for having remained too long with the abusive partner. When she feels better about herself and understands why she stayed, she will probably be able to mourn the loss of the relationship, and the rage will diminish.

If the woman becomes distressed about directing her anger at undeserving targets or aware that the intensity of the feeling paralyzes her, she may decide it is important to gain control over the degree and expression of her anger. She can begin by keeping track each day of the instances that cause anger, rage, or irritation. With the help of a counselor she can discover the other, more vulnerable feelings that accompany those feelings. Helplessness, hurt, rejection, and inadequacy are common and are often harder to face than anger.[6]

Once the woman recognizes the vulnerable feelings the anger has masked, she can reduce them by accomplishing tasks, making connections with other people, and appreciating the changes she is going through. As she does that, she will have to cope temporarily with feelings more painful than the anger, but gradually the anger will recede and she will have gained control.

THE SENSE OF A MORAL SELF

Some women remain with battering partners because of religious commitments or because it gives them a sense of moral righteousness. They experience a sense of pride — or even power — that they can endure, and that they are not being violent and abusive. Whether or not they have a deep religious commitment to remain married, whether or not they are even married, they may believe it is just and good to be loyal to their partners. After they leave, they may lose that moral sense of themselves; if that was a major source of self-esteem, they may experience depression and loss of hope.

You can help a woman in that condition maintain appreciation for the loyalty she demonstrated, if at the same time she develops an understanding that she owes loyalty and care to herself. It took a certain kind of moral strength to remain with the partner under threatening circumstances and it will take another kind of moral and psychological strength — which she has begun to demonstrate — to rebuild her life without the partner. If she has children, her duty to provide a safe environment for them should help her accept the righteousness of her decision.

Many women can benefit by examining their ethical and religious principles. They can evaluate the extent to which these principles are simply carry-overs from the teachings of childhood, whether they have been accepted as correct because the abuser insisted they were valid, or whether they have been thoughtfully considered from the perspective of a responsible adult.

A woman may also feel morally deficient because she has assumed that her church or the Scriptures on which she depends frown on leaving a violent partner. She will need to find out how her church leaders interpret Scripture and then decide whether she agrees with them. You can help the woman see herself as a deserving, moral person, one who has done her best to act on her highest principles under dire circumstances.

CONCLUSION

Somewhere in the formerly abused woman is a voice that says "Even though I have made mistakes, that is part of my humanity, and I am a valued and valuable human being. I am not the one who is wrong for being battered." You can help her nurture that voice. Your relationship is of great importance in helping the woman gain the confidence that she is a worthy and likable person. You can show her how to change her negative self-talk so she can reduce her feelings of helplessness, hopelessness, and self-criticism. You can encourage her to take small risks, step by step, and reassure her about moral decisions. Your concern and willingness to empathize, your refusal to blame her, and your counseling skills may make the difference between life and death.

NOTES

1. See H. Markus and P. Nurius, September 1986, "Possible Selves," *American Psychologist* 41 (9):954-969.
2. See G. NiCarthy, 1986, "Emotional Abuse," in *Getting free: A handbook for women in abusive relationships*, 2nd Ed. (Seattle: Seal Press), 285-304.
3. "Questions to Ask Yourself About a New Man," in *Getting Free*, pp. 227-229.
4. See the self-criticism reduction exercises in *Getting Free*, pp. 118-123.
5. See Evelyn C. White, 1985, *Chain Chain Change: For Black Women Dealing with Physical and Emotional Abuse* (Seattle: Seal Press); Myrna M. Zymbrano, 1985, *Mejor Sola Que Mal Acompanada: Para La Mujer Golpeada/For the Latina in an Abusive Relationship* (Seattle: Seal Press; text in Spanish and English); and K. Lobel (ed.), 1985, *Naming the Violence: Speaking Out About Lesbian Battering*, (Seattle: Seal Press).

When a shelter, group, or counselor designed to help women of specific ethnicity, sexual orientation, or belief system is not available, books can help women feel less alone.

6. See A. Ganley, 1981, *Court-Mandated Counseling for Men Who Batter: A Three-Day Workshop for Mental Health Professionals* (Washington, D.C.: Center for Women Policy Studies) 80-86. Although intended for men who batter, women who want to understand and control anger will find the log described here useful.

Fact Sheet: Alcohol Abuse and Domestic Violence

Many studies show a high rate of alcohol abuse among men who batter their female partners. Yet is there really a link between alcohol abuse and domestic violence? No evidence supports a cause-and-effect relationship between the two problems. The relatively high incidence of alcohol abuse among men who batter must be viewed as the overlap of two widespread social problems.

Efforts to link alcohol abuse and domestic violence reflect society's tendency to view battering as an individual deviant behavior. Moreover, there is a reluctance to believe that domestic violence is a pervasive social problem that happens among all kinds of American families. For these reasons, it is essential to emphasize what is known about the relationship between alcohol abuse and domestic violence.

- Battering is a socially learned behavior, and is not the result of substance abuse or mental illness. Men who batter frequently use alcohol abuse as an excuse for their violence. They attempt to rid themselves of responsibility for the problem by blaming it on the effects of alcohol.

- Many men who batter do not drink heavily and many alcoholics do not beat their wives. Some abusers with alcohol problems batter when drunk, and others when they are sober. For example, Walker's (1984) study of 400 battered women found that 67 percent of batterers frequently abused alcohol; however, one-fifth had abused alcohol during all four battering incidents on which data were collected. The study also revealed a high rate of alcohol abuse among nonbatterers.

- In one batterers program, 80 percent of the men had abused alcohol at the time of the latest battering incident. The vast majority of men, however, also reportedly battered their partners when not under the influence of alcohol.

- Data on the concurrence of domestic violence and alcohol abuse vary widely, from as low as 25 percent to as high as 80 percent of cases.

- Alcoholism and battering do share some similar characteristics, including:
  — both may be passed from generation to generation;
  — both involve denial or minimalization of the problem;
  — both involve isolation of the family.

- A battering incident that is coupled with alcohol abuse may be more severe and result in greater injury.

- Alcoholism treatment does not "cure" battering behavior; both problems must be addressed separately. However, provisions for the woman's safety must take precedence.

- A small percent (7 to 14 percent) of battered women have alcohol abuse problems, which is no more than that found in the general female population. A woman's substance abuse problems do not relate to the cause of her abuse, although some women may turn to alcohol and other drugs in response to the abuse. To become independent and live free from violence, women should receive assistance for substance abuse problems in addition to other supportive services.
- Men living with women who have alcohol abuse problems often try to justify their violence as a way to control them when they're drunk. A woman's failure to remain substance-free is never an excuse for the abuser's violence.

Information compiled from:

Flanzer, J. "Alcohol Abuse and Family Violence." *Focus on Family.* July/August 1984.

Rogan, A. "Domestic Violence and Alcohol: Barriers to Cooperation," *Alcohol Health and Research Word* 10(2). Winter 1985/6.

Sonkin, D., Martin, D., and Walker, L.E. *The Male Batterer: A Treatment Approach.* New York: Springer, 1985.

Walker, L. *The Battered Woman Syndrome.* New York: Springer, 1984.

Wright, J. and Popham, J. "Alcohol and Battering: The Double Bind." *Aegis,* Autumn 1982.

A Commentary on Violence against Women and Children in Rural Areas

Carol J. Adams and Marsha Engle-Rowbottom

Concerns about aiding victims of wife battering and childhood sexual abuse in rural areas have received insufficient attention to date. Community education about the problem is much needed but remains undeveloped. The transformation of rural areas into communities that can respond to the needs of battered women and survivors of childhood sexual abuse has yet to occur. Although there are now coalitions of rural task forces opposed to domestic violence, some rural communities have services, and various written resources have highlighted rural concerns, many rural communities have no contact with task forces or resources and no specific services for victims.

An analysis of specific concerns of those living in rural areas is essential if one is to understand the difficulties for both the survivors of battering and incest and those who wish to assist them. Unfortunately, it remains true that such understanding has been minimal because many of the advocates and legislators who are aware of the problem of violence against women and children share an urban bias. Clergy, especially, need to be alert to the problem

117

in rural areas because they are often the sole providers of service in such communities. This essay identifies some of the difficulties that individuals and groups encounter when addressing the problems of battering and childhood sexual abuse in rural areas. These concerns also apply to programs in cities or suburbs that are providing outreach to rural areas.

Any generalizations about rural areas will ultimately be compromised by the sharp regional differences that affect the experience of living rurally. For instance, in some areas of the Northeast, a rural community is geographically closer to urban areas than are many rural areas in the Southwest. The authors found that the assumption that something — anything — is within distance of the individual, is an assumption of someone from the Northeast. While in some areas of the country one might complain about insensitive medical and legal professionals, in other areas the concern would be that there simply are no medical and legal professionals at all.

ATTITUDES

A variety of attitudes exists in rural areas as elsewhere. Those who provide services in the country have identified the following attitudes as prevalent among the majority of inhabitants.

Healthy Country vs. Violent City

Rural communities have difficulty believing the worst — that is, the truth — about the offender or abuser. A contributing reason for this disbelief is that rural communities do not want to believe the worst about themselves. They perceive life in their environment as healthy compared to city living. Often they meet the mere suggestion that violence in homes occurs in rural areas with great resistance, disbelief, and/or ridicule.

Family Privacy

People in rural areas tend to rely on the family, even when it is dysfunctional, for problem solving, and they minimize the significance of violence when it does occur. They believe that whatever goes on in the home is the family's own business. Therefore, an assault of one family member on another is often not seen as a crime. Traditionally, public provision of human services in general is suspect; any form of service that by its very nature crosses the boundaries of the family and identifies violent intrafamily behavior is especially distrusted.

Inferiority

Rural areas, like urban areas, include persons from all socioeconomic and educational levels. As is true everywhere else, there are persons in rural areas who lack even the most basic education, as well as persons who are from extremely depressed socioeconomic situations. They may be totally or functionally illiterate. These circumstances may mean that survivors of battering may feel intimidated by persons in authority, who may include law-enforcement officers, physicians, and even local or regional human-services personnel. Add to this tendency the great distance many persons must travel to secure help, as well as the limited resources of many small-town social-service agencies, and it is not surprising that many victims do not seek help, even when they are aware of help that is available.

Racism

Unfortunately, racism is alive and well in many rural communities. Besides the fact that racism is inherently an evil that denies the personhood of some people because of race, it has a special effect on victims of battering and childhood sexual abuse. Those who benefit from the privilege of being white may believe that violence in the home is something that happens only to "those

kinds of people, and not to us." If they themselves are battered
or have been sexually abused, they have no perspective to interpret what to them — because of their racism — is anomalous
behavior. Furthermore, racism inhibits the development of resources for survivors who are women of color. For example, a
white medical professional attributed a Hispanic woman's problems to "craziness," discounting the evidence that a pastor held
in her hands — x-rays that showed three broken ribs caused by
the woman being pushed down the stairs. To this pastor it was
clear that racism impeded the delivery of medical service. Moreover, little faith can be placed in law-enforcement personnel who
are openly and unabashedly racist. Since many rural communities have no feminist organizations — many of which make
antiracism work central to their efforts — or civil rights groups
monitoring the police and other services, little effort is made to
dislodge the privileges of whites.

Local Loyalties

Residents of rural areas tend to hold different kinds of geographic
and community loyalties. Some people may be fiercely territorial
and thus feel highly threatened by any authority that they perceive as invasive of their personal property and their town.

In some rural areas, vulnerable women group together to protect themselves by forming communities of support. Kinship ties
may enhance their loyalty to the group, but loyalty comes chiefly
from sharing similar unfavorable socioeconomic situations, which
may include limited education, lack of job skills, and dependence
on the partner's income. Out of such dependent situations, resulting from having a lack of options, these communities of survival are born. They may be invaluable in times of crisis. Members
may rely on one another for food, lodging, transportation, child
care, and financial aid.

Engle-Rowbottom tells of one community of older women, in
which she served as pastor. She first assumed they had been wid-
owed but found out later that each woman had been battered.

When one finally said, "This is enough," and proceeded to get a divorce, the others felt emboldened to follow suit over the next few months and obtain divorces as well.

ROADBLOCKS TO LEAVING THE ABUSER

A variety of geographic, economic, and social circumstances makes it difficult for victims of battering and childhood sexual abuse who want to leave the abuser.

Isolation

Victims are often kept isolated from the rest of their family and friends by the person abusing them. Lack of transportation contributes to such isolation. Rural areas generally lack comprehensive public transportation. Private transportation may also be limited. A violent husband may deny his wife access to car keys or may damage the automobile to prevent her from using it. One victim reported that she has no car, no buses come within fifteen or twenty miles of her house, and there are no neighbors near enough to hear her scream when she is attacked.

In some rural areas, the isolation of victims of battering and childhood sexual abuse due to distance from a town or city is increased by the large amount of distance between the victim's home and a source of help. The greater the distance involved, the less likely it seems that the victim will seek assistance from resources in the nearest town. As to the related problem of transportation, not only might a victim not have access to a car, but she might also have never learned how to drive. There may be no forms of public transportation available to her. Such persons are dependent upon family and friends to provide transportation for them in order to undertake an escape plan. Some of these ties with others may have been broken by the abuser or by the victim as she attempted to prevent further abuse.

Consider the story of Leslie and her partner, Marshall, who lived in a trailer out of town, on a lake. There were no nearby neighbors. Leslie did not know how to drive a car. Marshall handled all the finances. While their relationship was at first romantic, it degenerated into slaps from Marshall, which soon became beatings. Marshall used various methods of torture. He would hit Leslie's legs and toes with a piece of firewood or a wooden mallet; he would choke her, put pillows on her head, whip her with rubber hoses and belts, burn her skin with a heating coil. When he went to work or to socialize with his friends, he would lock Leslie up in the trailer or seal the trailer's door from the outside to be able to check if she opened the door. Marshall told her that if she ran away, he would kill her, their children, and her family. Leslie became very isolated from her friends and family because of her feelings of shame and fear and because of the physical isolation Marshall imposed on her.

One day Leslie told a friend about her beatings. This upset Marshall; he took her into the bathroom and told her that the end was near, that God had talked to him and told him to kill her, the two children, and himself. In the middle of the night, Leslie shot and killed Marshall.

Lack of Privacy

Many residents of rural areas lack the privacy of anonymity. In a small community everyone knows everyone else's business. This situation can intimidate a battered woman, who may decide against joining a counseling group, filing a police report, or taking any other public action because she does not want the facts of her home life to be known and discussed by the residents of her small community. Lack of anonymity may, however, be a resource for a battered woman because service providers may have gathered a lot of information about the family from friends and neighbors, and she will not have to prove that she needs assistance.

A lot of intervention in rural communities often comes about not from trained service providers, but from nosy neighbors.

It is also true, however, that some persons have too much anonymity. They may be so isolated (geographically or by their husbands) that they are not known at all. Engle-Rowbottom reports that in the community she serves there are some houses that are occupied, but no one seems to know who lives there.

Lack of Communication

Word of mouth, or the grapevine, is an effective method of relaying information. The grapevine, however, may not be available in an emergency, and many rural homes do not have telephones or access to direct dialing. It may be a long-distance call to reach the nearest town with a shelter, services, or a crisis line. Victims may not be able to afford long-distance calls and probably do not want a record of the call on the bill, which the abuser might see. Party lines, which still exist in some areas, present their own specific problems: fear that someone may listen in when one is telephoning for help or unwillingness to ask someone else to get off the line so that one can call for help.

Problems with the Police and the Law

The police may be concerned and cooperative in situations of abuse but unable to be effective due to logistics. In a rural area there may be county sheriffs, state police, town police, and village police, which lack coordination. Police have neither the time nor resources to provide victims with transportation or to stay with them to insure their safety, even though both actions may be mandated by law. For example, the police often cannot cross town lines to transport victims to medical care or shelter because doing so would set a costly precedent or leave the town unprotected.

In addition, police response may be inconsistent. The diverse levels of police forces in an area are not trained together, and individual police officers may be unfamiliar with new legal developments that pertain to family violence. Some rural communities have no local law-enforcement body at all. Many have only one police officer, who may or may not be trained and certified. The sheriff may be located many miles away in the county seat.

Reporting procedures are rarely consistent among the various police forces, so any attempt to compile statistics is practically impossible. Battering might be variously listed as "lover's spat," "disagreement," "family trouble," "misunderstanding," "upset woman," "lady in distress," "uninvited guest," or "stolen laundry."

A victim of battering may be reluctant to report an assault to the police because "everyone will find out." The police she calls may well be her neighbor. The criminal charges filed against her husband are listed in the local paper. In addition, in many rural areas police scanners are common. Conversations between police and the dispatcher who instructs them to respond to a family-violence call become public knowledge to all those people who have a police scanner in their home or vehicle. On one occasion a victim's mother heard about her daughter's abuse over the police scanner, headed for her daughter's house, and arrived there before the police.

While it is mandated by law that professionals report signs of child abuse, some school personnel appear reluctant to do anything about the problem of sexual abuse of children. They make excuses for both their inaction and the father or stepfather's actions.

Lack of Social Services and Medical Care

Few social services are available to either abusers or their victims because rural areas frequently lack programs adequately staffed with trained personnel who can recognize and deal effectively with intrafamily violence. Moreover, it is difficult to obtain in-service training for existing mental-health professionals and other providers of social service.

Most medical services are located in urban areas. Some rural locations do not receive ambulance service. This lack can pose all sorts of problems, especially when persons must travel great distances to a hospital or clinic, personal vehicles are not available, and family and friends may not be supportive. Even when the victim reaches a hospital or clinic, it is most likely that her injuries will be treated while the cause of the injuries goes unaddressed. Victims of childhood sexual abuse and of battering may be reluctant to reveal their injuries to their family doctor (who may also be a friend or next-door neighbor). The lack of family-planning services in rural areas is accompanied by a high rate of teenage pregnancies and large families, which create additional stresses on family units.

Still another problem for victims is that many persons in rural communities do not speak English, and few of the helpers who do exist in these areas are bilingual.

Lack of Jobs, Housing, and Child Care

Rural areas generally lack job opportunities. The number or variety of jobs available may be very limited. Women trying to leave a violent home environment may have to confront the fact that the only possibilities for employment are in a factory or in other jobs for which they probably lack the requisite skills.

Rural areas often lack a supply of adequate housing. One-third of the people in the United States live in rural areas, but two-thirds of the inadequate housing is located there. The housing choices available to victims of abuse who want to move out of their abusive households may be limited and depressing.

In addition, rural areas generally lack provision for day care for children. That creates an additional burden for mothers attempting to work outside the home and support themselves independent of an abusive relationship.

Social Pressure and Family Stress

Two more roadblocks for victims are social pressure to maintain the family and a variety of stresses that weaken it.

Some rural areas put such emphasis on living as couples that separated or divorced people, especially women, are excluded from any positive social outlets and may even be socially ostracized.

Family tensions are intensified by stresses resulting from several factors that affect life in rural as well as urban areas:

- Alcoholism exacerbates family tensions and is often used to excuse violent behavior.
- Drugs, originally an urban problem, have made their way into the rural communities, even though many urban resources have not. They create a great deal of stress.
- Sporadic employment, in which people may be hired on a day-to-day basis or be employed for three weeks and then have two weeks off, can be extremely stressful.
- The presence of loaded guns in the house, kept for hunting, creates problems when the guns are used to terrorize other family members.
- Extremes of weather can also heighten stress, in that deep snow can make escape impossible, especially over roads that are not plowed, and excessive heat may be debilitating, especially in areas where there are no public facilities to offer a cool atmosphere when one's house is simply too hot.

PROVIDING SERVICES IN RURAL AREAS

Those providing social and medical services to rural families experiencing violence recognize the limits on their resources, yet they often try to create options for their clients, which in urban areas are provided by universities, YWCAs and women's centers. Providers of services attempt to give victims of family violence as many options as possible at the crucial moments when the family members are ready to take steps to end the violence. Rural areas offer some advantages in carrying on their work but also present many hindrances.

Organizing

A unique advantage of service programs in rural areas is that it is frequently easier than in urban areas for staff members to utilize other facilities in the community, for example, a church or a mental-health center. The fact that everybody knows everybody else's business can mean that various agencies can pool information (with the client's permission) and provide the most comprehensive services.

A drawback is that meetings are often difficult to arrange because the few service providers there are must travel long distances to reach one another, thus increasing their sense of professional isolation. Their colleagues in urban areas tend to have more opportunities to meet and support one another.

Staffing

Providers in rural areas often find it easier than do staff in urban areas to ask local residents for specific resources, such as a one-time safe home or two boxes of diapers. The smaller populations of rural areas, however, provide only a limited volunteer pool for long-term projects. Urban shelter programs may rely on student volunteers from local colleges and universities to help staff the program; rural areas usually lack these human resources. Unfortunately, the amount of work that needs to be done does not diminish in proportion to an area's population.

Funding

Funding sources seem to assume that rural areas require less money to combat family violence because they have smaller populations and smaller case loads. Consequently, rural programs for victims have access to few local funding sources, either government or private. Bottom-line operating expenses for these programs plus additional cost factors due to difficulties in providing services in a rural setting (for example, transportation) result in a higher cost per rural client than per urban client. Thus, funding agencies are often more inclined to allocate monies to urban areas, where a larger population base and reports of larger numbers of people served make a program appear more cost effective.

Many grants to family-violence programs are funded for only one to two years. It is difficult to establish credibility in rural communities in so short a time. Just as the credibility develops, the money ends.

Staff Privacy

It is difficult to maintain the anonymity of staff and volunteers who work with victims of family violence. Adams recalls one batterer whose wife had left him after a beating. He repeatedly called Adams' home number and left messages on her answering machine saying, "I know you have my wife. Where is my wife?" The lack of anonymity increases the risk of being attacked by violent family members who may seek retaliation.

Transient Populations

Some of the rural population consists of people engaged in seasonal or migrant labor. Since they may reside in an area for only brief periods of time, they may be unaware of services available in the community. Moreover, they can be difficult for service providers to identify or reach.

Media

A further hindrance is that rural areas may not have a local newspaper, radio, or TV station, a lack that increases the difficulty of broadcasting information about services available to area residents. Developing and maintaining productive working relations with active community members become even more critical in the absence of formal broadcast media.

Safe Homes or Shelters

A shelter for battered women and their children may not be available in the community where they live. Although service providers are developing safe homes and shelters in many rural communities, the safe homes may not remain anonymous in small communities, and their lifetime is short. Once a shelter is discovered by an abusive husband, the safety of all its residents may be jeopardized.

Referrals

In some rural communities it may not be prudent or appropriate to refer victims or offenders to local support services, such as mental-health centers, clergy, or police, when these services are unaware of the dynamics of battering and sexual abuse of children. It may be necessary to refer the client to services offered in another town or an urban area.

However, when an abused woman from a rural area is referred to, or avails herself of, a shelter in an urban area, she often experiences an "urban crisis" because she is confronted with a new environment and is away from her local supportive network.

Without intervention, abuse continues. The need for clergy in rural areas to be alert to signs of sexual abuse of children and battering and to respond to the victims and offenders becomes all the more urgent in the face of so many impediments to solution. Without intervention by clergy in rural areas where services and awareness are less than optimum, abuse will continue.

Carol J. Adams teaches a course at Perkins School of Theology called "Sexual and Domestic Violence: Theological and Pastoral Concerns." She is completing a book on pastoral-care issues and sexual and domestic violence.

Marsha Engle-Rowbottom is a United Methodist pastor in North Texas.

Reprinted with permission. Reprinted from *Violence in the Family: A Workshop for Clergy and Other Helpers* by Marie M. Fortune (Cleveland: Pilgrim Press, 1991).

Asian-American Patriarchies

The Rev. Dr. Brian Ogawa

Asian cultures have been described as essentially favoring a patriarchal system of male supremacy and rigidity toward women.
The inference has been that this sanctions violence against women.
Nilda Rimonte, the executive director of the Center for the Pacific Asian Family in Los Angeles, for example, outlines how this
"power imbalance" creates the potential for abusive behavior.
She states,

> A healthy family by Western standards has an
> open structure. Members are allowed to be
> individuals and to communicate their feelings
> freely. This ideal contrasts starkly with the
> controlled, conforming style of Pacific Asians, in
> which a high value is placed on one's strict
> accountability to the family. The Pacific Asian
> family has a closed structure. Communication is
> restricted and decision-making is vertical. Power
> in the marriage is hierarchical. . . . Studies have
> shown that the more closed the system is, the more
> disordered and dysfunctional the family becomes.
> They also show that men's limited ability to

express their feelings results in a continual state of
explosiveness and possible violence. (Rimonte,
pp. 329-30.)

Rimonte is primarily concerned that battered Asian women find
the strength and support to speak out concerning their abuse.
She qualifies her statements, however, by explaining that the
Pacific Asian family is not by nature dysfunctional, only that it is
"merely more responsive to the needs of men than to those of
women." She adds that although a certain amount of violence
directed at "women and children and other social inferiors" is
accepted and rooted in Pacific Asian culture, this does not mean
that the culture is itself the problem. It is of course the batterer
who must be held responsible. (*Ibid.*, pp. 330, 334.)

Asian cultures do appear to differentiate gender roles. This
does not necessarily mean that certain roles are subordinate to
others or that females are subordinate to males. The values placed
upon gender roles make them sexist or not. Different roles, in
other words, can have equal value. In Asian society, for example,
children are the threads of the social fabric. Mothers are *entrusted*
with their well-being and the proper inculcation of respect for
elders. This responsibility is *highly* regarded. The role itself is
not subordinate. It is only when this role is diminished by either
men or women, or the right of a particular woman to exercise
another role outside the home is disregarded or prevented, that
sexism enters the equation. As David Levinson, in his study of
the cross-cultural aspects of family violence, notes:

> The central premise of this study is that the
> concept of patriarchal society is too broad a notion
> for cross-cultural testing. Thus the strategy has
> been to define and conceptualize female status and
> power in very specific ways that are measurable
> with cross-cultural ethnographic data. When
> approached this way, it seems clear that there is no
> unidimensional relationship between female status
> and power and wife-beating. (Levinson, p. 84.)

According to Levinson, the key indicators of wife-beating are related to *inequality in decision-making*. If men unilaterally govern the family and have control over financial matters, and women are restricted in their freedom to divorce their husbands, the *possibility* of violence increases. In all cultures, in other words, the absence of choice is a predictor of domestic violence.

Persons, whether male or female, do not, moreover, perfectly represent the ideal formulation of their cultures, whether Asian-American or other. There are Asian males who mistakenly assume that gender roles were established only for their advantage and not for the benefit of the entire family. In any family there should be the atmosphere of respect for tradition and the allowance for changes based upon individual family preferences and circumstances.

Rimonte is correct when she suggests that Asians must learn to adapt to their new Western settings. There are pressures upon the Asian-American family which test former customs and practices. Debbie Lee, a women's advocate in San Francisco, concurs with Rimonte that cultural adjustment fosters an imbalance in traditional roles. Immigrant families, for example, may have both spouses employed out of economic necessity — a situation confusing domestic responsibilities. It may in fact be the collision of social and cultural values which have more to do with funneling frustrations and anger toward the incidence of domestic violence than deficits of traditional mores. When one emphasizes the Asian values of maintaining harmony and good relations in the home (and in the community) as well as the avoidance of direct confrontation and emotional outbursts, one begins to identify *non-violent* aspects.

Asian cultures, like the dominant American culture, in other words, are not inherently predisposed toward domestic violence nor can they absolutely safeguard women from all abuse. Sexism pervades many cultures and is not simply or exclusively the bedfellow of so-called patriarchal systems. Indeed, no matter how urgent and compelling it is to bring an end to abusive relationships, it must be done so that no element of any culture can be portrayed as historically justifying insult or injury to any one. All cultures are attempts to bring order, not disorder. All peoples are therefore accountable to this purpose.

REFERENCES

Levinson, D. (1989). *Family violence in cross-cultural perspective.* Newbury Park: Sage.
Rimonte, N. (1989). Domestic violence among Pacific Asians. In Asian Women United of California (Eds.), *Making waves: An anthology of writings by and about Asian-American women* (pp. 327-37). Boston: Beacon Press.

Battered Women: An African-American Perspective

Mary Alice Saunders-Robinson, MSN, MEd

This paper presents an overview of battered women. The initial statistics describe the magnitude of the problem — that a woman who is battered is at high risk for being murdered at the hands of her spouse or partner. The cycle of violence, the reasons for staying in such a dangerous environment and the profile of the battered woman are also discussed. The unique experience of the battered African-American woman will be incorporated throughout this paper as will be an overview of assistance for battered women. Finally, conclusions and implications for future research are presented.
Key Words: Battered Women

WHAT HAPPENS WHEN WOMEN ARE BATTERED?

Domestic violence inflicts pain and wounds both the physical body and the psychological being of the person (the emotions and the very spirit of the victimized woman). Physical and psychological abuse is a brutal and tragic experience for the woman who realizes that her injuries are being inflicted on a continual basis by the man she loves most with no regard for her health state. For example, pregnancy does not spare a woman from the ravages of a man who may suddenly become abusive (Walker, 1984). Indeed, when pregnant, a woman is especially at risk for abuse and the new mortal fear of the woman is for the life she carries within.

After many episodes of battering, a woman may come to believe the lie repeated by her battering partner who says, "This is your fault. Your behavior is causing me to lose control!" Wanting her relationship to work, the woman believes that if she tries harder and is more loving, the abuse will never happen again. When her efforts fail to ameliorate the situation, the woman may begin to believe that the problems in her relationships are her fault; therefore, she has no one to blame except herself for her unhappiness. This belief is reinforced by a society which provides tacit approval of this self-blame. It is not unusual to hear people say, "There must be something wrong with her if she stays," or "She must like it, otherwise she wouldn't tolerate that behavior." The cycle of pain is completed as the victim accepts responsibility for the violence she encounters.

REVIEW OF LITERATURE

The incidence of domestic violence is alarming. Every 15 seconds a woman is beaten in this country (National Coalition Against Domestic Violence [NCADV], 1987). Even more alarming is the number of battered women, 1 out of 4, who have attempted suicide (Stark et al., 1979; Campbell, 1986b). A study done by Gelles (1977) found that most acts of violence against women are place- and time-specific, that is, occurring in the kitchen between 8 pm and midnight.

A significant correlation has also been found between women who have been beaten by their partners and those who have been sexually molested as children. Walker (1984), in her landmark research on the battered woman, found that 67% of the women and 81% of the men in relationships of violence reported witnessing battering in their own homes as children. Other researchers with similar findings feel that witnessing the battering of their mothers often forms the basis of the learned behavior for women currently experiencing abuse (Gelles, 1977; Carlson, 1984; Duton & Painter, 1981). The gravity and extent of the problem, as documented by Campbell (1986b), show that of all females treated as emergency patients, approximately 20-50% are battered women.

The incidence of African-American women who are battered is almost identical to the rest of the population (Coley & Beckett, 1988). It is a myth that only lower class African-American women are the victims of domestic violence. African-American women who are in the high to middle socioeconomic class are not spared the beatings which poorer African-American women receive. Lockhart's 1987 study indicates that middle-class African-American women experience slightly more domestic violence than either upper- or lower-class African-American women. Additional research is needed to control for class and race factors. There is, however, no essential difference in the overall statistics for battery among all racial, cultural and socioeconomic groups of American women. The differences are seen in the cultural manifestations of battery experienced by the African-American. Specific cultural responses by the African-American woman will be discussed later. The most dangerous threat is encountered by all battered women at all socioeconomic levels.

Beyond the tragic physical, mental and emotional abuse that battered women experience is the grave risk to their mortality. Each year at least 4,000 women are killed by their partners (NCADV, 1987). The threat of death, therefore, is a very real one for many victims of violence. When murder is the final outcome of domestic violence, 95% of the victims are women. Male victims have almost always been perpetrators of violence prior to their being overcome by a woman acting in self-defense.

The risk of murder, however, is greater for some women than others. For instance, the incidence of murder at the hands of the batterer is greater among women aged 15-34, for women of a minority group and for those who are poor. A woman making plans to leave a relationship is also at greater risk for being murdered, especially if she has made clear that she intends to leave (Campbell, 1986b; Campbell & Sheridan, 1989).

Lenore Walker (1984), among the first to extensively research the battered woman, describes what she calls a "Cycle of Violence."

CYCLE OF VIOLENCE

Based on the findings of her research into the area of domestic violence, Walker (1984) noted a consistent pattern which she termed "Cycle of Violence." The initial phase of this cycle is described as one of tension building at the end of which is verbal abuse consisting of name-calling, demeaning and derogatory comments, slapping and pushing, complaints and frequently impossible demands. If a woman has been battered prior to this time, she knows the next phase is inevitable.

Acute battering is the next phase during which the male is likely to assault his partner with the same force he would use to injure a man. This beating, which may be severe and prolonged, may last from 15 minutes to one hour or longer, leaving the woman with broken bones, multiple injuries and frequently in need of emergency medical care. The length of the attack depends on the amount of tension the male discharges during this episode of battering.

After this discharge of tension, the male almost always regrets his behavior. He himself is shocked and stunned by his behavior after the first incident of battery. He explains specifically to his mate what she did to upset him, apologizes, begs forgiveness and promises that this will never happen again. His pleas are very eloquent. Because her memories of a loving and caring partner are strong, as are her desires for a successful relationship, battered women dare to believe that the first incident of battery will be the last.

Once the initial battery has occurred, however, the cycle will repeat itself with decreasing intervals of time between each cycle. Within each cycle, the length of time and the severity of acute battering increases (Campbell, 1986b). The cycle of violence is inevitable without assertive and intense intervention.

THE PROCESS OF ISOLATION

The process of isolation of the battered partner is an inherent component of the cycle of violence. One of the first things a potential batterer does is to isolate his partner (Benton, 1986). The method is, at first, often seductive and flattering since he begins by telling her how much he loves her. In addition, he says that he finds her company so special that he is reluctant to share her with anyone else.

Once the woman is seduced, whereby she sees herself as indispensable and very special to him, the batterer then moves toward greater control by demanding an accounting of her time. This rationale is viewed as charming, appealing and romantic by the woman who believes that her partner treasures her so completely that he moves heaven and earth to ensure that no one else will interfere with their relationship. Eventually, he literally times her at work and at everything she does so that her movements are completely and totally under his control. In addition, the woman does not see family or friends alone — the male partner is always present. Each of them at this point in the process adheres to a rigid sex-role stereotype for male/female relationships.

The underlying emotion on the part of the male partner is not love in any healthy sense; instead, it is indicative of a pathological dependence on his partner as well as a profound insecurity. The superficial picture, however, mirrors a woman who chooses to be in a painful environment. How is it that a woman becomes involved with such a man? Many women who are battered come to the relationship with low self-esteem which predisposes them to choose a man with this personality deficit as their partner.

Low self-esteem and fear are responses that many women including African-American women bring to their relationship with violent men. Sometimes these responses emerge as a result of the continued physical and verbal assault encountered in domestic violence. Often women who were gainfully employed are not permitted to continue their work because their partner does not approve. If they remain employed, their work is demeaned by him so that no matter what their occupation, he fails to acknowledge its importance (Benton, 1986).

The next calculated step in the systematic process used to isolate a potential victim is inconsistent behavior. For example, the male partner may accompany a woman to a social or family function and be alternately very charming and rude or verbally abusive. The woman, never knowing how her partner will behave, will choose not to go anywhere with him (Benton, 1986).

WHY STAY IN A PAINFUL RELATIONSHIP?

Like most women in a relationship in which battery occurs, the African-American woman stays in the relationship because she loves her spouse or partner. She responds to his remorse after the beatings and hopes with him that this will never happen again. She has already determined that she does not want to be like the degrading stereotypical negative image of the African-American woman: always complaining, never satisfied, never supportive of her partner, attempting to emasculate him by making all the decisions for the relationship without giving him a chance to do so.

Her attitude of support is reinforced by media messages from African-American leaders who state how important it is to support the African-American male, to not nag, to be patient, and above all, to not expose him to any more stressors than the ones he already has to confront. This belief system places the African-American woman in a unique position of knowing that if she does seek help, she may place the man she loves in grave danger of being brutalized by the police. For example, African-American men who are stopped for questioning on a traffic violation are randomly beaten in some locations. Police brutality against Black males is widely reported (Campbell & Humphreys, 1984). This knowledge places the African-American woman in tremendous conflict after a beating. Should she report the violence and provide some protection for herself and her children? Should she report the violence knowing that she may be condemning the man she loves to a justice system which is frequently a racist one? These are very difficult questions for an African-American woman seeking protection for herself and her children as well as help for her partner. Her choices are almost nonexistent.

Women in relationships of violence may be mothers; if so, they are forced to consider safety measures for their children who may have been threatened with death if the wife attempts to leave (Benton, 1986). Battered women are fearful that a partner who batters them may also hurt their children. Indeed, these fears are well founded because often men who batter their partners, also hit and abuse their children as well (Benton, 1986; Campbell, 1986a).

Women married to successful professional men are often afraid to leave because of the possibility of losing custody of their children. In some marriages, the charge of abandoning the children has been leveled at a woman who left to avoid being beaten. The battering partner frequently uses this ploy to make sure his partner does not leave and is a powerful control device that some men successfully employ (Benton, 1986).

Finally, a common reason given by many women who stay in an abusive situation is that they genuinely love their partner. When he is not abusive, the woman perceives him as a wonderful husband and continues to believe that the violence will stop if only she tries hard enough to comply with his requests (Benton,

1986). This belief prompts her to assume an inordinate amount of responsibility for making the relationship work.

The African-American woman is eager to see that her partner gets ahead and has the opportunities he deserves. She does not want to hinder him from assuming his role as a man who is free to claim all the rights he is entitled to have. She is often told to be patient when domestic violence occurs, and to try harder to understand the overwhelming stressors he experiences in this society.

She is repeatedly reminded that it takes two to have an argument and that if her partner is violent and abusive, it is difficult to imagine that she is an innocent victim. Therefore, she must have some role in precipitating that kind of extreme response. She is urged to keep the information about the beating in the family and try to work things out. She may be urged to seek counseling for herself so that she can learn to cope with her relationship in a more effective manner.

When counseling, or whatever effort she employs, fails to save her relationship, the battered woman begins to give up hope and to embrace despair. She has frequently tried in vain to share her pain with family and friends and begins to accept responsibility for the failure of her relationship. Her spirit is broken, and she gradually accepts the belief that nothing will ever change her situation. Finally, she gives up hope that the beatings will ever stop (Benton, 1986).

> As a survival mechanism, the woman may "desensitize" by ignoring or denying the violence problems. Her hope for the relationship, the belief that he will change and her life approach the ideal, give way to depression and anger. These emotions combine with the low self-esteem to sap many women of their motivation and the self-confidence necessary to make changes. They may feel change for the better is just not possible. (p. 409)

WHAT CAN BE DONE TO HELP?

A barrier which must be overcome before any help can be given is to challenge the negative attitude of a society which blames and punishes the victim. This attitude makes it difficult to hear the pain these women express for themselves and for their children. Society seeks logical explanations for these tragedies. However, the reasons for battery are complex and difficult to understand. Because of this, the victim is often labeled as sick, masochistic or depressed.

Some clues which indicate that the victim is being blamed might be to say: "I would never stand for that. The next time he hit me, I would see to it that he wished he had never been born." Another nonsupportive response would be: "It does take two people to make a marriage work." To ask, "Do you love him?" is not helpful.

Any of these negative responses increase the battered woman's sense of despair and hopelessness and deepen her sense of low self-esteem. This makes it even more difficult for her to reach out for help when the battering happens again.

The sheer numbers make it very likely that each of us will be touched in some way by this problem. The fact that children repeatedly witness such violence places them at risk for growing up to repeat the pattern of violence in their relationships. Male children learn that physical force is a way to relieve tension and frustration or to resolve conflict. A female child learns low self-esteem and is poorly equipped to parent children and teach them to value themselves.

How can we assist women who live in terror of their lives? We can begin by listening to what they have to say and taking their concerns seriously. We can also understand that they may be in grave danger if they remain in these relationships. Guidelines have been established to lessen some of the peril for the woman who makes the decision to leave. Sharing this information may save a life.

The following are nationally recognized guidelines for a woman who is considering leaving (Campbell & Sheridan, 1989).

> If she needs to leave home quickly in the face of threatened or actual abuse, she should plan to take the children with her. For herself and each child, she needs a change of clothing in the trunk of a car or at a friend's home. Essential documents (e.g., birth certificates, immunization records, rent receipts, prescription numbers, Medicaid certification) need to be placed together, ready to take at a moment's notice. She should talk to a neighbor about calling the police if there are sounds of violence. (p. 17)

Additionally, the Battered Women's Hot Line, 800-333-SAFE, will provide information about help at the community level.

CONCLUSIONS AND IMPLICATIONS FOR FURTHER RESEARCH

The implications for the future of a family racked with violence are chilling. The female partner who does not get help for herself is in danger of suicide or of being murdered. Her self-esteem is lowered as a result of the physical and psychological abuse she receives.

Society must determine that the violence will cease. Men must be taught to learn nonviolent ways of expressing frustration and anger. Women must learn to value themselves. Health professionals and educators who encounter members of violence-plagued families must learn how to provide effective intervention. We know that domestic violence exists in each and every class, race and socioeconomic group. However, additional research is needed to guide our understanding of how to help all women who are victims of battering, including the specific vectors influencing the situation of African-American women.

Lastly, our concern must become personal because the children born to a couple in such an unhealthy relationship are likely to grow up and repeat the cycle of violence. We can support legislation, education, therapy and all those measures which may free our women, men and children of the vicious cycle of domestic violence.

REFERENCES

Benton, D.A. (1986). Battered women: Why do they stay? *Health Care for Women International,* 7(6), 403-411.

Campbell, J. (1986a). A survivor group for battered women. *Advances in Nursing Science, 8*(2), 13-20.

Campbell, J. (1986b). Nursing assessment for risk of homicide with battered women. *Advances in Nursing Science, 8*(4), 36-51.

Campbell, J., & Humphreys, J. (1984). *Nursing care of victims of family violence.* Reston, VA: A Prentice-Hall Company.

Campbell, J., & Sheridan, D.J. (1989). Clinical articles on emergency nursing interventions with battered women. *Journal of Emergency Nursing, 15*(1), 12-17.

Coley, S.M., & Beckett, J.O. (1988). Black battered women: A review of empirical literature. *Journal of Counseling and Development, 66*(6), 266-270.

Gelles, R.J. (1977). No place to go: The social dynamics of marital violence. In M. Roy (Ed.), *Battered women, a psychosociological study of domestic violence* (p. 53). New York: Van Nostrand Reinhold Company.

Lockhart, L.L. (1987). A reexamination of the effects of race and social class on the incidence of marital violence: A search for reliable differences. *Journal of Marriage and the Family, 49,* 603-610.

National Coalition Against Domestic Violence (1987). *National Coalition Against Domestic Violence statistics paper.* Washington, DC: Women Together.

The American College of Obstetricians and Gynecologists (1989). *The American College of Obstetricians and Gynecologists fact sheet.* Washington, DC: Women Together.

Walker, L.E. (1984). *The battered woman syndrome.* New York: Springer Publishing Company.

Mary Alice Saunders-Robinson, MSN, MEd is assistant professor, Division of Nursing, Ursuline College in Pepper Pike, Ohio and is a Charter Member of ABNF.

Used with permission: Mary Alice Saunders-Robinson (Fall 1991) *The ABNF Journal* (an official publication of the Association of Black Nursing Faculty, Inc.), a copyright of Tucker Publications, Inc., P.O. Box 580, Lisle, IL 60532.

The Christian Abused Woman

Nancy Kilgore

The Christian abused woman presents a need for a particular understanding and should be spoken with skillfully. She has several messages that contribute to her guilt and not leaving:

- It is your Christian duty to forgive.
- The Bible instructs us to love each other. The family is very important to God.
- Sacrifice for your family. A wife is secondary to her husband.
- The Christian woman must keep her family together.
- Pray for a violent man. God can change him.
- Put your marriage in God's hands.

Be aware of Scripture that she will use to rationalize inexcusable abuse:

> Love your enemies, do good to those who hate you, bless those who curse you, pray for those who abuse you. To him who strikes you on the cheek, offer the other also. (Luke 6:27-29.)

> Let love be genuine; hate what is evil, hold fast to what is good. . . Bless those who persecute you;

> bless and do not curse them. . . Repay no one evil
> for evil. . . Beloved, never avenge yourselves, but
> leave it to the wrath of God; for it is written,
> "Vengeance is mine, I will repay, says the Lord."
> (Romans 12:9, 14, 17, 19.)

> Do what is right; then if men speak against you,
> calling you evil names, they will become ashamed
> of themselves for falsely accusing you when you
> have only done what is good. Remember, if God
> wants you to suffer, it is better to suffer for doing
> good than for doing wrong! Christ also suffered.
> (1 Peter 3:16-18.)

> Love is very patient and kind, never jealous or
> envious, never boastful or proud, never haughty
> or selfish or rude. Love does not demand its own
> way. It is not irritable or touchy. It does not hold
> grudges and will hardly even notice when others do
> it wrong. (1 Corinthians 13.)

It is extremely important to be acquainted with Scripture. She
can quote Scripture. You must be able to quote Scripture as well
and have comeback statements:

> The Bible is trying to teach us that we should not
> act out of vengeance. We should not seek to hurt
> the one who hurt us. To turn the other cheek
> means that we do not return abuse for abuse. We
> can walk away from abuse. The Bible does not
> endorse us to take abuse. There isn't anything
> loving when a man continues to destroy his family
> with violence. Violence is evil.

> You can pray for the man who abuses you. You
> can hope that he recognizes the harm that he is

doing. You do not need to stay there and be abused while you wait for him to make the decision to change his abusive patterns. You can get safe shelter for yourself and your children. You can pray for him while you're there.

You should not have to live in terror. Your home is your sanctuary. You have the right to feel safe. You are a child of God. If your house was on fire, you would call the fire department, wouldn't you? The fire department would help save your house. There are shelters that will provide help for an abused woman who is suffering from abuse. Your home is in crisis. Think of it this way: your home is on fire. You need to call for help.

And last but not least, be prepared for this Scripture:

Honor Christ by submitting to each other. You wives must submit to your husbands' leadership in the same way you submit to the Lord. . . .

You could reply:

This passage does not say that a woman is supposed to put up with abuse. It doesn't mean that a man is to lead a woman. This Scripture is the most misread part of the Bible. Read the next statement in the passage: *And you husbands, show the same kind of love to your wives as Christ showed to the church when he died for her . . .* This passage means that both men and women should show the utmost love and respect towards each other.

Excerpted from *Sourcebook For Working With Battered Women*, © 1992 by Nancy Kilgore. All rights reserved. To order, contact Volcano Press, Inc., P.O. Box 270 FVR, Volcano, CA 95689. (209) 296-3445.

When Love Is Not Enough: Spousal Abuse in Rabbinic and Contemporary Judaism

Rabbi Julie R. Spitzer

DOMESTIC VIOLENCE IN TODAY'S JEWISH COMMUNITY

Examples of abuse in Jewish homes have been described in studies and by the media. For example, Giller and Goldsmith describe an Orthodox couple, the husband a rabbi and the wife active in the Jewish community, who were going through divorce proceedings, mainly because of the psychological abuse of the wife. She had also reported physical abuse by her husband of both herself and the children. When the *Bet Din* completed the proceedings, the husband became so violently enraged that the wife and the rabbis locked themselves in the house and called the police for protection (1980, p. 140).

As described in a *Jewish Telegraphic Agency* article, an abused Jewish woman told participants at a conference that, in the first six weeks of her marriage, her husband slapped her and pulled her hair. Her husband apologized, but a week later he hit her hard enough to make her black and blue. The beatings consistently became more severe. She said she went to her rabbi, who said to her, "What did you do to deserve such a beating?" She went into hiding for five days and then, having nowhere else to go, returned home. She said her husband subsequently stomped on her, although she was two months pregnant (Gallob, 1982, p. 4).

Perhaps the most public case of abuse in a Jewish home began making headlines in the fall of 1988. In its wake, a little girl was dead, beaten to death over an extended period by an abusive father. She had been left vulnerable by a mother, who was herself a victim of abuse and violence inflicted by the same man. The names Joel Steinberg, Lisa Steinberg, and Hedda Nussbaum were particularly noticed by the Jewish community. They were, like so many members of the community, upper-middle-class, well-educated, professional people. Hardly the kind that most think about when such horrible accounts of abuse are detailed in the daily newspapers and news reports. More than any one case in recent memory, this tragedy took the Jewish community by surprise, giving many who had never thought of abuse as a problem among Jews reason to take notice.

These examples indicate that domestic violence is currently found within the Jewish community. The question is, to what extent does it exist? Researchers in the Los Angeles Jewish community investigated the following hypotheses:

1. Violence is not absent in synagogue-affiliated families.

2. Whatever violence occurs is not exposed to synagogue professionals by the families in which it occurs.

3. Rabbis have some knowledge of the problem of Jewish family violence.

4. Jews do not believe that family violence is a problem in the Jewish community.

(Giller and Goldsmith, 1980, p. 104)

Giller and Goldsmith's interviews with rabbis and Jewish social service professionals and surveys of 209 Los Angeles synagogue-affiliated Jews yielded some surprising findings. They report that the responses strongly support the first hypothesis, that violence is not absent among synagogue-affiliated families (p. 142), shattering the myth of the perfect Jewish family. The violence includes spouse and child abuse. Of the 22 reported incidents of spouse abuse, the husband abused the wife in 20 cases and in two cases the wife struck the husband.

When respondents were asked if they perceived family violence as a problem in the Jewish community, 39% said it was, and 61% said it was not, although 50% had reported actual instances of violence. On the other hand, 62% of those surveyed believed that family violence was a problem in the general community (Goldsmith, 1983-84, p. 21). Although many people reported cases of abuse, the problem was not considered significant in the Jewish community. Abuse in the Jewish community is denied; however, respondents encourage providing support services for victims of domestic violence.

Interviews with professionals in the field of human services also support Giller and Goldsmith's hypotheses. A worker in a rape crisis center was able to describe 21 cases of Jewish women (who clearly identified themselves as such) reporting violence in a six-month period. One worker in a hospital emergency room stated that approximately 20% incidence of wife battering in the Jewish community was equal to that of the general population (Giller and Goldsmith, p. 129). All of the psychiatrists and psychologists consulted in the study had seen Jewish women who had been battered.

Jewish family violence is also reported by social workers in Jewish agencies, such as Jewish Family Service. A survey conducted by the Jewish Board of Family Services in the New York area also found that of 2,600 families seen by the agency, one in 20 "have experienced incidents of physical abuse of the wife" (Gallob, 1982a, p. 4). The population for this study was about 70% Jewish. Moreover, in an interview in the Summer 1988 issue of *Lilith*, Barbara Harris, Director of the Transition Center, a kosher shelter for battered women and children in Queens, NY, reported that "there is domestic violence in 15-19% of Jewish homes in this country (deBeers, p. 6). As of 1995, Harris has been working on spousal abuse in the New York Jewish community for more than 14 years.

Why aren't abused women (and men) coming forward with their problems? If indeed abuse exists within the Jewish community, why aren't we hearing more about it? Why does the myth that such violence is absent from our homes and synagogues persist? In an article, "Family Violence Same as Non-Jews," in the *Jewish Post and Opinion*, Ellen Goldsmith writes:

> Violence in Jewish families is as prevalent as in the
> general population, . . . but it is the reluctance of
> Jewish victims to speak out that creates the myth
> that it is absent from the Jewish community.
> (1983a, p. 6)

The myth of the perfect Jewish family contributes to the silence of the Jewish community. Jewish families, according to this myth, are exceptionally close-knit, with loving fathers and doting husbands.

When abuse occurs, Jewish women often blame themselves (as do non-Jewish women) and see themselves as having failed a tradition of perfect Jewish family harmony. If a woman's upbringing was sheltered, she may be particularly shocked if her husband becomes abusive. The woman may derive her identity from her role as wife and mother, and as keeper of the peace in the home. This idea of domestic tranquility, of *shalom bayit*, often works against the woman in an abusive situation. She is told that she must bear her burden and appease her husband, because it is her job to keep the family together.

Another myth that discourages Jewish women from seeking help is that of the exalted standing of family values within the Jewish community. Betsy Giller points out, "Jews have the need to deny the occurrence of wife abuse because it is considered such a great *shanda* [shame] within our culture. This is related to our minority status within American society, and our subsequent need to prove and assert that we are 'better' than others" (Karlin, 1983, p. 6). The fear of damage to the Jewish community's reputation is one of the most debilitating factors in the fight against Jewish domestic violence. If everyone is afraid of admitting to a problem, then nothing can be done to control the problem. The irony is that the very emphasis Jewish tradition places on family values may be preventing us from recognizing that a problem exists.

Negative cultural images of the Jewish woman enable those hearing women's accounts of abuse to discount them. The stereotype "Jewish American Princess" (JAP) and attitudes, such as "JAPs are always complaining about something; it really can't be all that bad," conceal the problem of abuse. In addition, modern literary depictions of the Jewish woman henpecking her husband ("who couldn't harm a flea") contribute to the misconception that it is Jewish women not men who assert dominance and that Jewish men would never hurt their wives or children.

Many Jewish women fear they would damage their husband's reputation in the community if they were to come forward. This fear of coming forward to Jewish professionals helps to keep the awareness of spouse abuse in the community at a deceptive minimum. Giller and Goldsmith found that Jews are more likely to turn to mental health professionals in times of crisis, rather than synagogue or community professionals. Only four respondents of 209 reported speaking to a rabbi. Most often the respondents reported speaking to other family members and friends (Giller and

Goldsmith, pp. 162-63). However, although only 10 spoke to any synagogue professional (cantor, educator, or rabbi), 83% felt that synagogue professionals should be involved in trying to help with the problems of family violence (Giller and Goldsmith, pp. 162-63).

An important corollary to the respondent's view of the role of synagogue professionals in Giller and Goldsmith's study was their belief that more training in this area is needed (pp. 162-63). The need for training is also reflected in the following vignettes:

> Sarah had been beaten by her husband throughout their married life. She was 60 years old when she finally sought shelter at St. Joseph's House (a shelter for battered women in the Midwest), but then her rabbi telephoned and convinced her to go back home. When she returned to the shelter, she was bruised from another beating. The rabbi called again, and again he persuaded her to give her repentant husband another chance. The third time Sarah returned to the shelter, she had a broken rib. This time the rabbi called and said her husband was so repentant he wanted to take her on a trip to the Holy Land. (Papa, p. 1)

Another case involves a woman who went to her rabbi seeking a divorce from her abusive husband. The rabbi asked how many times her husband beat her in the past year. He supplied her answer. "Let's assume once a month. That's only 12 times a year. That does not make sense to get divorced" (Brown, 1982). The rabbis in the two cases above sought to maintain the marriages without responding to the pain and danger in which the women lived.

The rabbi plays a different role in the last vignette which concerns an upper-middle-class Jewish woman, a lawyer, whose fiancee beat her. She hid it, even at meetings of a program for abused women, Battered Women's Alternatives, where she was a legal advisor. She finally called the wedding off as the violence escalated. Her rabbi kicked the fiancee out of his study four days before the wedding because of the abusive treatment she suffered (Gallob, 1982).

In their study, Giller and Goldsmith interviewed a sample of rabbis in the Los Angeles Jewish community. All eight of the rabbis interviewed saw counseling as a part of their rabbinic role. When asked if family violence was a problem in the Jewish community, the replies were varied. One said, "Yes, anything a non-Jewish neighbor would do, a Jew would do. A Jew who seeks the uniqueness of being Jewish wouldn't do such things." A second answered, "Yes, but Jews have a better record than the general population." And a third said, "It might be, but I would be very surprised if there was anything like that going on in my congregation" (Giller and Goldsmith, p. 138).

Later, during the same interviews, the rabbis were asked what they would do if they were given information about a case of family violence in their congregation. Seven said they would become personally involved, one said he would "never shy away from problems, but would provide help for the family," and the last replied that he "didn't like to be intrusive" (Giller and Goldsmith, p. 140). All who said they would take action would talk first with the family.

If women and men are reluctant to speak directly to rabbis about domestic violence, rabbis will most likely remain unaware of its existence within the synagogue. Part of this is solved by making rabbis and other synagogue professionals aware of the extent of the problem. Part of the rabbis's lack of awareness may also be solved by listening more closely to what his/her congregants are saying about their relationships with one another. Giller suggests that, "rabbis may need to take such leading statements from female congregants as 'my husband has a terrible temper' to mean that their husbands vent their anger in a physical way" (Karlin, p. 10).

Additional factors which influence whether or not Jewish battered women and men seek help are related to the specific needs of Orthodox Jewish women. It is feared that in many such communities, especially among ultra-Orthodox and Chasidic Jews, rabbis generally counsel women to return to their husbands. Many women accept this advice without question. Special care must be taken to work with Orthodox women within their own frames of reference. The religious system of which they are a part can still be of some comfort to them (as it was for the more right-wing Christian women). It has been suggested that such women consider going to the rabbi's wife first. Perhaps she would be a sympathetic ear and yet have access to the power and authority of her husband. To some extent, the special needs of Orthodox Jewish women have increasingly been addressed by more facilities around the country. Several shelters, in large metropolitan areas, have arrangements for kosher food, others even have their own kosher facilities. It is fast becoming an irrelevant argument that shelters and safe home networks are unaware of the needs or unwilling to provide for the needs of traditionally observant Jewish women.

Another kind of factor comes into focus with abused women who are Holocaust survivors. For these women, the violence of the abusive relationship may pale by comparison to what they have already suffered. They may not even be fully aware of the extent of the violence in their own homes. Sunny Fischer of *Bitachon* in Chicago tells of a speaking engagement at which one woman challenged what she was explaining about spouse abuse (personal communication). The woman inquired, "Don't you think that a few beatings are worth it to save the marriage?" She was a Holocaust survivor. For her, marriage was paramount. It meant procreation, new life, someone who did care in between the beatings. It was as if the beatings were insignificant. Such women need to be heard and counseled with great sensitivity. Male survivors who are abusive may also have special needs. Knowing some background information on the abused women and their partners may be quite valuable for the counselor.

Two additional reasons for the Jewish women's reluctance to seek help or to leave abusive relationships have been suggested; in her article in the National Coalition Against Domestic Violence Newsletter, *Voice*, Liz Cramer suggests that some Jewish women don't even make the first call for help because of a "perceived indifference to their needs," or because they fear subtle anti-Semitism if they identify openly as Jewish women (Fall, 1990). "But You Can't Imagine," an op-ed piece in *The New York Times* written by an anonymous Jewish woman, indicates that she responds to the frequent question "why didn't you leave" by explaining that her batterer would follow her and beat her no matter where she was (Feb. 2, 1989). Even after a divorce or a separation, Jewish women, like other battered women, live in fear that the abuse will continue.

Research, surveys and interviews indicate that Jews do experience family violence in all segments of the Jewish population (across all socioeconomic, ethnic and religious lines). That families experiencing violence are not turning to synagogue professionals for help and violence is not acknowledged within the Jewish community (Giller and Goldsmith, p. 168). Moreover, the many burdens felt by Jewish women in abusive relationships help to explain, according to Barbara Harris, why Jewish women tend to live with the abuse longer; 8-10 years on average, while non-Jewish women come forward sooner, 3-5 years after the battering begins (Kuperstein, 1989, p. 10).

In the last several years, however, there have been some notable improvements. Although the numbers of Jewish women seeking help from synagogue professionals is still relatively small, there are more who are finding that their rabbis, cantors and educators are better informed than they previously were. Workshops and training sessions have been offered on both North American and regional levels. So too, the Jewish community as a whole has made rapid strides in responding to the issue of abuse in Jewish homes.

Battered Jewish women in Israel face problems: some of which are similar to those faced by Jewish women in North America, but also some problems which are based in the nature of Israeli society. A typical story is that of Nira and Yossi. Nira went to the rabbinate seeking help after suffering her husband's abuse for some time. They told her to stop provoking her husband. If he beat her, she must deserve it (Ben Shaul, 1983, p. 1).

The exact number of battered women in Israel is uncertain. Estimates range from 60,000 to 150,000, at least 10% of married Israeli women (Fein, 1983, p. 19; Yaron, 1984, p. 5; Ben Shaul, p. 2). Ruth Rasnic, director of the shelter for battered women in Herziliya, notes that her sources in the rabbinate tell her that four out of every five divorces contain complaints of physical abuse of the wife. She feels that up to 25% of married women in Israel are abused (Yaron, 1984, p. 5).

Israeli women report not only physical abuse, but sexual abuse as well. Helen Fein (1983) states that this includes marital rape, i.e., forced relations when a woman is ritually prohibited to her husband, which is particularly disturbing for Orthodox women. Social welfare workers are not always trained to counsel victims of such abuse. The rabbinate has been slow to take action, believing that *shalom bayit* must be upheld.

Ze'ev Falk, professor of law at Hebrew University, contends, "The principle of *shalom bayit* . . . has been turned into a euphemism for procedural steps to attain the opposite result" (Ben Shaul, 1983). According to Ruth Rasnic, "The policy of the rabbinate is *sh'lom bayit* and not what goes on in the house. The house is the man's castle—but why must it be the woman's dungeon?" (Yaron, p. 5). Jewish women in Israel must abide by religious law which allows only the husband to file for divorce. If a woman separates from her husband, as she may choose to do, she can be declared a rebellious wife and be denied child support payments. With finances as bad as they are in Israel, this is often a crucial factor in her decision to stay or leave. Additionally, the plight of the battered woman in Israel is profoundly affected by the experience of living in a society torn by war and terrorism. Violence is considered an acceptable alternative in settling many disputes; it does seem to exacerbate the problem of spouse abuse.

Battering is no longer the most underreported crime in Israel. Largely due to the efforts of several members of the Knesset, the government and the citizens are waking up to the problems of domestic violence in Israel. When MK Marcia Friedman first raised the issue in 1976, she was laughed at. MK Tamar Eshel brought up the issue again in 1979, with less argument. Today, government-sponsored symposia are held around the country. Shelters have been somewhat successful at changing public attitudes, but ironically, their funding from the Ministry of Welfare and Labor remains less than adequate. Considering the fact that battering affects the entire spectrum of Israeli society (middle and working classes, Ashkenazim and Sephardim) much more needs to be done.

Just as in North America, there have been strides taken in the response to abuse in Israeli homes. Some of these efforts are funded by the New Israel Fund, NA'AMAT and the Women's International Zionist Organization.

PROGRAMS IN ISRAEL

Since 1977, feminists have been organizing shelters for battered women in Israel. The oldest shelter is the one found in Haifa: Women for Women. Begun in November of 1977, it offered protection for battered women in all of Israel. Its short-range goals revolved around protection and counseling. Long-range goals emphasized public awareness. Each year the shelter provides refuge, support and counseling for women and their children. Following condemnation of their first location, women and men from the area staged a sit-in, embarrassing the government into funding a new home. Today, although financially troubled, the shelter is the largest in Israel.

In 1978, a shelter for battered women opened in Herziliya. It was named the Carmela Nakash Women's Aid Center in memory of a resident who was murdered by her husband at the front gate. Funding for the shelter comes in part from the government and

in part from private donations, but many volunteers are needed
to keep the operation running. An additional service of this shelter makes phone counseling available to women around the country. The director reports that the shelter is helped by good
relationships with the police and the local community.

Good relationships with one's neighbors have not always been
the case with Beit Tzipporah, the Jerusalem shelter for battered
women, which is housed in a religious quarter of the city. The
director has said, "I'm happy to say that the attitude of the neighbors has changed. They began bringing cakes and things for
Shabbat. And we've even had women in the neighborhood seek
shelter here—including a rabbi's wife" (Nevisky, 1984, p. 36).
Nevisky also notes that the shelter has raised public consciousness, simply by virtue of its existence. Hospitals, social workers,
police, and even cab drivers refer women to the shelter.

A fourth shelter was opened in Ashdod to serve the Negev
area which was to have opened in Be'er Sheva, but the mayor's
office was opposed to the idea. The shelters in Israel described
above were in place by 1985. Since then, a growing number of
resources have been developed to meet the needs of the abused
and abusers among Israeli families, including a court monitoring
program for cases of domestic violence and rape in Haifa (Shire,
December 1994, p. 22).

SUMMARY

The Jewish community is not immune to the pain of family violence, yet the denial myths continue to persist. Both in this country and in Israel, abused Jewish women are beginning to come
forward with their stories. They seek help from Jewish professionals who are often inadequately prepared to help them or their
abusive partners. They feel trapped in their relationships and
further trapped by a community which still may do little to acknowledge their pain and confusion.

Surveys conducted in the Jewish communities of New York and Los Angeles demonstrate that spouse abuse is a reality. Statistics from Israel do not challenge American findings. If such is the case, why are these women and men so reluctant to come forward? For some, it would be a greater problem to "embarrass" the community, than to publicly acknowledge their problems. Others are concerned with too many people finding out, so they seek help from those outside of the community, or keep it strictly "family business." Many are not sure that there is someone willing to help them, or have already met with denial and otherwise unsatisfactory results when they sought help. Myths about perfect Jewish families, Jewish mothers, and Jewish American Princesses only exacerbate the situation.

Many programs have been developed in the last 10 years to aid Jewish families with problems of abuse. In most major metropolitan communities, hotlines, counseling, and even shelters are provided by specially trained professionals and volunteers. National organizations are beginning to publicize information about domestic violence among Jewish families. The myths are slowly crumbling.

As seen throughout this chapter, during the past decade, activity has increased in the Jewish community in response to the problems of abuse in Jewish families. Despite all of the hard work, however, there are still far too many Jewish women who feel as if they are the "only ones" who suffer from abuse. One Philadelphia rabbi notes "the single most powerful factor contributing to domestic violence is the ability to get away with it" (Gluck, 1989, p. 49). And Dr. Samuel Klagsbrun, noted for his work with Hedda Nussbaum, told a group of New York rabbis, "Maintaining *shalom bayis* is hardly possible in the instance of domestic violence. . . . Be willing to call the authorities. Our obligation is to rescue the children and wives from an unchanging situation. Don't fall prey to the community impulse to keep the family together. Rabbis have to take a stand" (Gilman, 1989, p. 24). This is only the beginning. More work must be done, not only to help train rabbis and other synagogue and community professionals, but also to engender awareness within the Jewish community as a whole.

RECOMMENDED READING ON SPOUSAL ABUSE

General Works

Alpert, Jane (1994). Stop Violence Against Women: Strategies for Ending Violence Against Women. New York: Now Legal Defense and Education Fund.

Martin, Del (1981). Battered Wives. Volcano, CA: Volcano Press.

NiCarthy, Ginny (1989). *Getting Free: A Handbook for Women In Abusive Relationships.* Seattle: Seal Press. This book also comes in an easy-to-read handbook form, written by NiCarthy and Sue Davidson: *You Can Be Free* (1980). Seattle: Seal Press.

Walker, Lenore E. (1979). *The Battered Woman.* New York: Harper and Row.

Of Particular Religious and/or Jewish Interest

Bowler, Lee H. (1982, December). "Battered Women and the Clergy," *The Journal of Pastoral Care, 36*(4), pp. 226-235.

Commission on Social Action and Public Policy (1995). *Judaism and Domestic Violence.* New York: United Synagogue of Conservative Judaism.

Cuevas, C., Dankowski, K., Giggans, P. and Ledley, E. (1989). *Surviving Domestic Violence: A Safety and Empowerment Guide for Battered Women.* Los Angeles: The Los Angeles Commission on Assaults Against Women and The Family Violence Project of Jewish Family Service. (Available in English and Hebrew.)

Fortune, Marie M. (1991). *Violence in the Family—A Workshop Curriculum for Clergy and Other Helpers.* Cleveland: The Pilgrim Press.

Giller, Betsy, and Ellen Goldsmith (1980). *All in the Family: A Study of Intra-Familial Violence in the Los Angeles Jewish Community.* Unpublished master's thesis, HUC-JIR/University of Southern California, Los Angeles.

Gluck, Robert (1988). "Jewish Men and Violence in the Home: Unlikely Companions?" In Brod, Ed., *A Mensch Among Men.* Freedom, CA: Crossing Press.

Greenberg, Irving (1990, April). Abuse in Jewish Families. *Moment, 15*(2), p. 49.

Harris, Barbara (1981, October 16). "Helping the Abused Jewish Wife or Child," *Sh 'ma, 11*(219), pp. 145-6.

The Growing Problem of Spouse Abuse (1983, Summer). *The William Petschek National Jewish Family Center Newsletter, 3*(3). New York: American Jewish Committee.

Hispanic-American Battered Women: Why Consider Cultural Differences?

Sara Torres

Wife abuse occurs in families from all cultural and ethnic groups (Straus, Gelles, & Steinmetz, 1980; Walker, 1984), and intervention policies and practices in treating wife abuse should accommodate the diverse cultural backgrounds of battered women. However, information on the cultural aspects of wife abuse and how it differs between ethnic groups is sparse; most research on wife abuse has focused on the Anglo-American population. The majority of the literature on wife abuse ignores cross-cultural differences or acknowledges that cross-cultural differences in wife abuse have been minimally explored (Carrillo & Marrujo, 1984; Straus, et al., 1980).

An ethnic heritage is a manifestation of attitudes, values, personality, and behavior. Ethnic groups receive different societal opportunities and rewards, and they share certain attitudes and goals (Lystad, 1985). Though America is composed of many ethnic groups, the emphasis has been on assimilation — that is, conformity with Anglo-American values. Services rendered to ethnic groups are judged and categorized in accordance with adherence to white values. Ethnic and cultural diversity remains a reality and constitutes the "fabric" of American society (Cafferty & Chestang, 1976). Cultural factors are relevant in all aspects of the helping process if battered women are to be served effectively and sensitively.

Nurses and others providing services to battered women can incorporate cultural factors into plans of care. Nurses provide care to families in more health care settings than do any other health care providers and are thus in a position to help victims of family violence and to prevent, identify, and intervene in wife abuse (Campbell & Humphreys, 1984).

There have been few research studies investigating wife abuse in the Hispanic population. The comparative study reported in the following article obtained information on the cross-cultural aspects of wife abuse between Hispanic-American and Anglo-American victims (Torres, in press). Interviews were conducted with 25 Hispanic-American and 25 Anglo-American women residing in shelters for battered women. The study focused on women's attitudes towards wife abuse; their perception of what constitutes wife abuse; the nature, severity, and frequency of the abuse; and their response to the abuse. There were more similarities than differences in the manifestation of wife abuse among the Hispanic-American and Anglo-American battered women studied. There were some significant differences, however, with implications for treatment and other interventions. The following is a discussion of the most significant differences.

There were no significant differences between Hispanic-American and Anglo women in the severity and frequency of abuse, but there were some differences between the two groups in their attitudes towards wife abuse and their perceptions of what constitutes wife abuse. The Hispanic-American subjects were more tolerant towards wife abuse than Anglo-American subjects were. That is, such acts as hitting or verbal abuse had to occur more frequently to be considered abusive by Hispanic-American women. Furthermore, Hispanic-American women had a slightly different perception of what constitutes wife abuse. Some acts perceived as abusive by the Anglo-American women were not considered as abusive by the Hispanic-American women; they included verbal abuse and failure to provide adequate food and shelter. The perception of acts considered to be "physical abuse" was basically the same for Hispanic-American and Anglo-American women. For acts considered to be "emotional abuse," Hispanic-American women showed more tolerance than Anglo-American women.

The choices Hispanic-American women have in response to being abused were similar to those of most Anglo-American women. Should a Hispanic-American woman leave her home, she encounters the problems basic to all women. Nevertheless, one of the most important cross-cultural differences between the two groups was in the victim's response to physical abuse. This study showed that culture, family and religion were the major factors affecting the manner in which a Hispanic-American woman reacted to being battered.

The family was the most important factor that entered into a Hispanic-American woman's decision whether to leave or stay in the battering relationship. Hispanic women reported that they stayed in the relationship because of their children and threats to family members; Anglo-American women stayed because of love of the abuser and not having a place to go. Forty percent of Hispanic women compared with 20 percent of Anglo-American women said they left because of their children. Also, the reason most frequently given by Hispanic-American women for going back to their spouses was "the children." The Hispanic-American women in the study tended to stay longer than Anglo-American women in a relationship with an abusive spouse before seeking assistance, due to pressure from their families and for the sake of their children. Also, Hispanic-American women were hit more frequently in front of other family members than were Anglo-American women. Hispanic-American women left and came back to their spouses more times than Anglo-American women. Thus, it is important not to assume that because a Hispanic-American battered woman has asked for help, she may leave her home.

Therefore, in working with Hispanic-American battered women, it is necessary to be aware of the family roles, traditions, and expectations that are peculiar to the Hispanic culture. The attitudes a woman's culture holds towards sex roles will affect a woman's self-image. Also, a Hispanic-American woman is likely to be especially sensitive and react to criticism or perceived non-acceptance of herself, her family, culture, language, husband (or other male relative), economic situation, level of education, consciousness, and/or degree of dependence/independence. In addition, some of these women may be victims of racial prejudice, which makes family and community ties increase in importance.

Catholicism, the predominant religious experience for Hispanics, considers the maintenance of the family unit to be of primary importance, at times, even at the expense of the woman's well-being. This also can affect a woman's reaction to being abused. A higher percentage of Hispanic-American women surveyed had sought assistance from religious organizations before coming to the shelter. In addition, some Hispanic-Americans practice "curanderismo," the art and science of using herbs, prayers, and rituals to cure physical, spiritual, and emotional ills. Before some of the Hispanic women sought help from agencies they had practiced curanderismo first.

Other factors that may affect the reaction of Hispanic-American women to abuse are their immigrant status and their knowledge of the English language. Being of immigrant status is stressful, and if a woman is in this country illegally, this may further inhibit her from seeking help. Also, immigrants often leave family and friends — their major sources of psychological and financial support — behind. Intervention could be focused on assisting these individuals to become familiar with resources in the community and to develop support groups, that is, church, a battered woman's support group, and so forth.

Inability to speak English provides its own constraints. English-speaking nurse advocates need to be aware of possible language difficulties. Even though a woman may be bilingual, it is difficult to express oneself in a second language while under stress.

She may not understand professional jargon, so when possible, treatment should be conducted in the individual's native language. In conclusion, intervention policies and practices in treating wife abuse should accommodate the diverse cultural backgrounds of battered women. Nurses have a responsibility and an obligation to deliver services to all battered women without regard to racial or ethnic origins. At the same time, we need to recognize the probability of important differences between cultural groups and be careful about assumptions.

REFERENCES

Cafferty, P. S. J., & Chestang, L. (Eds.) (1976). *The diverse society: Implications for social policy.* NASW.

Campbell, J., & Humphreys, J. (1984). *Nursing care of victims of family violence.* Reston, VA: Reston Publishing.

Carrillo, E. A., & Marrujo, R. (1984). Acculturation and domestic violence in the Hispanic community. Unpublished manuscript.

Lystad, M. H. (1985). Family violence: A mental health perspective. *Emotional first aid.* Unpublished manuscript.

Straus, M. A., Gelles, R. J., & Steinmetz, S. K. (1980). *Behind closed doors.* New York: Anchor Books.

Torres, S. (in press). A comparative analysis of wife abuse among Anglo-American and Mexican-American battered women: Attitudes, nature, severity, frequency, and response to the abuse. *Victimology.*

Walker, L. E. (1984). *The battered woman syndrome.* New York: Springer.

Sara Torres, RN, PhD, is Assistant Professor in the Division of Nursing at Florida Atlantic University.

Reponse: To the Victimization of Women and Children, Vol. 10, No. 3 (October 1987). Reprinted with the permission of Response, Inc., 4136 Leland St., Chevy Chase, MD 20815. Phone/fax: (301) 951-0039.

Some Common Characteristics of Children in Abusive Homes

Families under stress produce children under stress. If you are being abused and have children, they are affected by your abuse. Moreover, spouse abuse is a form of child abuse. Hurting someone the child loves also hurts the child. Children in abusive homes may experience the following:

SEE, HEAR VIOLENCE

Children hear frightening noises, threats, and screams. In addition, they often experience the same abusive behavior used against the spouse, i.e., the abusive parent may embarrass, hit, or threaten them.

FEEL POWERLESS

Children of abuse feel a complete sense of powerlessness. They cannot stop the abuse; they cannot fix the abusive relationship; and they cannot save the parent or siblings who are abused. Younger children are powerless to leave situations which are (or are seen as) life-threatening.

FEEL FEAR

Just as a fetus can hear music and respond to familiar voices outside the womb, the fetus can hear arguing and be jolted or awakened by it. The fetus also experiences the mother's fear and her injuries during the battering. The fetus also may sustain damage to its brain and developing nervous system as a result of physical abuse, verbal punches, and other repeated assaults on the mother.

Infants and young children are immobile, defenseless, and without language skills. They may experience a terrifying "storm of angry energy" around them during abuse. Their first and most lasting impression is that the world is a frightening place. Issues of personal safety, abandonment, and betrayal result. These feelings often follow the child into adulthood.

Older children may experience pain or fear for their lives. They also fear what will happen to them if mother is hurt or if father goes to jail. Children also become caretakers, comforting the abused parent and/or siblings. In addition, children may become "crutches" for the abused parent, e.g., the parent may turn to the child for companionship instead of resolving the troubled marital relationship. This is not a child's role.

EXPERIENCE EMOTIONAL ABANDONMENT

Fighting parents cannot attend to the child's emotional needs. Often, the ups and downs of abusive homes are ignored: the child feels anxiety and agitation as the tension builds up; the child feels fear and helplessness during the battering; and then the child feels guilt and shame afterward. Without intervention, these feelings are never resolved.

DEVELOP LOW SELF-ESTEEM

Children of abuse do not develop healthy self-esteem. They often blame themselves for the arguments and the violence. They may believe that it is their own failing that they receive little love. Violence also creates low self-worth. For example, if a parent does not realize what happens to the child who witnesses the abuse, the child may believe that, "My feelings (of fear or pain) are ignored, and my needs (for peace and comforting) are not being met, therefore, I must not be important."

DEVELOP BEHAVIORAL PROBLEMS

Children of abuse learn to abuse themselves and others. They are at risk of alcohol and drug abuse. They also may develop eating and sleeping disorders and other symptoms of traumatic stress. Moreover, many boys learn to abuse, and girls learn to accept and expect abuse. Moreover, children of abuse do not have good role models for resolving conflict, communicating their feelings, or for building close relationships.

DEVELOP PROBLEMS WITH ANGER

Many boys learn how to lash out or "go off" on others. They may take out their frustration in school by bullying others. They may become aggressive, rebellious, turn to crime, or act out sexually. Girls may become very angry with their mothers for not protecting them. They also learn to turn their anger inward or may become abusive themselves. Also children may feel anger toward the abusive parent and then blame themselves for hating the batterer.

FEEL ISOLATED

Violence represents betrayal. It interferes with the child's ability to get close to his or her parents. In addition, because trust in the parents has been violated, a child of abuse is frequently unable to trust others. Closeness equals emotional or physical devastation, and the child's deepest fear is that others will beat them, torture them, abandon them, or emotionally destroy them the way their parent(s) did. This feeling of isolation can create profound loneliness and an unwillingness to risk sharing themselves with others.

TAKE ON ADULT ROLES PREMATURELY

Girls may become super-responsible, taking on tasks which parents neglect. The child may spend a lot of energy trying to make peace. He or she may separate the fighting parents, call the police, or try to "save" the abused parent or abused siblings. These are not a child's jobs.

EXPERIENCE DEPRESSION AND FLASHBACKS

Children of abuse often experience low-grade, long-term depression. Abused children also experience flashbacks of the violent episodes they have witnessed. They may also block out violent scenes for years.

The Rod of Guidance

A phrase often bantered about as though it were sacred is "spare the rod and spoil the child." That is not a quotation from the Bible, but is based on Proverbs 13:24, "He that spareth his rod hateth his son, but he that loveth him chasteneth him betimes [KJV]." There are people who use this verse as a mandate for corporal punishment of their children. Is that what the Bible really teaches?

Scripture is often quoted, misquoted, or applied in a manner contrary to its intent because the words and/or the context of their use are not understood. Portions of the Bible taken out of context have been used to substantiate both sides of a given argument. Poor scholarship may be the culprit.

One of the most popular portions of the Bible is Psalm 23. Verse 4 reads, "Your *rod* and your staff they c*omfort* me [NRSV, emphasis added]." The assurance of comfort is not easily reconciled with corporal punishment.

The Hebrew word for "rod" used in both the Psalms and Proverbs passages is *shabat*. A *shabat* is specifically the rod used by a shepherd in caring for sheep. The *shabat* has five common practical uses: (1) it is the symbol of the shepherd's guardianship of the sheep; (2) it can be thrown with great accuracy just beyond the wandering sheep to send the animal scurrying back to the flock; (3) it can be used to ward off an intruder and protect the sheep from any animals that may attack; (4) it is used to count the sheep as they pass under it; and (5) it is used to part the wool in order to examine the sheep for disease, wounds, or defects, which may then be treated. There is no evidence that the rod is ever used to strike the sheep.

A biblical scholar notes that the rod may symbolize correction, that is, firm yet kindly discipline and instruction. The five uses of the shepherd's *shabat* may be interpolated into parental guidelines. Parents should provide (1) security — let the child know he or she is loved, cared for, accepted; (2) guidance — teach the child and keep him or her from going astray; (3) protection — not allow outsiders to hurt the child; (4) evaluation — make the child feel he or she counts and monitor his or her progress; and (5) diagnosis — look for signs of anxiety or pain in the child and seek out treatment and healing.

The rod *is* a comfort to the sheep. Similarly, loving, firm discipline can be a comfort to the child. In the second half of Proverbs 13:24, the Hebrew word *yasar*, given as "chasteneth" in the KJV, is more accurately translated "disciplines." *Yasar* has both a positive and negative connotation, each equally balanced. It does mean "to chasten, correct, punish," but it also means "to admonish, exhort (build up), instruct." The use of *yasar* in the verse injects a thought of love and a thought of appropriateness.

Another biblical scholar commenting on Proverbs 23:14, describes a well-moderated, loving correction as follows. (1) It should be carefully related to the offense. (2) It should never be administered in the heat of temper, but rather in the calmness of conviction. (3) It should be free from physical violence — possibly a look of reproach, a scolding, or a wisely chosen exclusion from some appreciated privilege. (4) Such correction should be fair, always leaning over in consideration of the child, on the theory that one unjust infliction will do more harm than many just ones will do good. (5) Finally, it should be occasional and of brief duration, since nothing defeats its own purpose more certainly than perpetual fault-finding, constantly repeated punishment, or penalty that is too severe.

Let those who are eager to follow biblical principle not forget the words addressed to fathers in Colossians 3:21, "Do not provoke your children to anger lest they be discouraged." The original Greek word *athymeó,* that is translated "discouraged" implies a broken spirit. This has been called "the plague of youth." Discipline must always be balanced with encouragement. That is a good principle of child psychology. That is a good principle of Judeo-Christian teaching.

That is a good principle.

References: Howard Bedmond, Whitworth College, *The New Layman's Parallel Bible; The Funk and Wagnalls Pulpit Commentary;* The Barclay Study Bible Series; Phillip Keller, *A Shepherd Looks at Psalm 23* (Zondervan, 1976).

Revision of an article by Sue Hille.

Reprinted with permission. Reprinted from *Violence in the Family: A Workshop for Clergy and Other Helpers* by Marie M. Fortune (Cleveland: Pilgrim Press, 1991).

Battered Women of Age: The Experiences of WEAVE

by Pat Friedkin

As the battered women's movement goes forward into the 1990s and as we focus on freedom through unity and diversity, it is imperative that we include and celebrate women who, up to now, have been kept pretty invisible: battered/formerly battered women of age. My purpose in writing this paper is to establish that older battered women do have issues and needs that are unique and to stimulate discussion and action on the implications these differences have for battered women's programs. My hope is that by sharing some of what I've learned from battered women of age over the past two years, other battered women of age will feel freer to come forth and say, "We have unique needs and issues that have not been adequately addressed by the battered women's movement. Hear our voices!"

Please keep in mind that what is written here is based on heterosexual experiences of approximately 50 women, all of whom are white, working and middle class, and live in rural or urban areas of the Midwest. While the issues may be the same for other women of age, so little work has been done in this area that it is not possible to extrapolate from this small group to a larger and more diverse population of battered women.

All material presented in this paper was generated by the incredible women of WEAVE, Inc. (Women Ending Abuse Via Empowerment), a grassroots organization in which all policy decisions are made by battered/formerly battered women of age and all direct service is provided by battered/formerly battered women of age. The ideas presented are by no means inclusive or exclusive or the last word. They are, rather, concepts that the women of WEAVE have found important to be aware of in order to do empowering work with older battered women. Some of the issues we consider unique and important include:

- Who are "older" battered women? It has been our experience that "older" is best self-defined by what issues a woman is dealing with, the social value system under which she grew up and where she is in her life process rather than a rigid adherence to "over 40," "over 50," "over 60," or whatever.
- The social norms and values in place when she grew up are different for an older woman than for one who is younger. The socialization of women in the 1920s, 1930s, and 1940s was much different than now. Women didn't get divorced; the social stigma was too intense. Women were raised with the idea that some abuse was normal and you just learned to live with it. Career options for women were few in number. You worked as a secretary, nurse or teacher until you got married and settled into the career for which you were created: wife and mother. (The reality was that many women did work outside of the home but at menial jobs that were considered women's work and not careers.)
- Older battered women have frequently been abused by the mental health system. Not too many years ago it was fairly easy to commit

people to mental hospitals against their will. The abuser didn't have much difficulty convincing a doctor or judge (usually white males) that a battered woman was crazy or delusional and needed to be locked up "for her own good." Once she was committed, the abuser, as the responsible next of kin, had the legal and moral authority to make decisions for her, decisions like subjecting her to electroconvulsive therapy ("Shock Treatment"), deciding who could visit her, what doctor she would have, and so on. Even though laws have changed so that in most places it is now very difficult to commit a person against her will, an older battered woman who was previously committed as a result of her husband's testimony lives in terror that he can and will do it again.

- A woman who has invested 20, 30, or 50 years in a relationship has more to lose if she leaves her abuser. One example might be a woman who has worked and sacrificed for years and now the house she has lived in for most of her adult life is just about paid for. The apple trees she has nurtured as seedlings are now laden with fruit. Her garden is finally just the way she wants it. Her house is finally furnished the way she always hoped it would be. These things are all a part of her that she could stand to lose if she leaves the abuser.

- An older battered woman who wants to leave her abuser can meet with tremendous resistance from her adult children. It is not uncommon for them to put great pressure on her to "stay and take care of Dad. He won't be able to make it without you." Her selfishness rather than his abuse becomes the family problem.

- While an older battered woman who has made the decision to leave her abuser may feel tremendous anger and bitterness toward him, she doesn't necessarily have a desire to humiliate him or ruin him professionally. She wants to end the relationship in a way that preserves her sense of dignity and integrity. We must respect and support her in this.
- While fear of being alone is a very real obstacle for all battered women, it is particularly difficult for older battered women. We fear being alone as we age and worry about who will care for us if we become ill.
- While older battered women usually are not dealing with issues related to dealing with young children, they often are dealing with teenagers who have adopted the abuser's behaviors and who are usually larger and stronger than the woman. Not only is she subjected to continuing verbal, emotional and, sometimes, physical abuse from her teenagers, but she also is often dealing with feelings of guilt and remorse: "Would my child be acting this way if I had left my abuser, or if I had left him sooner?"
- It is usually much more difficult for a battered woman of age to reach out for help. She grew up in an era when family problems stayed within the family at all cost. In addition, she was socialized to hold herself responsible for the emotional health and stability of her family. Failure of her family life is totally devastating.

This paper has made no attempt to address the very real social and economic problems faced by battered women of age. Nor have we attempted to give concrete suggestions for how programs can make themselves more accessible to older battered women. It is our hope that all battered women's programs will begin to consider the unique needs of battered women of age and develop the responses that are most empowering to their particular consumers.

Reprinted with permission from the National Coalition Against Domestic Violence (NCADV). Individual memberships $20; supportive organizations $100. For more information, contact NCADV at P.O. Box 34103, Washington, DC 20043-4103, phone: 202/638-6388.

Elder Abuse:
An Unspeakable Shame

By Mike Payne

Truth is not only stranger than fiction, it's much harsher. Follow any Ohio adult protective service worker into any area of the state.

• Butler County — A 79-year-old woman is admitted to a hospital with broken ribs, head lice and sores that expose her spine. Open wounds on the 82-pound woman's body are covered with maggots. Metal pins from a 1986 hip joint replacement protrude more than an inch from her hip. Her son and daughter are charged with criminal neglect.

• Franklin County — Covered with urine and feces, a 76-year-old woman is found sitting on her front porch in a disoriented, obviously confused state. She is dehydrated and malnourished. Her home is filthy and roach-infested. The only thing in the refrigerator is a dead brown mouse. An investigation reveals the woman's landlady, supposedly looking after her finances and affairs, has been using the money for herself and failing to adequately provide for the victim.

• Lucas County — An 83-year-old emaciated woman with Alzheimer's disease enters a hospital, from a home she shared with relatives, with deep bruises on her chest. She has several broken bones that have gone without treatment, and the bottom of her feet are a solid black and blue. Signs of sexual abuse are also noted.

What goes on in Ohio goes on in every state in the union — an estimated 1.5 to 2 million times every year. And it often goes unreported and unpunished. In 1985, the skeletal body of a blind, demented elderly woman was found on the floor of her Texas home. She had literally starved to death in a decrepit environment where excrement was found on the floor and furniture. Charges against the woman's 26-year-old son were dropped because there was no law in the state specifically addressing neglect of the elderly. Had the victim been a dog, the state could have prosecuted.

A host of similar horror stories has been compiled in "Elder Abuse: A Decade of Shame and Inaction," a 1990 federal House of Representatives report by the chairman of the Subcommittee on Health and Long-Term Care of the Select Committee on Aging. As the title of the report suggests, little has been done to effectively stem the rising tide of elder abuse in this country since the late Rep. Claude Pepper and his Select Committee on Aging first brought the problem into national focus more than 10 years ago. Despite repeated attempts at such legislation, Congress has yet to enact a plan for national coordination of elder abuse programs and funding. The 1990 Subcommittee report states that elder abuse continues as a "shocking national problem of increasing proportions . . . a national disgrace."

As with child abuse, elder abuse is directed at those too weak, frail or otherwise incapacitated to defend themselves. It also parallels child abuse in that it is inflicted upon, by most accounts, approximately 5% of the applicable age category; i.e., one out of every 20 persons 60 and older. But, elder abuse is far less apt to be reported than child abuse. While one out of three child abuse cases is reported, according to the Subcommittee's report, that figure is only one of eight for elder abuse. Other research has found that ratio to be as low as one of 14.

Elder abuse often goes unreported because it often occurs in an isolated setting. And, unlike children who attend day care or school, the abused elderly may never come into contact with a segment of society outside of their own dwellings. Also, they may be too incapacitated, mentally and/or physically, to escape or report the conditions. When the abuse is coming from a close family member, the victims may be too ashamed to bring it out into the open. "It is hard to imagine what could cause somebody more shame than suffering the abuse of one of their own children," notes University of New Hampshire elder abuse researcher Karl Pillemer, Ph.D. Another big factor here is intimidation. The abused elderly may be kept in line by the abusers' threats — or just the thought — of being placed in a nursing home or other institution.

But even when outsiders suspect or are aware of abuse, they are hesitant to report it. "One reason it's not reported, especially physical abuse, is because it's traditionally considered as a family affair, people don't want to get involved," says Georgia Anetzberger, Ph.D., program director at Case Western Reserve University's Geriatric Education Center. Anetzberger, a member of Governor Richard F. Celeste's Task Force on Family Violence and the Ohio Coalition for Adult Protective Services, affirms that, despite reporting requirements, doctors, lawyers, and even clergy are among the least likely to report elder abuse. They are rooted in the traditional client-attorney, doctor-patient, clergy-layperson confidentiality, and are usually not well linked for referrals to the available network of appropriate social services, she explains.

Despite underreporting, advances have been made nationally in tracking cases of elder abuse, thus aiding in the understanding of its causes. Ten years ago, only 16 states had mandatory provisions for the reporting of elder abuse. That figure now stands at 42, including Ohio.

Using reports from Ohio's 88 county departments of Human Services, the Ohio Department of Human Services (ODHS) has been keeping statistics on abuse of Ohioans age 60 and over since the mid-1980s. Cases are categorized as "abuse," "neglect," or "exploitation," as defined in Ohio's 1981 Adult Protective Services Law (Ohio Rev. Code 5101.60-5101.71):

Abuse — ". . . the infliction upon an adult by himself or others of injury, unreasonable confinement, intimidation, or cruel punishment with resulting physical harm, pain, or mental anguish."

Neglect — ". . . the failure of an adult to provide for himself/ (herself) the goods or services necessary to avoid physical harm, mental anguish, or mental illness or the failure of a caretaker to provide such goods or services."

Exploitation — ". . . the unlawful or improper act of a caretaker using an adult or his/(her) resources for monetary or personal benefit, profit, or gain."

More than once every hour of every day of the year in 1989, an Ohioan reported a case of elder abuse. The 9,132 total reports break down as follows:

Type of Abuse	Number of Reported Cases	Percent of Total
Self-neglect	3,845	42.1%
Neglect	3,394	37.2%
Total Neglect	7,239	79.3%
Abuse	1,082	11.8%
Exploitation	811	08.9%
Total — All Types	9,132	100.0%

Of these 9,132 investigated cases, 5,670 warranted protective services. Protective services are any of a number of services provided by the county for the prevention, correction, or discontinuance of abuse, neglect or exploitation. Eight hundred (14%) of the protective services cases were considered emergencies — i.e., ". . . conditions which present a substantial risk of immediate and irreparable physical harm or death. . . ."

These figures go back to 1986, rising by about 16% the first two years, then, curiously, going down 4% in 1989 (see chart below). The 1990 federal Subcommittee's report and other national research have found elder abuse cases to be steadily rising across the country. Anetzberger, who did much to bring about Ohio's elder abuse legislation, does not interpret Ohio's recently falling numbers in a positive light. "The decrease in reports of elder abuse," she warns, "reflects a lack of continuing community education and, in some cases, diminished credibility of adult protective service systems in the state." The actual incidence of elder abuse in Ohio continues to climb, she asserts; there has just been a decline in reporting.

Elder Abuse Reports*

Fiscal Year	Abuse	Neglect	Exploitation	Total
1986	1,017	5,325	707	7,050
1987	1,154	6,199	849	8,202
1988	1,363	7,259	966	9,588
1989	1,082	7,239	811	9,132

compiled from 88 reporting counties

Henry Jenkins, ODHS division chief of Adult and Child Care Services, does not altogether agree with Anetzberger's assessment. He suggests, instead, that Ohio's reduction in elder abuse reports may be attributed to public awareness campaigns in certain counties. "Through increasing public awareness," he says, "referral sources are becoming better able to distinguish between abuse, neglect and exploitation, and basic adult needs."

ODHS, which has overseen adult protective services in Ohio since 1981, is striving to further increase community awareness with $5.7 million in first-time state funding received in the 1990-1991 Ohio biennium budget. Previously, even though Ohio's 1981 Adult Protective Services Law charged the ODHS with overseeing adult protective services in the state, no state funds were allocated and the actual services were funded strictly through federal Title XX block grants to the counties. Not until the most recent budget did the Ohio Legislature finally provide for line-item funding at the state level.

The $5.7 million is being distributed among Ohio's 88 counties. Each county receives a base amount of $20,000. The remaining dollars are allocated to the counties on a per-capita basis, determined by each county's 60-plus population. Counties may use the money for their individual adult protective service programs as they see fit, though the ODHS' intent is to add to the state's current total of 630 adult protective service workers. "Our commitment is to provide each county with the resources needed to combat the problem at every level," says Jenkins. Though the state funding is certainly appreciated, Jenkins adds, still more money is needed to effectively keep up with elder abuse reports as Ohio's aging population continues to grow.

While acknowledging criticism for not providing more uniformity in standards for county departments of Adult Protective Services, Jenkins explains that, while ODHS issued adult protective service guidelines in 1982, the department was not given rule-making authority until this year.

ODHS is attempting to bring some standardization into the field through recently developed statewide competency training for adult service workers. Regional training sites are in Hamilton, Franklin, Summit and Lucas counties. "The program is geared toward the needs of the worker," Jenkins says. "There is a lot of stress due to the lack of resources and the severity of the cases. Also, emphasis on the client's rights produces situations where the answers are unclear, particularly when the client's choice must be weighed against health and safety issues.

"We're pretty excited about the training," Jenkins continues. "Our goal is to give the workers the best possible tools for the job; an understanding of the problems they'll encounter, a sensitization to cultural diversity and a look at some of the particular problems of the aged."

They will be encountering all kinds of people and problems, as elder abuse is a problem that crops up in all segments of society. Different types of abuse, however, are more likely to occur among different income groups. Anetzberger observes that lower-income groups are at a higher risk for neglect — especially self-neglect — than their counterparts. On the other hand, those with higher incomes are more open to financial exploitation. Physical abuse, she says, is inflicted upon the rich and poor alike, with no documented distinction in incidence.

Some helpful information comes from the National Aging Resource Center on Elder Abuse (NARCEA) in Washington, D.C., which compiles information from a number of states, Ohio among them. (As the 50 states still do not have uniform reporting methods, NARCEA bases its data on compatible figures from 15-27 states.) According to NARCEA statistics from 1986-1988, females suffer abuse at about twice the rate of men (63% to 37%). This can partly be explained by women's longer life expectancy; also, women are traditionally less likely to resist abuse and are more vulnerable to sexual exploitation. NARCEA figures, based on reporting from the five rural states and five urban states with the highest incidence rates, indicate that elder abuse is more prevalent — at least more often reported — in urban areas. The 1988 urban rate was 3.77 reports per 1,000 elders; the rural rate was 2.60.

The federal Subcommittee's report, while emphasizing that no one part of society is immune, does caution that certain characteristics or circumstances of older people can make them especially vulnerable to abuse:

- Isolation — Geographic and social isolation impede detection and intervention
- Female — Larger in population; sexual abuse
- Advanced Age — Linked to physical and mental impairments, making it harder to resist abuse
- Dependency/(Poverty) — Studies correlate dependency with abuse; economic dependency may arouse hostility among family members
- Intergenerational (Long-Standing) Conflict — Problems between a parent and child may become intensified by parental dependency; the same holds for problems among other relatives

While these specific observations do not cover self-neglect, as mentioned before, research puts self-neglect and poverty hand-in-hand. Anetzberger holds that self-neglect is predominantly found in impoverished, impaired older women living alone. The potential for this problem is alarmingly brought out in U.S. Census figures showing that approximately 1.7 million (19%) of the elderly living alone live beneath the federal poverty level, which, in 1987, was a pitiful $5,393 for an elderly single person.

Poverty also plays a significant role in general neglect cases. Brenda Lovenshimer, an Ohio Department of Aging (ODA) employee who worked five years with adult protective services in Allen County, saw a lot of homes where people simply did not have the resources to care for themselves or their elderly relatives. "The majority of the cases I went out on were neglect," she recalls. "With some, it was more irresponsibility than anything else. With others, they had kind of edged by for years without any real preparation in case something went wrong. A lot of these people had worked all their lives, lived through the depression without taking charity, and they weren't going to start taking it now."

Income and other personal factors are important in relation to elder abuse because so much of the abuse starts so close to home, inflicted and suffered most by those with close family ties. Although nursing homes tend to grab the headlines, institutional abuse constitutes only a small fraction of overall elder abuse cases. In Ohio, for example, incidents of elder abuse in nursing homes and other institutions (575) account for barely 6% of the total reports. According to the American Association of Retired Persons (AARP), for every older person in a nursing home, there are two severely dependent elderly people receiving care at home.

NARCEA numbers, based on reports from 15 states, show that adult children of the abused are implicated in 30% of elder abuse cases. "Other relatives" was the category next most likely responsible for abuse (17.8%), followed by spouses (14.8%). Service providers were involved in 12.8% of the cases.

Preventing Elder Abuse

(From the AARP publication: "Domestic Mistreatment of the Elderly," Washington, D.C., 1988)

"The time to think about prevention is not when the caregiver's ability begins to be inadequate: this may be too late."

1. Be aware of the prevalence of the problem, and the factors contributing to it. Make family, friends and/or attorney aware of your concerns.
2. Plan ahead. Ensure family members or other caregivers have the physical, emotional and financial resources to provide adequate care. Anticipate situations in which mistreatment may occur.
3. Have at least one plan for alternate care in the event that the first plan does not work out.
4. Remain sociable as you age; participate in community activities as much as possible and maintain or increase your network of friends.
5. Develop a "buddy system" with a friend or friends outside your home to check up on each other and provide mutual reassurance.
6. Keep regularly scheduled medical, dental and social appointments. These professionals can be helpful and, in special cases, can be used to attest to your level of competency.
7. Ask friends and relatives to regularly visit you where you live. Even brief visits will allow friends to check on your environment, well-being and attitude.
8. Have your own telephone and post box, and make sure you open your own mail. If you suspect mail is being intercepted, contact postal authorities.
9. Make others aware that you are keeping track of your affairs and that you know where everything is supposed to be.
10. Let others know that you expect your personal records, accounts and property to be available for examination, either by you, or someone you trust.

The federal Subcommittee report profiles a typical abuser of the elderly as a close relative of the abused who ". . . will usually be experiencing great stress. Alcoholism, drug addiction, marital problems and long-term financial difficulties all play a role. It is interesting to note that the abuser, in many cases, was abused by the parents as a child. Further research suggests that for most abusers, the abuse is not a one-time episode; rather, it is of a repeat nature in 95% of the cases."

Anetzberger took a close-up look at those who abuse their elderly parents in her doctoral dissertation, "The Etiology of Elder Abuse by Adult Offspring: an Exploratory Study" (Case Western Reserve Univ., 1986). Her study examined 40 cases of elder abuse among northeastern Ohioans, with in-depth interviews of the abusers. The most interesting finding, Anetzberger stresses, is that pathology, e.g., alcoholism, mental illness, mental retardation, existed in most of the cases. Additionally, in some families, the elderly victims were being cared for by adult children brought up in authoritarian environments she describes as "strict and restrictive." About 80% of the abusers saw their parents as demanding while growing up. Among other characteristics, Anetzberger found the abusers tended to be:

- Male
- Socially isolated
- Living with the abused (in 38 of 40 cases)
- Dependent (psychologically and/or financially on the abused)

Surprisingly, Anetzberger's research did not often detect a history of family violence. "One of the feelings I came away with was that in some of the cases, in some ways, the abusers were victims themselves. I doubt that a lot of them have the ability to re-channel their anger like you or I would, for instance. This is not to agree with or condone their conduct, but I sometimes found myself feeling sympathetic with them as well."

Often compounding the personal problems related to elder abuse is the paucity of government health programs and social services for the elderly needing in-home assistance. Medicare doesn't pay for the nonmedical care the dependent/elderly may need to safely remain in their homes. Medicaid is designed primarily to cover the costs of institutional care, offering little in the way of in-home assistance. (The Medicaid waiver recently granted to ODA's PASSPORT program is an exception.)

Adult Protective Services*

- Counseling/Casework Services
- Mental Health Services
- Provision of Food, Clothing or Shelter
- Housing-Related Services
- Placement Services
- Homemaker Services

- Medical Care
- Home Health Care
- Fiscal Management
- Guardianship Services
- Legal Services

* Services may vary from county to county

Services provided at the state and county levels, such as Home-Health Aide, Nutrition and Transportation, may not reach all the people who need them; and they may not always be known to those who need them most. "In a lot of the cases I handled, the people just weren't aware of what was out there, they didn't know the programs existed," says ODA's Lovenshimer. "The services need to be better advertised." (See sidebar above.)

Without sufficient assistance, many families can all too easily end up in the position of taking on more than they can reasonably handle when they take on the care of a dependent relative. The care may be required for an extended period not anticipated by the family. The AARP points out that the average length of home care for the severely dependent elderly over 70 years of age is almost six years. The in-home care of the impaired and dependent elderly frequently imposes unmanageable physical, emotional and financial burdens on even the best prepared friends and relatives. The medical costs of caring for the elderly, coupled with the stress of providing them continuous assistance in the routine of daily living, can often become overwhelming and lead to neglect and/or physical abuse. And sometimes, as with elderly spouses, the person providing the care and assistance may be nearly as old — or older, with impairments of their own — as the person they are attempting to provide for. Complicating the matter is that, partly by culture, people are often reluctant to ask for help.

Even the abused or neglected themselves hesitate to report their conditions, fearing further abuse in retaliation or that they may be placed in an institution. "I'm sure that's something that hangs over their heads," notes Judy Baughn, an Adult Protective Services administrator with the Franklin County Department of Human Services. "The elderly are terrified of nursing homes; they're even afraid of hospitals."

Lovenshimer saw that fear constantly, and makes it clear that institutional placement was very rarely the outcome in her adult protective service case work. "I think we really need to educate people that institutionalization is the last resort; that there are a lot of alternatives out there; that the protective service workers are there to help them any way they can. We want to maximize their independence."

That is emphasized in Ohio's Adult Protective Services law, which specifies that: "The court shall not order an institutional placement unless it has made a specific finding entered in the record that no less restrictive alternative can be found to meet the needs of the individual."

Only in the most severe cases of abuse — including self-neglect — do the county courts resort to restraining orders or guardianship for the protection of the abused or neglected. According to Anetzberger, the courts use the involuntary provisions of Ohio's Adult Protective Service Law in only about 2% of the cases, and Ohio law has lately stiffened the requirements and occasions for guardianship to better protect the rights of the elderly. In the 1989 reporting year, only 18 restraining orders were issued, according to ODHS data.

The reporting requirements of Ohio's Adult Protective Services law (Ohio Rev. Code 5101.61) allow any person, anonymously or otherwise, to report elder abuse to the appropriate agency. In Ohio, reports are taken by the county department of human services within the county where the abuse occurs. All 88 counties have such an office. While everyone is encouraged to report suspected cases of abuse, a number of legal, health and social service professionals are required to do so. As the law reads, they must "immediately report" whenever they have "reasonable cause to believe that an adult is being abused, neglected, or exploited. . . ." (See sidebar below.)

Ohio Revised Code 5101.61 (A)
Duty to Report Suspected Abuse of Adult

Any attorney, physician, osteopath, podiatrist, chiropractor, dentist, psychologist, any employee of a hospital as defined in section 3701.01 of the Revised Code, any employee of an ambulatory health facility as defined in section 1739.01 of the Revised Code, any employee of a home health agency as defined in section 1739.01 of the Revised Code, any employee of an adult foster care facility as defined in section 5103.30 of the Revised Code, any peace officer, coroner, clergyman, any employee of a community mental health facility as defined in section 1739.01 of the Revised Code, and any person engaged in social work or counseling having reasonable cause to believe that an adult is being abused, neglected, or exploited or is in a condition which is the result of abuse, neglect, or exploitation shall immediately report such belief to the county department of welfare. This section does not apply to employees of any hospital as defined in section 5122.01 of the Revised Code.

When an Ohio county department of Human Services receives a report on elder abuse, it is obliged to investigate within 24 hours if the situation qualifies as an emergency. Otherwise, the investigation can be initiated within three working days of the first report. Reports may be made orally or in writing, though some departments may request certain reports to be put in writing.

Ohio's recent $5.7 million infusion of state dollars into adult protective services obviously comes none too soon. This first-time funding, along with the ODA's continuing expansion of in-home services to the elderly and preventive support services provided locally through Title XX funding, puts Ohio in a minority of states increasing efforts to confront elder abuse. In the opening section of its 1990 report, the Subcommittee proclaims: "Sadly, at a time when the incidence of elder abuse is on the rise, the Congress and the states are doing less."

It is generally agreed that the most important, single action regarding elder abuse would be the passage by Congress of H.R. 220, legislation which parallels the federal Child Abuse Prevention, Identification and Treatment Act of 1974. This legislation would provide for a coordinated national effort, giving federal funds to states with mandatory reporting systems. It also would create a national clearinghouse for elder abuse information and data, as well as a national hotline. Another critical measure, recommended by the Subcommittee, would be passage of H.R. 2263, Congress' Long-Term Home Care legislation. This legislation would provide federal funding for long-term, in-home care services to chronically ill elderly and disabled persons.

While Ohio is definitely taking steps in the right direction, by most accounts it will still be a struggle just keeping up with the proliferating elderly abuse problem.

We are a violent society — increasingly so. A front-page report last summer has the United States as the most murderous industrialized nation on earth, with more than 10 times the violent crime rate of some European countries. While that news may not come as a major surprise, the violence that goes on in the privacy of the American home might. In a 1980 study of domestic violence, "Behind Closed Doors: Violence in the American Family," Richard Gelles and Suzanne Steinmetz estimated that every other household in America is the scene of a violent family episode at least once a year. The authors further conclude that: "Americans run the greatest risk of assault, physical injury and even murder in their own homes by members of their own families."

The chances of this national tendency toward violence being taken out on the elderly are increasing because, among other reasons, the elderly in this country are increasing. There are now more than 30 million Americans 65 or older. At the turn of the century, only 4% of the population was over 65. Today, those 65 and over account for 12.4% of the population, and that percentage is expected to go on increasing — up to 18% by the year 2000.

Other factors aggravating the elder abuse problem will include a declining pool of caregivers to meet the rising in-home needs of the elderly. Women, who most often assume the caregiver role, continue to enter the work force in higher numbers. Moreover, as the baby-boom generation ages, it will find itself with a shortage of offspring to supply care. Approximately 30% of the baby boomers have no children.

Pervading all this, sometimes subtly, sometimes not, is the fact that America is becoming more and more an ageist society — a society where the elderly are too often looked upon as something less than human. Some of this may be due to a heritage too quick to equate tangible productivity with human worth. We may also point in the direction of Madison Avenue and its relentless premium on youth — but then we're the ones buying it all.

A telling cultural comparison comes by the way of a conversation Anetzberger recalls with a Japanese social-work exchange student: "We were talking about elder abuse, and she said they don't have that problem in her home country. It's not a part of their lifestyle. They don't even have words for it."

Unfortunately, we, as a nation, can't find enough words for it — or even enough concern to effectively deal with what is becoming an unignorable national disgrace.

Reprinted with permission. Mike Payne (Autumn 1990). "Elder Abuse: An Unspeakable Shame," *Ohio's Heritage* magazine. Columbus, Ohio: Ohio Department of Aging.

Elder Mistreatment: A Call for Help

Georgia J. Anetzberger, PhD; Mark S. Lachs, MD, MPH;
James G. O'Brien, MD; Shelley O'Brien, MS;
Karl A. Pillemer, PhD; Susan K. Tomita, MSW

Abuse of the elderly is a relative newcomer to the
domestic violence scene. This practical approach
to its complex issues focuses on awareness,
treatment, and prevention.

Express Stop

Prevalence and importance: Elder abuse and mistreatment affect anywhere from 1 to 2 million persons a
year. Detection is often difficult, especially since older
people sometimes tend to be relatively isolated. Physicians are well situated to detect, treat, and even prevent many cases. To do so, however, you must first
increase your awareness and understanding of the
problem and acknowledge your role in detection, reporting, and intervention.

Elder abuse and neglect, sometimes referred to more broadly as
elder mistreatment, is gaining increased attention as a serious
and potentially life-threatening problem that may afflict 1 to 2
million elderly persons a year. It is a problem that transcends

racial, ethnic, and socioeconomic boundaries, and it is usually the outcome of a complex and troubled situation in which a wide range of medical, psychosocial, economic, and interpersonal factors converge. Unfortunately it is also the form of domestic violence about which the least is known.

From the start, the development of a knowledge base in this area has been hindered by disbelief, misinformation, underdetection, and a scarcity of well-designed research. Physicians, most notably, have been uninvolved in helping to fill this void, in sharp contrast to their early leadership role in child abuse research and education.

There are no national prevalence data on elder mistreatment for the United States. There have been several localized studies, however, including a 1988 report based on data collected in the Boston metropolitan area (see "Uncovering abuse: Results of a random-sample survey," page 205).* This study yielded a lifetime prevalence rate of 3.15%, which is comparable to other findings from well-run studies on elder mistreatment. Based on these reports, the national prevalence rate for elder mistreatment is believed to be 2-5%.

The Boston area study found physical abuse the most prevalent form of mistreatment, although community and state registries of actual reported cases contain far more reports of neglect. The overwhelming majority of elder abuse cases are unreported. It is in this unreported segment that you are likely to find currently hidden cases of physical abuse, psychological abuse, exploitation, and even sexual abuse and assault.

Elder abuse and neglect are probably not the most common — or even the most critical — problems facing older Americans. They are less prevalent than cognitive impairment and poverty in the elderly, child abuse, and nonelderly spouse abuse. But, based on numbers alone (and with expected increases due to the aging of the United States population), they are certainly not trivial. And the significance of the problems, particularly to the primary care physician, extends beyond that of sheer numbers.

---

* Pillemer, K., Finkelhor, D.: The prevalence of elder abuse: A random sample survey. *Gerontologist* 1988;28:51-57.

Uncovering abuse: Results of a random-sample survey

The 1988 prevalence study conducted in the Boston metropolitan area by article consultant Karl A. Pillemer, PhD, was the first large-scale, random-sample survey designed to assess the prevalence and nature of elder mistreatment in a community.[*] Before that, most of the research dealing with prevalence came from samples of reported cases, which could not be relied on as representative of the community at large.

In the Boston area study, more than 2,000 elderly residents were selected at random and interviewed to determine if they had been the victim of mistreatment since turning 65. The identified categories of mistreatment were physical violence, chronic verbal aggression, and physical neglect.

The researchers found an overall prevalence rate of 3.15% (roughly 32 cases per thousand, with a 95% confidence interval of 25-39 cases per 1,000). Physical violence was the most common form of mistreatment, and it was also the most common type between spouses. The investigators surmised this was simply because the elder was most likely to be abused by the person with whom he or she was living. Furthermore, men were found to be at higher risk of abuse than women, in contrast to earlier studies based on reported cases alone. But, when husbands abused their wives, the injuries were reported to be more severe, perhaps a reason for higher numbers of reports among women.

This is not the first study to uncover large percentages of spousal abuse in elderly populations. Such abuse may represent a continuation of abuse from an earlier undetected or unresolved problem, or it may be a new phenomenon precipitated by the stresses of aging or by changing dependencies — and physicians need to be aware of it.

And yet, the actual prevalence of elder mistreatment may be even higher. Certain forms of abuse that are thought to be quite common — such as financial exploitation and acts of omission — were not included in this study. Therefore, for an overall prevalence estimate, 3.15% may be too low.

The main points of the study, however, remain undisputed. First, well-designed and well-conducted research must continue to be done because reliable and reproducible data are needed to understand the problem; second, a large percentage of elder mistreatment in the community may in fact be spousal abuse, and this possibility should not be ignored in identifying cases and selecting interventions; and third, a large unreported segment of abuse in the community can be uncovered by surveys of this type. The final point is that elder abuse — though not the most common problem experienced by the elderly — may be one of the more treatable.

[*] Pllemer, K., Finkelhor, D.: The prevalence of elder abuse: A random sample survey. *Gerontologist* 1988;28:51-57.

Because the elderly are much more likely to be socially isolated than children or nonelderly adults, abuse or neglect is far less likely to be detected. In fact, as a doctor, you may be one of the few individuals whom your elderly patient regularly sees. Elder mistreatment, while manageable, is also very difficult to resolve and can vary widely in severity. Just because you have not seen serious cases of abuse in your practice does not mean they do not occur.

To intervene effectively, you must increase your awareness of the problem, from its most subtle and insidious presentation to its most blatant. Recognize your responsibility to participate in detection, reporting, assessment, and treatment. Foremost, realize that elder mistreatment does occur, even in the most unexpected of circumstances.

Express Stop

Defining the problem: Research, and therefore knowledge, about elder mistreatment has been hindered by the lack of clear and consistent definitions. The greatest area of concern for you, as a clinician, is the safety and well-being of your patient. You also need to be fully knowledgeable of how your state defines elder mistreatment so that you may comply with the law. Underreporting — for whatever reasons — is a serious problem.

The lack of clear and consistent definitions of precisely what constitutes elder mistreatment has been a great hindrance to researchers in generating reliable data on this matter. The full range of ethnic variations in the definition of abuse is just beginning to be explored. From a clinical perspective, however, your most important concerns are the care and well-being of your patient and the legal definitions of abuse and neglect in your state.

Categories of abuse and neglect

Physical abuse An act of violence resulting in pain, injury, impairment, or disease. Examples include pushing, punching, slapping, burning, improper use of physical restraints or medications, sexual coercion, or assault. The improper use of physical restraints or medications is of particular concern in institutional settings, according to the following definition:

> **Failure to carry out a plan of treatment or care** Unauthorized use of physical or chemical restraints, administration of medications or isolation as punishment or for convenience of staff, or as a substitute for treatment and in conflict with a physician's order.

Physical neglect Failure to provide goods and services necessary for optimal functioning or avoidance of harm. Examples include withholding of care, medication, food, hydration, assistance with hygiene; failure to provide physical aids such as eyeglasses, hearing aids, false teeth; failure to provide safety precautions, and access to medical care. This can be intentional (for example, as punishment), or unintentional (for example, due to ignorance or the caregiver's inability to meet the patient's needs).

Psychological abuse Acts that result in psychological distress or emotional anguish. Examples include verbal aggression, denigration, harassment, intimidation, threats of punishment, or deprivation.

Psychological neglect Failure to provide social stimulation. Examples include social or physical isolation, leaving an elder unattended or without needed supervision for long periods of time, restricting access to news or community events, and threatening to abandon or place an elder in a nursing home.

Financial abuse or exploitation Unauthorized use of an elder's funds, property, or resources. Examples include taking an elder's Social Security check and cashing it for drugs, taking or misusing an elder's property including medications, stealing money or food stamps, and coercion into signing or changing legal documents such as wills. Exploitation can have a direct impact on care, as the patient may be deprived of medications or access to medical treatment.

Financial neglect Failure to use available funds and resources necessary to sustain or restore an elder's health and well-being. (Although recognized as real, this category is not generally used in classification.)

Violation of personal rights Failure to allow an elder who is otherwise able to do so to make his or her own decisions. Examples include depriving an elder of right to privacy, self-determination, voting, worshipping, and receiving mail. An elder may even be evicted from his own home or placed prematurely in a nursing home.

In general, elder mistreatment is defined as an act of commission or omission that results in harm or threatened harm to the health and welfare of an older adult, and it does not include steps, however unpleasant, necessary to maintain the quality of life. The umbrella term, elder mistreatment, refers to suffering imposed by means of abuse and neglect, whose definitions are typically divided into several categories (see "Categories of abuse and neglect," page 207). Adult protective services workers around the country include self-neglect as a separate category, and it is probably the most common form of mistreatment that they see.

To comply with jurisdictional requirements, you must have at least some working knowledge of your state's elder mistreatment laws, including the definitions and circumstances under which you are required to report. Beyond legal considerations, clinical judgment is also needed in evaluating suspected cases, especially where individual and family norms are in question. As the primary care physician, however, you must always ensure that the patient's overall needs are being met and that he or she is not being harmed by what the caregiver or family perceives as the norm.

Underreporting — especially by physicians — is considered significant, with as many as 13 cases unreported for each case that comes to light. In a 1991 study looking at reporting patterns, investigators surveyed a national sample of direct practice workers in area agencies on aging to find out who helps them the most in the discovery and treatment of new cases.[*] Out of 14 occupation groups listed, physicians ranked just tenth in helping to discover new cases and only sixth in helping to treat. Clearly there is need for improvement.

The issues surrounding physician underreporting are complex. Among the reasons given are lack of recognition of cases, lack of knowledge or awareness of mandatory reporting requirements, issues of confidentiality, poor expectations as to outcome

---

[*] Blakely, B.E., Dolon, R.: The relative contributions of occupation groups in the discovery and treatment of elder abuse and neglect. *J Gerontol Soc Work* 1991;17:183-199.

and the related belief that reporting may actually harm the patient, lack of faith in the system, and fear of liability despite immunity provisions in most state laws. You may also feel reluctant to report less severe cases of abuse or neglect for fear that it may damage your relationship with the patient or family.

Most of these issues can be resolved by a better understanding of the laws and by improved capabilities of detection. On the positive side, mandatory reporting may actually help to facilitate effective referrals, which can be critically important to the success of a coordinated intervention effort.

Express Stop

The validity of risk factors: A great deal of controversy has surrounded risk factors for elder mistreatment, especially with regard to victim versus caregiver biases. The only factors that seem to hold up consistently in studies are abuser deviance and dependency, a shared living situation, and social isolation. The notion of caregiver burden, while credible to clinicians in the field, has yet to be adequately documented. Your best bet in this area might be to remain cognizant of potential risk factors while taking nothing for granted.

Studies before the mid-1980s characterized the elder abuse victim as typically female, old old, frail, and cognitively and functionally impaired. Studies since then find men as likely to be abused as women, young old as likely to be abused as old old, and cognitively intact as likely to be abused as cognitively impaired, when the broad range of abusive and neglectful behaviors is considered. The area of risk factors is highly controversial, and here, in particular, methodologic issues (such as different definitions of the problem and poorly designed studies with lack of adequate controls) seem to account for some of the discrepancies seen in published reports.

Research carried out by social scientists has tended to link elder abuse and neglect more closely with abuser characteristics than with victim characteristics.* Clinicians, however, have a hard time discounting the potential for elder abuse and neglect in situations where the elder is frail, incontinent, behaviorally or cognitively impaired, or acts aggressively toward the individual who is largely responsible for providing care.

The notion of caregiver burden as a risk factor (see "Caregiver burden: A myth that won't die," page 211) is still being explored, although no study has shown that abused elderly are more likely than nonabused elderly to be dependent on the person abusing them. In fact, the majority of abusers who engage in physical or financial abuse (but not necessarily psychological abuse) have been found to be heavily dependent on the person they are abusing for things like money, child care, and housing. Other risk factors associated with the abuser include substance abuse, psychopathology, and a history of abuse or institutionalization.

The abuser is also likely to be living with the elder whom he or she is abusing and controlling the victim's access to friends or family, with resultant social isolation. Issues of control also surface in other forms of intrafamilial violence, where the abuser feels powerless and seeks to counterbalance the situation with harmful acts toward the victim. Changing dependencies may also surface in elder spouse abuse cases, such as those in the 1988 study in the Boston area.

A special circumstance may be that of dementia (see "Alzheimer's patients and caregivers: Two-sided stories," page 212). There is some indication that caregivers of the demented elderly may be more likely to be abusive or violent to the patient, particularly if the caregiver is depressed, and that the demented elder is also more likely to be abusive or violent to the caregiver.

---

* Pillemer, K., Finkelhor, D.: Causes of elder abuse: Caregiver stress versus problem relatives. *Am J Orthopsychiatry* 1989;59:179-187.

Caregiver burden: A myth that won't die

Many clinical researchers feel that family violence research on elder abuse and neglect perhaps places too much emphasis, or even blame, on the abuser. Along with this viewpoint is the feeling that, in at least some cases of elder mistreatment, the needs of the patient — which may place great physical, financial, and psychological strain on the caregiver — play a significant etiologic role.

Blanket acceptance of this viewpoint is reminiscent of victim-blaming biases that were known to plague early work in child and spouse abuse. Even more troubling is the notion that frail or dependent elder abuse victims may themselves embrace this viewpoint and delay seeking help for fear of the consequences.

Clinicians who treat frail and demented elderly patients also find it difficult to dismiss the notion of caregiver burden as a contributory factor in at least some cases of abuse or neglect. Stress and conflict may be most likely to emerge when a single relative has been designated the primary caregiver, when there is little support from other family members, when the caregiver and patient have had a strained relationship to begin with, and when caregiving needs are great. The stressed caregiver may well have financial or other needs that keep him or her from exploring alternatives. Or it may simply be that the caregiver is living up to a promise never to let the patient go to a nursing home.

To date, the evidence specifically linking caregiver burden to elder abuse or mistreatment is largely anecdotal. But caregivers of chronically ill or demented patients have high rates of depression and low self-esteem. Serious cases of caregiver stress should probably not be overlooked since they can lead to inadequate care of the elder, if not outright neglect.

In the clinical setting, it's a good idea to evaluate the caregiver of an elderly patient for signs of depression, stress, and feelings of being overburdened or lacking time to themselves. Very simply, you can ask the caregiver to describe a typical day. For example:

• How many hours a day do you spend caring for the elder?
• Do you get enough sleep at night?
• What do you actually do and how often?
• How do you feel about your caregiving responsibilities?
• Are there times when you just cannot meet the elder's needs?
• Do you feel angry at the elder or frustrated?
• How do you deal with those feelings?

Additional questions about the caregiver's financial situation, health status, and family support system can also help you to identify feelings of overburden. The jury is still out on whether interventions directed at decompressing caregiver stress, or treating depression, will serve to prevent any cases of abuse or neglect of the elderly. But, at the very least, they are likely to benefit the caregiver.

Alzheimer's patients and caregivers: Two-sided stories

A recent study on the prevalence of severe violence in caregiving situations for community-living Alzheimer's disease patients shows a higher than usual risk of violence — for both patients and their primary caregivers.[*] The researchers interviewed 184 primary caregivers of Alzheimer's patients living in the community to corroborate previous findings of abuse by caregivers and of aggressive and disruptive behaviors by patients. The investigators were especially interested in the interactive nature of these findings and the possibility of identifying risk factors for severe violence.

They found that significant violence does indeed occur in Alzheimer's caregiving situations in the community, with an overall prevalence rate of 17.4%. Specifically, 15.8% of patients had been violent toward their caregivers, 5.4% of caregivers were violent toward the patient, and 3.8% of patients and caregivers were mutually violent. These rates, which are greater than anything previously reported in the community, take into account only severe violence and not the full range of abusive behaviors.

The variables most often associated with violence were caregiver depression — at near clinical levels — and type of living arrangement. Caregiver depression is a particularly important finding, given that as many as half of all Alzheimer's caregivers may be clinically depressed. The researchers also cite a recent report in which significant levels of depression were found in abusive caregivers of demented and stroke patients.[**] If these findings hold up, clinical depression in caregivers of demented or Alzheimer's patients may prove to be a phenomenon worth noting — and a possible risk for abuse.

Another study examines feelings in caregivers and might lead to actual violence.[†] The researchers looked at 236 family caregivers of Alzheimer's and other patients with nonreversible dementia. They found that interactional stressors (physical aggression by the care recipient and disruptive behaviors) made caregivers more likely to think about becoming violent. Low self-esteem was also correlated with violent feelings, but it was not known whether it preceded the feelings of violence or occurred in response to them. A third variable, shared living situation, was also a predictor of violent feelings on the part of the caregiver.

The study also looked at instances in which violent feelings in the caregiver had led to actual acts of violence. Though this subsample was relatively small, the researchers described some interesting findings: Spouses were more likely than other relatives to engage in actual violence, as were older compared with younger caregivers. Lastly, violence by the caregiver was again related to violence by the patient.

[*] Paveza, G.J., Cohen, D., Eisdorfer, C., et al: Severe family violence and Alzheimer's disease: Prevalence and risk factors. *Gerontologist* 1992;32:493-497.

[**] Homer, A.C., Gilleard, C.: Abuse of elderly people by their carers. *BMJ* 1990;301-1359-1362.

[†] Pillemer, K., Suitor, J.J.: Violence and violent feelings: What causes them among caregivers? *J Gerontol* 1992;47:S165-S172.

Future studies may show at least some cases of abuse or neglect to be positively correlated with specific medical findings in the victim, perhaps in combination with specific intrafamilial or caregiver characteristics. Your knowledge of risk factors may best be used proactively, rather than reactively, to avert potentially risky situations or to understand cases once they occur. The clinical hazard of relying too heavily on risk factors as a diagnostic tool is that cases that do not fit the mold may be missed.

REFERENCES

for Anetzberger, G.J., Lachs, M.S., O'Brien, J.G., O'Brien, S., Pillemer, K., Tomita, S.K.: Elder mistreatment: A call for help. (J.N. Travalino, ed.). *Patient Care,* June 15, 1993, pp. 93-130.

1. American Medical Association: *Diagnostic and Treatment Guidelines on Elder Abuse and Neglect.* Chicago, 1992.
2. American Medical Association white paper on elderly health. Report of the Council on Scientific Affairs. *Arch Intern Med* 1990;150:2459-2472.
3. Beth Israel Hospital: *Elder Assessment Team (EAT) Elder Abuse/Neglect Protocol.* Boston, 1991.
4. Blakely, B.E., Dolan, R.: The relative contributions of occupation groups in the discovery and treatment of elder abuse and neglect. *J Gerontol Soc Work* 1991;17:183-199.
5. Bloom, J.S., Ansell, P., Bloom, M.N.: Detecting elder abuse: A guide for physicians. *Geriatrics* 1989;44:40-68.
6. Butler, R.N., Finical, S.I., Lewis, M.I., et al.: Aging and mental health, part 3: Prevention of caregiver overload, abuse, and neglect. *Geriatrics* 1992;47:53-58.
7. Clark-Daniels, C.L., Daniels, R.S., Baumhover, L.A.: Physicians' and nurses' responses to abuse of the elderly: A comparative study of two surveys in Alabama. *J Elder Abuse and Neglect* 1989;1:57-72.
8. Ehrlich, P., Anetzberger, G.: Survey of state public health departments on procedures for reporting elder abuse. *Public Health Rep* 1991;106:151-154.
9. Godkin, M.A., Wolf, R.S., Pillemer, K.: A case-comparison analysis of elder abuse and neglect. *Int J Aging Hum Dev* 1969;28:207-225.

10. The Harborview Medical Center, Department of Social Work: *Protocol for Identification and Assessment of Elder Mistreatment.* Seattle, 1992.

11. Homer, A.C., Gilleard, C.: Abuse of elderly people by their carers. *BMJ* 1990;301:1359-1362.

12. Jecker, N.S.: Privacy beliefs and the violent family. Extending the ethical argument for physician intervention. *JAMA* 1993;269:776-780.

13. Johnson, T.F.: *Elder Mistreatment. Deciding Who Is at Risk.* New York: Greenwood Press, 1991.

14. McCarthy, M.J.: Grim prospect. Older people will do anything to avoid life in a nursing home. *The Wall Street Journal.* December 3, 1992; page A1.

15. McDonald, A.J., Abrahams, S.T.: Social emergencies in the elderly. *Emerg Med Clin North Am* 1990;8:443-459.

16. The Mount Sinai/Victim Services Agency Elder Abuse Project: *Elder Mistreatment Guidelines for Health Care Professionals: Detection, Assessment and Intervention.* New York, 1968.

17. National Aging Resource Center on Elder Abuse: *Elder Abuse Questions and Answers. An Information Guide for Professionals and Concerned Citizens,* ed. 2. Washington, DC, 1992.

18. National Eldercare Resource Center on Aging and State Long Term Care Ombudsman Programs, unpublished material.

19. O'Malley, T.A., Everett, D.E., O'Malley, H.C., et al.: Identifying and preventing family-mediated abuse and neglect of elderly persons. *Ann Intern Med* 1983;96:996-1005.

20. Paveza, G.J., Cohen, D., Elsdorfer, C., et al.: Severe family violence and Alzheimer's disease: Prevalence and risk factors. *Gerontologist* 1992;32:493-497.

21. Pillemer, K., Bachman-Prehn, R.: Helping and hurting: Predictors of maltreatment of patients in nursing homes. *Research on Aging* 1991;13:74-95.

22. Pillemer, K., Finkelhor, D.: Causes of elder abuse: Caregiver stress versus problem relatives. *Am J Orthopsychiatry* 1989;59:179-187.

23. Pillemer, K., Finkelhor, D.: The prevalence of elder abuse: A random sample survey. *Gerontologist* 1988;28:51-57.

24. Pillemer, K., Moore, D.W.: Abuse of patients in nursing homes: Findings from a survey of staff. *Gerontologist* 1989;29:314-320.

25. Pillemer, K., Suitor, J.J.: Violence and violent feelings: What causes them among caregivers? *J Gerontol* 1992;47:S165-S172.

26. Tomita, S.K.: The denial of elder mistreatment by victims and abusers: The application of neutralization theory. *Violence and Victims* 1990;5:171-184.

Article Consultants

Georgia J. Anetzberger, PhD, adjunct professor, Case Western Reserve University School of Medicine; and associate director, Benjamin Rose Institute, Cleveland.

Mark S. Lachs, MD, MPH, assistant professor of medicine, Yale University School of Medicine; and attending physician, Yale-New Haven Hospital, New Haven, Conn.

James G. O'Brien, MD, professor, department of family practice, and director, programs on aging, Michigan State University College of Human Medicine; medical director, geriatrics division, St. Lawrence Hospital and Healthcare Services, Lansing, Mich.; and director, Geriatric Education Center of Michigan.

Shelley O'Brien, MS, Regional Ombudsman, State of Connecticut Department on Aging, New Haven.

Karl A. Pillemer, PhD, associate professor of human development and family studies, Cornell University, Ithaca, N.Y.

Susan K. Tomita, MSW, associate director of social work, Harborview Medical Center; and clinical associate professor, School of Social Work, University of Washington, Seattle.

NOTE: The pages as they appear in this manual are an excerpt from the longer article. Those pages pertinent to spousal abuse and/or considerations have been reprinted here.

When I Call for Help: A Pastoral Response to Domestic Violence against Women

Bishops' Committee on Marriage and Family Life;
Bishops' Committee on Women in Society and in the
Church. Affirmed by the NCCB/USCC General
Membership, November 1992; National Conference of
Catholic Bishops.

*When I Call for Help: A Pastoral Response to
Domestic Violence against Women* is a collabora-
tive statement of the NCCB Committee on Marriage and Family Life and the NCCB Committee on
Women in Society and in the Church. It was
prepared in the Secretariat for Family, Laity,
Women and Youth under the supervision of the
above committees. Publication was approved by
the Administrative Committee in September 1992.
The statement is further authorized for publication by the undersigned. — Monsignor Robert N.
Lynch, General Secretary, NCCB/USCC, September 30, 1992.

> She told the psychotherapist that she was living in the doghouse because her husband locked her out when he was in a rage.
>
> He told the abuse counselor in group therapy that after the first couple of beatings, he didn't have to beat her up again. All he had to do was raise his fist.

INTRODUCTION

As pastors of the Church in the United States, we join bishops in other countries, notably Canada and New Zealand, in stating as clearly and strongly as we can that violence against women, in the home or outside the home, is *never* justified. Violence in any form — physical, sexual, psychological, or verbal — is sinful; many times, it is a crime as well.

Abuse is a topic that no one likes to think about. But, because it exists in our parishes, dioceses, and neighborhoods, we present this statement as an initial step in what we hope will become a continuing effort in the Church in the United States to combat domestic violence against women. This statement is our response to the repeated requests of many women and men around the United States to address the issue.

We write out of our desire to offer the Church's resources to both the women who are battered and the men who abuse. Both groups need Jesus' strength and healing. We also write out of an awareness that times of economic distress such as the present, when wage-earners lose their jobs or are threatened with their loss, often are marked by an increase in domestic violence.

Though we focus here on violence against women, we are not implying that violence against men or against youths or violence against the elderly or the unborn is any less vicious. In fact, violence against any person is contrary to Jesus' gospel message to "love one another as I have loved you." When violence toward women is tolerated, it helps to set the stage for violent acts against other groups as well.

Violence against women in the home has particularly serious repercussions. When the woman is a mother and the violence takes place in front of her children, the stage is set for a cycle of violence that may be continued from generation to generation.

Domestic violence counselors teach that violence is learned behavior. In many cases, men who become abusive and the women who are abused grew up in homes where violence occurred. In such a situation, a child can grow up believing that violence is acceptable behavior; boys learn that this is a way to be powerful. Abuse counselors say that a child raised in a home with physical abuse is a thousand times more likely to use violence in his own family. At the same time, 25 percent of men who grow up in an abusive home choose not to use violence.

We agree with the bishops of Quebec, Canada in calling on the Christian community to "join forces with and complement the work of those associations and groups that are already involved in preventing and fighting this form of violence." [1]

We also agree with the Canadian church leaders, who stated that when men abuse women, they "reflect a lack of understanding in our society about how men and women ought to relate to each other. They violate the basic Christian values of justice, equality, respect, dignity, and peace; they go against the call to practical kindness, gentleness, faithfulness, mutual support, and to love one another as ourselves." [2]

THOSE WE ARE ADDRESSING

Recognizing the seriousness of the problem, we are addressing this statement to several audiences:

- to women who are victims of violence and who may need the Church's help to break out of their pain and isolation;

- to pastors, parish personnel, and educators who often are a first line of defense for women who are suffering abuse;
- to men, especially to those men who as abusers may not know how to break out of the cycle of violence — or who may not realize that it is possible to do so; and
- to society, which slowly is recognizing the extent of domestic violence against women.

NOTE: This is not meant to be an all-inclusive statement on violence against women. Because violence has many dimensions and ramifications, this statement is intended to be an introduction along with some practical pastoral suggestions of what parishes can do now.

**Domestic Violence
in the United States**

An estimated 3 to 4 million women in the United States are battered each year by their husbands or partners.*

Approximately 37 percent of obstetric patients of every race, class, and educational background report being physically abused while pregnant.*

More than 50 percent of the women murdered in the United States are killed by their partner or ex-partner.*

In 1987, 375,000 abused women and children were served by shelters and safe houses, but shelters can accept only about 60 percent of those who need help.**

---

*Journal of the American Medical Association
**National Women's Health Report *(see Bibliography for citations)*

DIMENSIONS OF THE PROBLEM

"Evidence collected over the last twenty years indicates that physical and sexual violence against women is an enormous problem. The high prevalence of violence against women brings them into regular contact with physicians; at least one in five women seen in emergency departments has symptoms relating to abuse."[3] Domestic violence is the most common form of violence in our society and the least reported crime.

What is *abuse?* It is any kind of behavior that one person uses to control another through fear and intimidation. It includes emotional and psychological abuse, battering, and sexual assault. Abuse is not limited to a single group. Cutting across racial and economic backgrounds, it occurs in families from every ethnic, economic, religious, and educational background.[4]

Because violence usually occurs in the privacy of people's homes, it often is shrouded in silence. People outside the family hesitate to interfere, even when they suspect abuse is occurring. Traditionally, the abuse of a wife by her husband has been considered "not only a family matter but virtually a husband's prerogative."[5] Even today, some people — mistakenly — argue that intervention by outside sources endangers the concept of the sanctity of the home.

Yet, "abuse, assault, or murder are not less serious because they occur within the family. . . . Violence, whether committed against family members or strangers, is antithetical to the Judeo-Christian messages of love and respect for the human person."[6]

As we have said, "a woman's dignity is destroyed in a particularly vicious and heinous way when she is treated violently. It shocks us to learn that currently one woman in four will be sexually assaulted in her lifetime."[7]

WHY MEN BATTER

Some psychiatric opinion holds that in a very small percentage of cases a psychophysical disorder may trigger violent behavior. However, in the majority of cases, other reasons can explain men's abusive behavior. Men who abuse women convince themselves that they have a right to do so. They may believe that violence is a way to dissipate tension and to solve problems — a view that society often supports. Battering and other forms of abuse occur in a society saturated with violence, where violence is glorified in books, in movies, and on television. Often, violence is portrayed as an appropriate way for people to respond to threatening situations.

Violent men tend to be extremely jealous, possessive, and easily angered. For example, they may fly into a rage because their spouse called her mother too often or because she didn't take the car in for servicing. Many try to isolate their wives by limiting their contact with family and friends.

Often, abusive men have low self-esteem and feel vulnerable and powerless. They are "more likely to have witnessed or experienced violence in childhood, to abuse alcohol, to be sexually assaultive to their wives, and to be at risk for violence against children."[8] Typically, they deny that the abuse is happening, or they insist that it happens rarely. Many try to pin the blame for their abusive behavior on someone or something other than themselves — their wives, the job, and so forth. Alcohol is an especially serious presence in many domestic-violence incidents. Alcohol and drugs lessen inhibitions and can heighten anger, impair judgment, desensitize, and increase the amount of force being used.

Many abusive men hold a view of women as inferior. Their conversation and language reveal their attitudes toward a woman's place in society. Many believe that men are meant to dominate and control women.

WHY WOMEN STAY

No answer fully explains why women stay with their abusers. Psychiatrists report that abusive relationships usually start out like other relationships; initially, they are loving and rewarding to both parties. Down the road, when the first violent act occurs, the woman is likely to be incredulous and willing to believe her spouse when he apologizes and promises that he will never repeat the abuse.

As time goes by and the abuse is repeated, many women come to believe they somehow are to blame for their husband or partner's actions; that if they just acted differently, the abuse would not occur. In time, as their self-esteem plummets, they feel trapped in the abusive relationship, especially if they have children and no other means of support.

Many abused women are isolated and alone with their pain. Even if they would like to seek help, they do not know where to go. In addition, many women are deeply ashamed to admit what is happening. They may believe that they are responsible for the success or failure of the marriage. Accordingly, many women are ashamed to admit that the man they married and with whom they have children, the one they love, is the one who is terrorizing them. "Violence at home typically leaves no place in which defenses can be let down."[9]

Finally, many battered wives are vulnerable economically. They may not believe that they can support themselves, much less their children. Accordingly, they do not see how they can escape. The result is that they become passive, anxious, and depressed. Most are unable to visualize a different future for themselves.

Over time, abuse escalates, though it may not always involve ongoing physical violence. Often, the threat of physical abuse is enough to terrorize women. For some victims, the final outcome of abuse is murder.

TOWARD A CHURCH RESPONSE TO DOMESTIC VIOLENCE

Scriptural Teaching

A theme throughout Scripture, beginning with Genesis, is that women and men are created in God's image. As John Paul II has said, "Both man and woman are human beings to an equal degree."[10] In the New Testament, Jesus consistently reached out to those on the fringes of society, those without power or authority, those with no one to speak on their behalf. He taught that all women and men are individuals worthy of respect and dignity.

Jesus unfailingly respected the human dignity of women. John Paul II reminds us that "Christ's way of acting, the Gospel of his words and deeds, is a consistent protest against whatever offends the dignity of women.[11] Jesus went out of his way to help the most vulnerable women. Think of the woman with the hemorrhage (see Mk 5:25-34) or the woman caught in adultery (see Jn 8:1-11). By his actions toward women in need, Jesus set an example for us today. Like him, we are called to find ways to help those most vulnerable women in our midst. We also need to find ways to help the men who want to break out of the pattern of abuse.

As a Church, one of the most worrying aspects of the abuse practiced against women is the use of biblical texts, taken out of context, to support abusive behavior. Counselors report that both abused women and their batterers use Scripture passages to justify their behavior.

Abused women say, "I can't leave this relationship. The Bible says it would be wrong." Abusive men say, "The Bible says my wife should be submissive to me." They take the biblical text and distort it to support their right to batter.

As bishops, we condemn the use of the Bible to condone abusive behavior. A correct reading of the Scriptures leads people to a relationship based on mutuality and love. Again, John Paul II describes it accurately: "In the 'unity of the two,' man and woman are called from the beginning not only to exist 'side by side' or 'together,' but they are also called to exist mutually one for the other." [12]

Even when the Bible uses traditional language to support the social order common in the day, the image presented is never one that condones the use of abuse to control another person. In Ephesians 5:21-33, for instance, which discusses relationships within the family, the general principle laid down is one of mutual submission between husband and wife. The passage holds out the image to husbands that they are to love their wives as they love their own body, as Christ loves the Church. Can you imagine Jesus battering his Church?

WHAT WE CAN DO TO HELP

Presented here are some practical suggestions to implement in your parish and diocese.

For Abused Women

- Begin to believe that you are not alone. Women have reached for help and found a way to a new life for themselves and their children.
- Talk in confidence to someone you trust: a relative, a friend, a parish priest, a deacon, a sister, a lay minister. Though it is distressing to talk about intimate family matters, trust them with the truth about yourself.
- If you must stay in the situation at least for now, set up a safety plan of action for when you think another episode of abuse is near. *This includes:* hiding a car key somewhere outside the house; keeping a small amount of money in a safe place; locating somewhere to go in an

emergency. When you fear another episode of violence is near, leave the house at once and do not return until you think it is likely to be over.

- Check out the resources in your area that offer help to battered women and their children. Your doctor or local librarian can refer you to the appropriate groups. Your diocesan Catholic Charities Office or Family Life Office can help. Catholic Charities Offices often have qualified counselors on staff and can provide emergency assistance and other kinds of help.
- The telephone book's yellow pages list Shelters for Abused Women in your area. 911 is the universal number to call the police.

For Men Who Abuse

- Have the courage to look honestly at your actions in the home and especially toward your wife. Begin to believe that you can change your behavior if you choose to do so.
- Acknowledge the fact that abuse is your problem; it's not your wife's problem. Do not look for excuses to batter.
- Be willing to reach out for help. Talk to someone you trust who can help you look at what is going on. Contact Catholic Charities or shelters in your area for the name of a program for abusers.
- Keep in mind that the Church is available to help you. Part of the mission Jesus trusted to us is to offer healing when it is needed. Contact your parish.
- Find alternative ways to act when you become frustrated or angry. Talk to other men who

have overcome abusive behavior. Find out what
they did and how they did it.

For Pastors and Pastoral Staff

- Make your parish a safe place where abused
  women and men who batter can come for help.
- Learn as much as you can about domestic
  violence. Be alert for the signs of abuse among
  parish women.
- Join in the national observance of October as
  "Domestic Violence Awareness Month." Dedi-
  cate at least one weekend that month to educate
  parishioners about abuse and its likely presence
  in your parish.
- Make sure that parish homilies address domestic violence. If abused women do not hear
  anything about abuse, they think no one cares.
  Describe what abuse is so that women begin to
  recognize and name what is happening to them.
- If you suspect abuse, ask direct questions. Ask
  the woman if she is being hit or hurt at home.
  Carefully evaluate her response. Some women
  do not realize they are being abused, or they lie
  to protect their spouses.
- In talking to an abused person, be careful of
  your language. Don't say anything that will
  bolster her belief that it is her fault and that she
  must change her behavior. The victim is not to
  blame. The abuser must be accountable for his
  behavior.
- In marriage-preparation education sessions,
  check couples' patterns of handling disagree-
  ments and their families' problem-solving
  patterns. Suggest postponing marriage if you
  identify signs of abuse or potential abuse.

- In baptismal-preparation programs, be alert that the arrival of a child and its attendant stress may trigger violent behavior.
- Keep an updated list of resources for abused women in your area.
- Have an action plan in place to follow if an abused woman calls on you for help. Build a relationship with police and domestic-violence agencies. Find a safe place for abused women.

For Educators and Catechists

- Make sure all teachers and catechists receive training in how to recognize abuse.
- Insist that teaching and texts be free of sexual stereotyping. Battering thrives on sexism.
- Try to include shelters for abused women and children on lists of service for confirmation classes and other service groups.
- Include information about domestic violence in human-sexuality and family-life classes.
- Sponsor parish workshops on domestic violence.

Ultimately, abused women must make their own decisions about staying or leaving. It is important to be honest with women about the risks involved. Remember: Women are at a most dangerous point when they attempt to leave their abusers. Research indicates that "women who leave their batterers are at a 75 percent greater risk of being killed by the batterer than those who stay." [13]

For Liturgy Committees

- In parish reconciliation services, identify violence against women as a sin.
- Include intercessions for victims of abuse, for the men who abuse women, and for those who help both victims and abusers.
- Strive to use inclusive language in liturgical celebrations, as authorized.

For Commissions on Women and Other Women's Groups

- Include a list of names and telephone numbers of parish contacts in parish bulletins and directories for abused women to call.
- Work to see that women as well as men are represented in parish leadership positions (e.g., on parish finance and pastoral councils).
- Offer free meeting space to support groups for abused women and for men who abuse.
- Spearhead education in your parish/diocese on crimes of violence against women.
- Look for resource people in your parish who can offer their expertise.

A CONCLUSION AND A PRAYER

This statement has addressed the problem of violence against women in their homes. Such violence has repercussions on all residing there, even to the extent of setting up a situation for repeating violence in successive generations. Accordingly, we encourage all parents and all educators and catechists to teach children from the earliest ages that abuse is not appropriate behavior. As pastors of the Church, we are dedicated to encouraging all that nurtures and strengthens family life.

One of the sources of healing we have in our lives as Christians is prayer. The psalms in particular capture the depth and range of human anguish and hope and reassure us of God's help. Psalm 31 may be an especially apt prayer for women who are dealing with abusive situations. With all of you we pray:

Have pity on me, O LORD, for I am in distress;

with sorrow my eye is consumed;

my soul also, and my body.

———————

I am like a dish that is broken. . . .

But my trust is in you, O LORD;

I say, "You are my God."

(Ps 31:10-15)

END NOTES

1. Social Affairs Committee, Assembly of Quebec Bishops, *A Heritage of Violence: A Pastoral Reflection on Conjugal Violence* (Montreal: L'Assemblee des eveques du Quebec, 1989).

2. Canadian Church Leaders, "Violence against Women." Testimony given by an ecumenical coalition to the Canadian Panel on Violence against Women. *Origins* 21:47 (April 30, 1992):789-790.

3. Council on Scientific Affairs, American Medical Association, "Violence against Women," *Journal of the American Medical Association (JAMA)* (June 17, 1992):3184-3189.

4. The Women's Commission, *A Pastoral Response to Domestic Violence* (Richmond, VA: Catholic Diocese of Richmond, n.d.).

5. Commission on Women in Church and Society, *A Pastoral Response to Domestic Violence against Women* (Buffalo, NY: Catholic Diocese of Buffalo, n.d.).

6. United States Catholic Conference, Office of Domestic Social Development, *Violence in the Family: A National Concern, A Church Concern,* Barbara Ann Stolz, ed. (Washington, DC: USCC Office for Publishing and Promotion Services, 1979).

7. Ad Hoc Committee for the Pastoral on Women in Society and the Church, National Conference of Catholic Bishops, *Called to Be One in Christ Jesus,* third draft (Washington, DC: United States Catholic Conference, 1992), p. 46.

8. *JAMA, ibid.*

9. *Ibid.*

10. John Paul II, *Mulieris Dignitatem (On the Dignity and Vocation of Women),* Apostolic Letter (Vatican City: Polyglot Press, 1989), 6, 7.

11. *Ibid.*, 15.

12. *Ibid.*, 7.

13. National Coalition Against Domestic Violence, 1990.

RESOURCES

Catholic Social Services, Diocese of Green Bay, Box 23825, Green Bay, WI 54305-3825. Telephone: 1-414-437-7531.
Family Affairs Commission, National Council of Catholic Women, 1275 K Street, Washington, DC 20005. Telephone: 1-202-682-0334.

BIBLIOGRAPHY

Pamphlets/Brochures

Catholic Social Services. Diocese of Green Bay. *The Cycle of Violence*. Green Bay, WI.
Commission on Women in Church and Society. Diocese of Buffalo. *A Pastoral Response to Domestic Violence against Women*. Buffalo, NY.
National Women's Health Resource Center. National Women's Health Report: Domestic Violence as a Health Issue. Washington, DC.
The Women's Commission. Diocese of Richmond. *A Pastoral Response to Domestic Violence*. Richmond, VA.

Articles/Statements

Ad Hoc Committee for the Pastoral on Women in Society and in the Church. National Conference of Catholic Bishops. *Called to Be One in Christ Jesus*. Third Draft. Washington, DC, 1992.
Brody, Jane. "Personal Health." Health Section, *New York Times*. March 18, 1992.
Canadian Church Leaders. "Violence against Women." *Origins* 21:47 (March 27, 1992):789-790. Testimony to Canadian Panel on Violence against Women.
Catholic Commission for Justice and Peace. New Zealand Catholic Bishops' Conference. "Women in the Church." *Dossier* 3:6, pp. 262-274.
Council on Scientific Affairs. American Medical Association. "Violence against Women." *Journal of the American Medical Association*. June 17, 1992. A Report of the Council.

National Council of Catholic Women. "Can We Help Heal the Hurt?" *Catholic Woman* (Nov./Dec. 1991).

National Women's Health Resource Center. "Violence against Women." A Center-sponsored Conference Report, Washington, DC. June 21, 1991.

Office for Domestic Social Development, United States Catholic Conference. *Violence in the Family: A National Concern, A Church Concern.* Barbara Ann Stolz, ed. Washington, DC. 1979.

Social Affairs Committee. Assembly of Quebec Bishops. *A Heritage of Violence: A Pastoral Reflection on Conjugal Violence.* Quebec, Canada. 1989.

Crux Special: To Live Without Fear

Here is the complete text of the statement issued June 13, 1991 by the Canadian Conference of Catholic Bishops Permanent Council on Violence against Women.

INTRODUCTION

On May 13, 1991, the Federal Government announced in the Speech from the Throne, its intention to appoint a "blue ribbon panel of concerned Canadian men and women to inquire into the serious problem of violence against women in our society." This is a significant and most welcome initiative.

Every year at least one million women are physically, sexually, or psychologically abused by their husbands or common law partners. Two women are murdered by their male partners every week. Fifty-six percent of urban Canadian women as compared to eighteen percent of men feel unsafe walking alone in their neighborhoods after dark.[1]

A SIN AND A CRIME

Violence against women breaks the fifth commandment. It is a sin, a crime, and a serious social problem. It is not only an individual, private or family matter.

Many of our ecumenical partners[2] and the Social Affairs Committee of the Assembly of Quebec Bishops[3] have prepared statements and workshop materials that include an analysis of the social and individual causes and dynamics of violence against women. It is not our intention to repeat the good work that has already been done.

The purpose of this statement is to express our deep concern about violence against women and to identify some of the ways the Catholic community, in collaboration with others, can work for short-term and long-term solutions.

PASTORAL APPROACHES TO DOMESTIC VIOLENCE

Since clergy and pastoral workers are often among the first people to be contacted by an abused woman, there is a significant opportunity for them to do real good or real harm. Some of the pastoral approaches that have been identified as harmful or helpful are listed below.

Harmful Approaches

1. Being Uninformed
The dynamics of family violence are very specialized and very explosive. It is critical that everyone in ministry become informed about these dynamics by attending seminars or workshops, visiting emergency shelters, or reading the available literature. Failure to understand the situation could be lethal. It is also important to be prepared to discern signs of abuse among people who seek counseling.

2. Premature Reconciliation
Counseling premature reconciliation minimizes the woman's pain, suffering, and danger. Moreover, it will not stop the abuse, protect the victim, or provide any healing. Only the man can stop the

violence by accepting responsibility for it and changing his behavior.

In an abusive situation, the priority must be the safety of the woman. This may involve a marital separation. True reconciliation can occur only after the woman has been protected, the man has been held accountable for his actions, and he has genuinely repented. Acceptance of responsibility for the abuse and a firm purpose of amendment are integral to authentic repentance. It is therefore important that the man, even when he has expressed regret, be encouraged to seek professional help.

3. Silence

The abused woman is often very isolated; church may be the one place she is still able to go. If she never hears a homily on this topic, her sense of isolation may be increased or she may not feel free to approach the pastor or a member of the pastoral team.

4. Misuse of Scripture

The misuse of Scripture to justify the domination of women is unacceptable. Clearly, men and women are created equally in the image of God and are one in Christ.

Pope John Paul II says that it is a sinful situation when a woman is "the object of domination and male possession." [4] He affirms that the passage at 3:16 of Genesis ("Your desire shall be for your husband and he shall rule over you") does not mean that men are created to rule over women. On the contrary, the "ruling over" that we have seen in history is the result of sin and broken relationships between God and humanity and among people.

If we as Christians believe that the relationship between God and humanity has been restored through Jesus Christ, then should we not also believe that the relationship of equality between men and women has also been reaffirmed? Anything less diminishes both men and women.

Helpful Approaches

Through the richness of its tradition and its commitment to community, the Church can help to end violence against women. The following are some pastoral approaches that have been found to be effective:

- taking the woman seriously when she discloses abuse;
- avoiding sentimental clichés;
- following up after the initial contact;
- acquiring an ability to detect abuse;
- becoming informed of the available community resources (medical, legal, shelter, counseling) and working with them;
- being ready to deal with the profound spiritual questions that arise concerning the woman's relationship with God and her worth and dignity as a person; and
- creating a parish atmosphere where clergy and laity can discuss the question of violence against women openly and sensitively in homilies and other forums and offer concrete support.

PREVENTION OF VIOLENCE AGAINST WOMEN

Helpful, compassionate and just responses to women who are victims of violence are important and needed. Long-term strategies for prevention are critical. Each sector in society must contribute their expertise and energy to finding long-term solutions. Governments, communities, social, religious, and educational institutions have a role to play. As bishops, we shall work, in collaboration with others, for prevention by:

- providing catechetical programs that teach the equality of all persons;
- developing marriage preparation programs that stress the fundamental equality of men and women, avoid sexual stereotypes, deal with the issue of violence against women, and teach nonviolent methods of communication and resolving disputes;
- offering programs or pastoral messages on human sexuality that celebrate the equality and dignity of men and women;
- encouraging local diocesan structures to deal with this important issue;
- urging the Catholic community to support social policies and programs that enhance the equality of women and address the long term (e.g., child care, emergency shelters and second-stage housing, affordable housing, affirmative action, pay equity, legislation against violent and degrading pornography);
- encouraging theologians and other scholars to reflect and write on the root causes of violence against women;
- giving seminarians and priests information on the equality of men and women and the dynamics of violence against women; and
- supporting the involvement of women in the formation of seminarians and continuing education of priests.

VIOLENCE DESTROYS ALL THAT IS HUMAN

A healthy and creative society cannot tolerate any form of violence. When this violence is based on the erroneous and insidious premise that men are entitled to dominate women, it is particularly abhorrent and dangerous. This attitude and behavior are capable of destroying all that is life-affirming and beautiful in society. As Pope John Paul II said on his visit to Canada: *"Human beings live by wisdom, by culture and by morality. Violence is in complete contradiction to such a life. Violence creates the justifiable need for defense. And at the same time, violence threatens to destroy the sources of human life. Not only does it threaten to kill human beings, millions of men and women, but it threatens to destroy all that is human."* [5]

Let us work together as men and women of faith for a truly nonviolent society that respects the equality, integrity and dignity of all persons. Let us break the cycle of violence and enable women to live without fear.

Canadian Conference of Catholic Bishops
Permanent Council
June 13, 1991

REFERENCES

1. Linda MacLeod, *The City for Women: No Safe Place*, 1989. (A study commission by the Secretary of State).
   Health and Welfare Canada, The National Clearinghouse on Family Violence, *Wife Assault*, January 1990.
   Linda MacLeod, *Battered But Not Beaten: Preventing Wife Battering in Canada*, Ottawa: Canadian Advisory Council on the Status of Women, 1987.
2. The Catholic Women's League of Canada has prepared an annotated bibliography of these resources.
3. Social Affairs Commission of the Assembly of Quebec Bishops, *A Heritage of Violence: A Pastoral Reflection on Conjugal Violence*, 1989. A bibliography is included.
4. John Paul II, *On the Dignity and Vocation of Women*, 1988, no. 10.
5. John Paul II, Ottawa, September 20, 1984.

Breaking the Silence: A Biblical Reflection

by Mitzi Eilts

> Direct your heart to her,
> take counsel and speak.
> — Judges 19:30

The stories of violence against women and children are every-where. Tales of abuse in the family are so common we are practi-cally deaf to their recurring terror. Scripture itself is a landscape dotted with telltale signs. Women, only a few of them even named, are abused, rejected and raped by brothers, husbands and strang-ers. Daughters are traded and sacrificed. A concubine wife is sliced into pieces by the master who had traded her body for his own safety (Judges 19).

Where is justice? Where is God? Where is the church? Where are we? We have been silent and deaf to the recurring terror. Silent, and the silence is deafening.

Who's going to hear? When will action be taken? Justice be done? Will the silence ever be broken?

There are some who hear now — the battered women's shelters, the sexual trauma centers, the child abuse workers, and sometimes a family member, friend or pastor. Yet, there are too few to deal with the numerous incidences of battering, incest, and rape. Seldom are those who do hear and respond to those of us in the church. Too often we are ready to believe that our religious values insulate our families from such goings-on, or that our faith will protect and heal and nothing else is needed.

Meanwhile, the overarching silence is deafening, disabling.

Silence is a conspiracy. It conspires to cover our complicity in the violence and to conceal our impotence in defeating it. The more we don't talk about it, don't listen to the victims of it, don't see the evidence all around us — the longer it will continue. The longer we take to face squarely the reality of this demon in our midst, the bigger will be our fear of confronting it and the harder it will be to make better all our lives.

Study after study indicates that the violence and abuse are horribly widespread. One out of every two women is battered by an intimate partner in their lifetime. One out of every three girls and one out of every seven boys is sexually abused by a family member or family friend.

These are horrible facts to hear and consider. But they are even more horrible things to live through. Our silence doesn't make it go away. We'd like to pretend that none of this occurs at all and to avoid thinking that it can or has occurred. But silence about violence is a conspiracy which allows it to go on and on, undetected. It just goes on; it doesn't go away. Those who are its victims will tell you that. The silence is a door locked against justice and mercy.

The violent story of abuse and murder found in Judges 19 offers, however, a Word for us in the church as a whole. From this story comes the Word for the church about the silence. The concluding command which follows the telling of the horror tells us all to "consider it, take counsel, and speak." Thanks to the work of Phyllis Trible, biblical scholar, we can know that this command is an even stronger and more personal Word. The original

Hebrew says not just "consider it" but *"direct your heart to her, take counsel and speak. "* It is the silence, the unwillingness or the inability to acknowledge the violence, the horror, which leaves victims isolated and thwarts healing. To tell each other that we know it exists; to speak of battering and incest and rape from our pulpits and in our educational programs — is to challenge violence's right to exist. We are commanded to break the silence; to give credence to the stories; to be the door that opens to the victim's/survivor's knock.

There are things to be done, ways to respond, and when we "take the stories to heart" we will each know what it is we can do. It might be to volunteer for the local shelter or rape crisis center; to help raise funds or give money; to lobby the city or county to support such programs; to talk about the issues with people where we work; or to assist secular professionals to deal with the faith questions which violence and abuse bring up. It may be to allow our own stories to surface and find support and healing.

It is time. It is time that we of the church take the stories of violence against women and children to heart, and then speak out against them.

Reprinted with permission from *Common Lot* (Autumn 1990), p. 10. (Available from UCC Coordinating Center for Women, United Church of Christ, 700 Prospect Avenue, Cleveland, Ohio 44115.)

Ministry in Response to Violence in the Family: Pastoral and Prophetic

Marie M. Fortune

The Saturday before Easter found a pastor in his
study at the church. The woman who appeared at
the door was bruised and bloody and asking for
help. As the pastor took her in and inquired about
her injuries, she asked that he call the police. Her
three-year-old son was still at home, she said. Her
husband, who had beaten her, had also threatened
her son. She feared for her child's safety.

    After calling the police, the pastor called me.
"There is a woman here who has been beaten by her
husband," he told me. "Will you talk with her?" In
our very brief conversation, I encouraged her to
seek medical care and to go immediately to the
shelter for battered women. I gave her the phone
number there. Then the police arrived and our
interchange ceased.

There are two lessons about ministry to be learned from this incident. First, the battered woman came to a church near her home
— a church to which she did not belong and which she had never
entered before. She came seeking sanctuary as she literally ran
for her life. Her expectation that she would find safety by coming

to a church was legitimate. Fortunately, she found someone there to take her in. The church's historic role as a place of safety for those who are in danger and at risk of suffering further harm makes it an appropriate place for battered women to come seeking help.

Second, when the woman arrived at the church, she found a pastor whose compassion and desire to help were apparent. However, she also found a pastor who was ill prepared to assist her in this crisis. He cared deeply for her and did not turn her away, but he did not know how to minister to her. Instead, he called me to provide what he should have been prepared to offer. The church as an institution and its people in ordained and lay ministry are, by and large, ill prepared to respond to victims or abusers in the midst of family violence.[1]

PASTORAL SILENCE AND NEGLECT

The result of this lack of preparation has been silence and neglect in the face of a widespread social problem — a problem that has manifested itself in the lives of individuals and church families for many years. In addition, many pastors — blinded by cultural norms and by the common practice of blaming the victim — have exacerbated situations that came to their attention by advising behaviors that never challenged the violence and that perpetuated the abusive environment. "Go home and try to be a better wife," some might say, or "Submit to your husband as Scripture says," or "Pray for your husband; God will protect you."

The parable of the good Samaritan (Luke 10:29-37) provides a paradigm through which to view the common responses to victims of family violence. The priest and Levite saw, but did not see, a battered person by the side of the road. This person, clearly injured and in need, had not merely fallen from his donkey. He had been assaulted by someone. The priest and Levite denied that they saw him, denied that they saw his injuries, denied that they saw his need and passed by him there. The Samaritan, who was regarded as an outcast in the community, also came by this injured man, but his actions were different. He stopped, attended to the man's wounds, took him to a safe place, and provided financial support for his care and recovery.

Why did the priest and Levite pass by? Why did they ignore this person in need before them — in contradiction of their own values expressed in the hospitality code that required care for the sojourner?

> First, they were afraid. They recognized that the injured man was a victim of assault, and they did not know if the assailant was still in the vicinity. They feared that should they stop and attend to this victim, they might make themselves vulnerable to attack as well.
>
> Second, they were not prepared. They did not know what to do. No one in seminary had taught them about victimization or explained how to help in such a crisis. They lacked the confidence to respond, and this increased their anxiety.
>
> Third, they did not know what other resources might be available to help this victim. So they felt isolated, faced with the possible burden of caring for him alone.
>
> Finally, they blamed the victim. They assumed that somehow this person had brought his suffering on himself. After all, what was he doing out traveling alone, anyway (just as they were)?

All these typical reactions to a victim of violence allowed the priest and Levite to dissociate themselves from the injured man and to avoid the empathic response that they might otherwise have felt. The Samaritan simply responded without hesitation. He did what he could with the resources available to him.

Up until very recently, it has been the secular community, through the Battered Women's Movement, that has played the good Samaritan and responded to the victims of violence in the family. The church and its ministers have passed by, just as the priest and Levite did — and for the same reasons.

Lack of Preparation

The vast majority of seminarians still do not receive instruction regarding ministry in situations of family violence. They are seldom even alerted to the fact that they will see family violence in whatever form of ministry they pursue. A working knowledge of this problem (as contrasted with a specialist's knowledge) is necessary if one is to do effective ministry with individuals and families. The absence of this knowledge base is translated into an absence of skills and confidence in responding to the victim or abuser.

Denial and Minimization

The common response to evidence of violence in the family is minimization and denial. This response is the individual's emotional distancing, used as a means of coping with a reality that is distasteful, disquieting, and generally overwhelming. The response is common for victim and abuser alike as well as for all manner of helpers, friends, family members, and ministers. The things that victims of abuse will hesitantly describe to a minister are often unbelievable. However, this does not mean that they are untrue. In an effort to make the situation manageable and tolerable, there is the temptation to minimize and deny the particulars. This temptation, while ever present, should be resisted.

Solo Ministry

Traditionally, the pastor, priest, or rabbi has the self-perception of being a solitary helper and one-person resource to a congregation. It is assumed that the minister carries the responsibility of providing for all the needs of the congregants. The minister's ability to do this becomes the measure of ministerial success. In addition, some ministers may have a long-standing distrust of secular resources, whether they be the counseling profession or the legal system. Because of these two factors, a minister may sometimes be hesitant to refer a congregant to a secular professional or program. The noncooperation that results further reinforces the isolation of victims or abusers. They have sought help from their minister but have found that the church has generally not provided for their needs.

The minister in a local church setting is a generalist. In this role, ministers are expected to know a little about a lot of areas. When it comes to addressing violence in the family, this is a reasonable expectation. Ministers should know enough to avoid perpetuating the problem, by (1) identifying the problem clearly; (2) making appropriate referrals; and (3) providing the resource that they are best qualified to provide: pastoral intervention and support. Ministers should not attempt to provide long-term counseling to victims or offenders (unless this is an area of special training they have received).[2] But ministers should be available to assist with the issues of faith that so often accompany the crisis of the disclosure of abuse.

Ministers need to look to other professionals and paraprofessionals with expertise in the field of family violence as appropriate referrals. These peers are invaluable resources. They enable the minister to respond with confidence to a crisis situation and to bring to bear specialized pastoral care as a complement to the services provided by the shelter worker, police officer, counselor, or child protection worker.

Theological Confusion

The minister has often faced the violent family in theological confusion. This confusion, at best, has stymied a much-needed pastoral response to the individuals involved and, at worst, has exacerbated the situation. The resulting theological rationalization for ignoring the violence has meshed with the social and cultural rationalizations. It has left the violence and its destruction of the family virtually unchallenged.

Even on the brink of the twenty-first century, it is not surprising to read these instructions given to priests in the fifteenth century to guide their counsel of husbands.

> Scold your wife sharply, bully and terrify her. If this
> doesn't work, take up a stick and beat her soundly,
> for it is better to punish the body and correct the
> soul than to damage the soul and spare the body. . . .
> Then readily beat her, not in rage but out of charity
> and concern for her soul, so that the beating will
> redound to your merit and her good.
>
> — Rules of Marriage

It cannot be assumed that substantial progress beyond this theological perspective has been achieved.

For example, a theology that allows a victim of wife abuse to explain her condition by viewing herself as a suffering servant — someone whom God has called to suffer at the hands of her abuser in the hope of bringing him to salvation — is in fact a doormat theology. It serves only to justify the abuse and the domination of one person by another and to maintain the status quo of coercion and violence in a marital relationship. It denies the abused wife the comprehension of her condition that might allow her to seek release from this bondage.

Likewise, a theology that maintains the priority of obedience to the authority of the father in the family — even when that father is molesting his children — denies the suffering of the children at his hands and reinforces the misuse of parental power to the detriment of those vulnerable to it.

Theological assertions of the rightness of women's unquestioning submission to men in marriage merely reflect the practices of a worldly, sexist culture and undergird the societal permission given to abusive men to persist in their mistreatment of women. This theology does not challenge the practices of this world with a vision of the kingdom in which justice and mutuality are normative. Yet such theologies continue to be promulgated.

They give permission to abusers to abuse, just as they deny victims the opportunity to question or resist their victimization.

Since many of these theological assertions are, supposedly, Scripturally inspired, perhaps the place to begin to question this practice is with the hermeneutical norm itself. How should Scripture be interpreted? The minister or congregant who seeks to be faithful to Scripture reads that Scripture through a particular lens. The lens is shaped by experience and by some vision or expectation of the way life should be. Hence the question, "Where are you coming from?" determines what you see and hear, preach and counsel.

It is important for that vision also to be shaped by Scripture. Susan Thistlethwaite asserts: "No authority except that of the Bible itself can challenge the image . . . of woman as silent, subordinate, bearing her children in pain, and subject to the absolute authority of her husband." [3] Hence the following Scriptures provide a basis for understanding and interpreting those Scriptures that address marriage and family relationship in particular.

> The thief comes only to steal and kill and destroy. I came that they may have life, and have it abundantly.
>
> — John 10:10

> Do you not know that you are God's temple and that God's Spirit dwells in you? If anyone destroys God's temple, God will destroy that person. For God's temple is holy, and you are that temple.
>
> —1 Corinthians 3:16-17

> I have set before you life and death, blessings and curses. Choose life so that you and your descendants may live.
>
> — Deuteronomy 30:19

> "The spirit of the Lord is upon me, because God has anointed me to bring good news to the poor. God has sent me to proclaim release to the captives and recovery of sight to the blind, to let the oppressed go free, to proclaim the year of the Lord's favor." [Jesus reading from the prophet Isaiah in the temple.]
>
> —Luke 4:18-19

Hence Scripture-based adages, such as spare the rod, wives be subject, honor your father, or God hates divorce must be understood through these Scriptures and not in isolation as justification for violence in the home.

Clarity of one's Scriptural interpretation can support clarity of one's theological perspective on family violence and give direction to one's pastoral intervention.[4]

Confession

Any discussion of ministry in response to violence in the family should begin with confession. There have been times for every person in ministry when we looked but did not see, listened but did not hear, and so passed by the victim of family violence. Confession that we were hesitant, ill prepared, anxious, unaware, unavailable, or insensitive is a step in our preparation for ministry in response to violence in the family. The purpose of this confession is not to instill guilt, which leads to further immobilization. Rather it is to acknowledge our previous experiences and resolve to prepare ourselves for the next occasion when we are called upon to minister to victims or offenders.

PASTORAL RESPONSE

The initial response by a minister to the disclosure of any form of violence in the family will be a pastoral intervention. This intervention can take many forms, depending on the circumstances. The complexity of the issues that are revealed through disclosure can easily lead to confusion for the minister who attempts to respond. In the midst of often chaotic circumstances, it is valuable to have a means of maintaining clarity as to one's goals in intervening. Enhanced by a general understanding of the problem of violence in the family, the following three goals provide a framework for response. They can guide the minister through the confusion to effective intervention.[5]

1. Protection of the victim or victims from further abuse.

Although the form of this response will depend on the degree of danger faced by the victims, it is the number one priority in response to battering or child sexual abuse. The immediate safety of the person harmed must be secured. For the battered wife, this may mean encouraging her to go to a shelter for battered women or taking her there yourself. Or it may mean supporting her desire to go to visit her sister in a neighboring state for a few weeks. Or, if you are on the telephone with her and she is calling from her home where she is in the process of being beaten, it means calling the police immediately to intervene.

2. Stopping the abuser's violence.

Again the circumstances will dictate the form of response. This goal encompasses two dimensions: immediate cessation of the abusive behavior and calling the abuser to accountability for it in order to prevent its continuation. Immediate but temporary cessation may be accomplished by helping the victim get to a safe, secret place. But the abuser's violent behavior must also be confronted. Arrest is one of the most effective means by which to begin the process of stopping an abuser's violence. It may be for the abuser the first time that anyone with authority has made it clear that this behavior is criminal and intolerable. The authority of the pastoral office can well be used to reinforce this message. But the weight of the criminal justice system is an important resource to bring to bear. Research now suggests that arrest is the single most effective deterrent to future abusive behavior.[6] Court-mandated treatment following conviction also seems to be the most effective rehabilitative resource.

3. Restoration of the family relationship or mourning the loss of the relationship.

The third goal of ministry with victims and abusers presents the possibility of reconciliation and healing of individuals and of relationships. But this goal is entirely dependent on the successful accomplishment of goals #1 and #2. Restoration of a relationship is impossible prior to the authentic accomplishment of these more urgent goals.

It is possible to create the appearance of restoration at an earlier point, as by encouraging a couple to live together in the same house and to attend church together. But genuine restoration is not accomplished by such superficial signs.

The process of achieving goals #1 and #2 may take months or years. Even so, any circumvention of this agenda will prevent family members from reaching goal #3 and will result in the ultimate loss of the relationship. Restoration cannot be based on partial success or on the promises of the abuser. It is dependent on clear evidence of change in the abuser's behavior. Even then, there is only the possibility of restoration. There are no guarantees. The outcome depends on how severe the damage has been to the relationship.

The abuser's violence has broken apart the family or marriage relationship and has destroyed the safety and trust that make for intimacy and covenant. The certainty and the evidence that coercion and violence are no longer part of an abuser's repertoire in relationships are prerequisites for considering the possibility of reconciliation.

If, for whatever reason, goals #1 and #2 are not accomplished, then the option remaining is mourning the loss of the relationship. This amounts to an acknowledgment that the positive dimensions of the relationship and its future possibilities are irretrievably lost. Hence grief will result for the victim, the abuser, and the community of which they are a part. Still, out of this loss comes the possibility for the victim of healing and of a new life.

If one of the priorities of ministry is to restore what was broken and to reconcile the rupture of relationships, then our sincere attention to protecting the victim and calling the abuser to account are the means by which we may help people accomplish restoration. To ignore goals #1 and #2 would preclude any possibility of a genuine healing of the relationship.

COOPERATION AND CONSISTENCY

Ministers have neither the time nor the expertise to provide all that is needed by victims and abusers. Multiple resources are required. Professionals and paraprofessionals in the secular community are allies with specialized skills much needed by victims and abusers. An informed and cooperative approach to these resources makes possible a comprehensive response to a victim or abuser.

Consistency is equally important in response to victims and abusers. The victim needs consistent support and advocacy from all the resource people she encounters. The abuser needs consistent confrontation and expectations of accountability. It does no good for a mother to notify Child Protective Services when she finds her husband molesting her child, for the CPS worker to gather evidence, and for the prosecutor to file charges and bring the case to court, if the man's pastor is going to arrive and testify on his behalf, claiming that it is impossible for this man to have molested his child because he teaches Sunday school and sings in the choir. Instead, this pastor should know that it is very possible that the same father who otherwise appears to be an upstanding member of the community could well have molested his child. This is a common rather than an uncommon situation. The proper pastoral response should *not* be to try to help an incest offender avoid the consequences of his behavior.

PARTICULARITIES OF THE PASTORAL ROLE

The unique and particular resource that ministry can bring to both victim and abuser is that of pastoral care in the context of their faith. In addition to the multifaceted crisis wrought by violence in the family, there is, for many people, also a crisis of faith.

In this immediate experience of fear, suffering, anxiety, and confusion there are a multitude of spiritual themes and concerns that rise to the surface.

> Why does God let this happen to me?
> Suffering servant/my cross to bear
> Separation and divorce
> Honor your father
> Forgiveness
> Roles of husband and wife
> Abandonment by God

For many, these themes and concerns are of ultimate importance because they have to do with meaning and purpose, salvation and eternity. The presence and counsel of the minister and congregation in giving attention to these issues is critical.[7]

But the reality is that this pastoral presence can either help or hinder the victim or abuser in dealing with the violence. The teachings of the church — and Scripture itself — will be a part of the questions that face victims and abusers. These aspects of faith will either be a resource that will support and encourage the victim or abuser in dealing with the violence or they will be a roadblock that will prevent their dealing with the violence. The faith issues will never be neutral or irrelevant. Here are some examples.

> A battered woman, who was still living in the abusive relationship after ten years, viewed her abuse as God's punishment for the fact that she had had sex with her boyfriend on a single occasion when she was sixteen years old. Her interpretation of the meaning of her abuse prevented her from questioning it and seeking a safe refuge. Thus her misinterpretation of her faith served as a roadblock preventing her from dealing with her abuse.
>
> A woman discovered her husband molesting her children and had him arrested and removed from the home. She protected her children from further abuse and called him to accountability. The response of her church was to forbid her to teach Sunday

school and to forbid her children to attend Sunday school anymore. Nothing was said to the male incest offender by the church. Instead of supporting her, this woman's church became a potential roadblock to her fulfilling her responsibility to her children. Her choice then was to leave the church.

An incest offender facing prosecution went to his pastor begging forgiveness. The pastor prayed with the offender, assured him of forgiveness, and sent him home. No report was made and no help was provided, either for the victims of the man's abuse or for him. The incest continued. The pastor's response created a roadblock for the offender. It did not help him stop his abuse of his children.

A battered wife who had survived twenty years of abuse was a Christian and active in her local church. One day her abusive husband told her that he did not want her going to church anymore. That was the last straw for her. Her faith was central to her life and she refused to allow him to take it from her. The importance of her faith and the strength which it gave her became a resource that finally made it possible for her to seek to protect herself from further abuse.

A mother of two small children who was abused in her marriage separated from her husband and divorced him after it became clear that he had no intention of changing his abusive behavior. Her church supported her financially for six months until she could find stable employment. In the custody hearing, her pastor and head deacon both testified on her behalf so that she could retain custody of her children. Her church was the resource she needed to protect herself and her children. It helped her to begin to heal from the pain she had known.

An incest offender came to his pastor, confessing his sin and promising never to harm his child again. The pastor assured him that God is a forgiving God but that God expects sincere repentance and amendment of life. The pastor then instructed the offender to telephone Child Protective Services and to report himself. The man complied. The pastor

then told the man that he wanted to see him each
week for prayer and Bible study in conjunction with
the treatment program in which he would be placed.
This offender's pastor and church became a
resource for him in confronting his abuse, and they
supported him in stopping it.

The task of ministry in response to family violence is to provide the resources of faith and of the church to help people accomplish the three goals listed above. The task is also to minimize the roadblocks that a person's faith and church can raise as a result of distortion, misinterpretation, and misdirection.

Pastoral Agenda

Each of the three goals presents a practical agenda for intervention in a situation of family violence. In addition, however, they present a pastoral agenda. The minister's role combines the two.

1. Hospitality and sanctuary for victims (protection)

Pastorally, there are two mandates from the Jewish and Christian traditions that call for hospitality and sanctuary in response to victims. From Jewish ethics and practice there was the hospitality code that required the community to protect the widow, orphan, and sojourner in their midst. The intent of this practice was to provide for those left vulnerable by circumstance and those who were without resources to provide for themselves. Certainly the abused adult or child today fits the category in being vulnerable and in need of hospitality and protection. In addition, the practice from Christian tradition of providing sanctuary for those in danger of further harm is a clear ethical mandate for ministry in the face of family violence.

2. Repentance for the abuser (accountability and stopping the abusive behavior)

Jesus instructs the disciples on how to respond to the brother who sins:

"Be on your guard! If another disciple sins, you
must rebuke the offender, and if there is repentance,
you must forgive. And if the same person sins against
you seven times a day, and turns back to you seven
times and says, 'I repent,' you must forgive."

— Luke 17:3-4

After taking care of oneself (goal #1), the response to the
abuser is to rebuke or confront him. Then *if* he repents, forgive
him. Repentance, when found in both the Hebrew and Greek references, very clearly refers to turning around, a change of self:
"Repent and turn from all your transgressions. . . . Get your-
selves a new heart and a new spirit! . . . Turn, then, and live."
(Ezekiel 18:30-32). This is the kind of total change that is necessary for an abuser to stop the abusive behavior. Forgiveness depends on this total repentance.

3. Healing the brokenness of victims and relationships: becoming survivors (justice and restoration)

Beyond the immediacy of hospitality and sanctuary is the pastoral task of helping make justice for the victims of family violence.[8]
Justice making begins with clear acknowledgment of the fact of
the victim's experience of abuse. The acknowledgment and belief
of the victim's story on behalf of an institution like the church is
a powerful beginning in the victim's process of healing. It is an
important counterexperience to the disbelief in and blaming of
the victim that most victims experience initially. The appropriate
response of the legal system may provide a measure of justice for
the victim. The abuser's repentance, which begins with his acknowledgment of what he did and the consequences for those
around him, can be an experience of justice for the victim.

The experience of justice on the part of the victim is the beginning of the process of healing and becoming a survivor of abuse.
It can potentially free the victim to be able to forgive — to let go
of the immediacy of the pain caused by the abuse and to place it
in perspective. Forgiveness can never be forced from the outside
or accomplished out of obligation. It is a means of healing for the

victim and will be available when the victim is ready. Survivors have scars rather than wounds — memories that inform them and protect them but do not revictimize them every day. The task of the minister is to help bring victims to the place where forgiveness and healing can come forth and victims can become survivors.

The restoration of the relationship previously broken by abuse is the goal that most victims and abusers long for together. It will be possible if there is the absence of fear for the survivor, true repentance for the abuser, justice, and forgiveness. From these authentic experiences it will be possible to recovenant in a relationship — this time with a very different set of expectations concerning what is normative in a relationship. Forgiveness allows the pain to be left behind but never forgotten or explained away. The relationship can now take on a new heart and a new spirit as a place of safety, trust, respect, shared power, mutuality, and love.

When this restoration is not possible because the repentance is not real or the damage was simply too great, then the grief work in the face of the loss of the relationship (divorce) becomes the priority. No matter how bad the situation was, there was some good that held the victim there. This good must be grieved for. But also what is lost is the illusion about what is really possible. In spite of the promises, the genuine good intentions, and the desire that it never happen again, the abuse continued. In such cases, the only means to survival is to grieve the loss and to restore oneself to wholeness. Out of the experience of loss can come new life.

Pastoral Cautions

Beware of abusers' conversions. It is not uncommon for a batterer or incest offender to suddenly "come to the Lord" when faced with criminal charges of assault. The abuser who sees himself as a reborn Christian will frequently use this experience as a way of deflecting court action that would require treatment for him. "I've found Jesus and I'll never molest my daughter again," he may say. If this is a genuine experience of conversion, then it can lead to repentance and can be an excellent resource to the abuser as he undertakes the long, slow process of therapy. The task of the minister is to guide this conversion, clearly indicating to the abuser that it is the first step rather than the last. If it is *not* a genuine experience, but rather one more way that the abuser is seeking to avoid responsibility for his violence, then the minister is in the best position to confront his charade, disallowing his manipulation of the authorities who would hold him accountable.

Beware of quick forgiveness. A group of twenty-three Christian incest offenders in treatment all said that the thing that was least helpful to them had been how quickly their pastors had forgiven them. They were very clear that this "cheap grace" had prevented them from confronting their abusive behavior and dealing with it. The minister's role is to guide the process of forgiveness, using this occasion of confession and plea for forgiveness as a means of confronting the abuse and getting the help that is needed. This can be accomplished, for example, within the Catholic practice by the withholding of absolution until the offender has reported himself and engaged in therapy to assure that he will not repeat his abusive behavior. Forgiveness handed out by the minister in a vacuum never leads to repentance or restoration.

Report child abuse. The legal requirement for clergy to report suspicion of child abuse (physical abuse, sexual abuse, or neglect) differs from state to state. However, regardless of the presence or absence of a mandatory reporting requirement, it is important for the clergy to be aware of the services provided by Children's Protective Services in their state. This is the agency in every state that is mandated to protect children from abuse and that is authorized to remove a child from a dangerous situation. In addition to this crisis intervention resource, CPS also provides the counseling that the child victim, the abuser, and other family members need. CPS is much better prepared to do both these things than are those who serve as generalists in a ministry setting.

If a child or teenager comes to a minister and discloses information that gives cause to suspect that there is child abuse, Child

Protective Services should be notified immediately by the minister. It is not the responsibility of the minister to investigate nor to have conclusive evidence; that is the job of CPS. Utilizing this agency as a resource makes possible quick and effective intervention into a situation where a child may be harmed.[9]

PROPHETIC RESPONSE

Social ethicist Beverly Wildung Harrison has said that ministry is responding to the private pain of individuals and making that pain a public issue. Making the private pain of violence in the family a public issue is necessary if we are to do more than put Band-Aids on injured bodies and spirits. The agenda amounts to creating a major shift in the cultural norms of our society — away from the tolerance of family violence as acceptable and normative familial behavior.

Currently the tide of public acceptance runs strongly in the direction of violence in the family as normative. There are significant, although still relatively few, exceptions to this reality. Only now (and slowly) is the voice of the church beginning to be heard to counter this tide. Still too often Scriptural and doctrinal legitimation is given to coercion and domination in family relationships, and the priority of "keeping the family together" is touted in the face of family brutality as the "Christian" response. The church has been slow to step into the public arena and lay claim to the issue of violence in the family.

BREAKING SILENCE

The prophetic act of breaking silence is a potentially powerful antidote to the existing cultural and religious norms. Breaking silence means to speak openly about violence in the family — naming it for what it is and naming it as a sin before God. To do so is to acknowledge the secrets of abuse in families that keep those secrets quiet, in conspiracy. The abuses are not hidden, but they are secrets. The secrecy is what sustains the suffering for so long. Speaking openly from the pulpit or in committee or on the editorial page about violence in the family is prophetic and necessary.

There is a powerful pastoral dimension to this prophetic courage as well. When victims and abusers hear their minister speaking about an experience that they know very well, they then have permission to seek help from their church. Until they hear this message, they will very likely hesitate to come to their pastor or priest for help. Believing that they are alone in their experience and that the church cannot deal with such matters, they may seek help elsewhere or not at all.

An Episcopal priest was attending a four-week seminar on violence in the family and came into the fourth session very upset. He had become aware in the previous three weeks of two incest cases and a rape in his small, suburban congregation. In discussing this situation, he recalled that, on the first Sunday after he began the seminar, he had mentioned from the pulpit that he was taking this course and so would not be in the office on Wednesday mornings. These three situations then presented themselves. His brief, passing comment had been the signal to his congregation that he was prepared and available to deal with this subject. Any minister who breaks silence in a congregation should be prepared for disclosures from congregants.

EDUCATION FOR PREVENTION

The church is an ideal setting for education at all age levels — education that can support healthy, just familial relationships and that can prevent abusive ones. The opportunity is there at significant points in the life cycle to provide healthy norms and expectations for relationships and to provide skills through which to maintain familial intimacy in a nonabusive environment.

> Children need prevention education to prepare them to deal with the strong likelihood of attempted sexual abuse. Teaching them self-respect and self-confidence and giving them permission to say "no" to any adult who would harm them is both a practical and a theological priority.[10]
>
> Teenagers who are exploring their sexuality and their relationships need straightforward information about both in order to have expectations of mutuality, choice, and respect in a relationship. Providing them with communication and assertiveness skills and with support for their development within a context of religious values is a priority.[11]
>
> Adults who are approaching marriage or commitment face an excellent opportunity to reflect carefully on their expectations of each other and of their relationship. In addition to a long list of other concerns, the minister can, and should, raise questions concerning conflict, expression of anger, previous experiences of coercion or abuse in relationships and experiences in the young people's family of origin when they were growing up. To provide an opportunity for this discussion as a preparation for commitment is vital and is much appreciated by couples.
>
> Adult children who are facing the illness or disability of an adult parent also need information, resources, and support that the church can provide. The open discussion of ways to deal with the stress that such a family crisis can create can militate against the possibility of elder abuse or neglect.

Perhaps more than any other institution in our communities, the church is in a position to provide these kinds of educational resources within its educational ministry. Thus it can be a primary means of prevention of violence in the family.

By breaking silence and by taking the initiative in the development of prevention education at the local church level, ministers are announcing the good news that there is an alternative to the generational cycle of abuse in families. This self-consciously prophetic act is risky, but it is crucial in our time if we are to redeem family life and restore it to a place of abundant care, respect, safety, and support for its members.

NOTES

1. The author will use the generic references of feminine pronouns for victims and masculine pronouns for abusers in this article. Although victims and abusers in family violence can be either male or female, the vast majority of victims are women and children and the vast majority of abusers are men; hence these generic references are adequate. Persons in ministry will be referred to as both female and male.

2. Ideally, a faith community should have pastoral care resources that could provide shelter and support groups for victims of that faith and long-term treatment for abusers. This would make it possible for people to deal with issues of the violence and of their faith together. However, this would require that people with a strong pastoral counseling background also be specifically trained to work with victims or abusers.

3. Susan Brooks Thistlethwaite, "Every Two Minutes: Battered Women and Feminist Interpretation," in *Feminist Interpretation of the Bible,* ed. Letty M. Russell (Philadelphia: Westminster Press, 1985).

4. See Marie M. Fortune, "A Commentary on Religious Issues in Family Violence" in this volume.

5. Any effective intervention presupposes that counseling of couples is not an appropriate response to spouse abuse and should never be attempted as a means of stopping the violence. Victims need safety and support to recover from the violence. Abusers need confrontation and treatment to stop their abusive patterns. Counseling of couples may be utilized as a part of goal #3.

6. See study by Sherman and Berk, 1983, carried out by the Minneapolis Police Department.

7. See Marie M. Fortune, *Keeping the Faith: Answers for the Abused Woman* (San Francisco: Harper & Row, 1987).

8. See Marie M. Fortune, "Justice Making in the Aftermath of Woman Battering" in *Violence in the Family: A Workshop for Clergy and Other Helpers* (Cleveland: Pilgrim Press, 1991).

9. See Marie M. Fortune, "Confidentiality and Mandatory Reporting: A False Dilemma?," *Christian Century* 103, no. 20 (June 18-25, 1986).

10. See Kathryn Goering Reid with Marie M. Fortune, *Preventing Child Sexual Abuse — A Curriculum for Children Ages 9-12* (New York: United Church Press, 1989).

11. See Marie M. Fortune, *Sexual Abuse Prevention: A Study for Teenagers* (New York: United Church Press, 1984).

Reprinted with permission from *Violence in the Family: A Workshop for Clergy and Other Helpers* by Marie M. Fortune (Cleveland: Pilgrim Press, 1991).

A Commentary on Religious Issues in Family Violence

Marie M. Fortune

THE IMPORTANCE OF RELIGIOUS ISSUES: ROADBLOCKS OR RESOURCES?

The crisis of family violence affects people physically, psychologically, and spiritually. Each of these dimensions must be addressed, both for the victims and for those in the family who abuse them. Approached from either a secular or a religious perspective alone, certain needs and issues tend to be disregarded. This reflects a serious lack of understanding of the nature of family violence and its impact on people's lives. Treatment of families experiencing violence and abuse requires integrating the needs of the whole person. Thus, the importance of developing a shared understanding and cooperation between secular and religious helpers to deal with family violence cannot be emphasized too strongly.

Occasionally, a social worker, psychotherapist, or other secular service provider will wonder, "Why bother with religious concerns at all?" The answer is a very practical one: religious issues or concerns that surface for people in the midst of crisis are *primary issues*. If not addressed in some way, at some point, they will inevitably become roadblocks to the client's efforts to resolve the crisis and move on with her or his life. In addition, people's religious beliefs and community of faith (church or synagogue) *can* provide a primary support system for them and their families in the midst of an experience of family violence.

For a pastor, priest, rabbi, lay counselor, or other person approaching family violence from a religious perspective, there is little question about the relevance of religious concerns. These are primary for any religious person. Rather, the clergy may doubt the importance of dealing with concerns for shelter, safety, intervention, and treatment. "These people just need to get right with God and everything will be fine." This perspective overlooks the fact that these other issues are practical and important as well. Family violence is complex and potentially lethal; these seemingly mundane concerns represent immediate and critical needs.

When confronted with a personal experience of family violence, as in the case of any other crisis, whether chronic or sudden, most people also experience a crisis of meaning in their lives. Very basic life questions arise and are usually expressed in religious or philosophical terms. Questions such as, "Why is this happening to me and my family?" or "Why did God *let* this happen?" or "What meaning does this have for my life?" are all indications of people's efforts to understand, to make sense out of experiences of suffering, and to place the experiences in a context of meaning for their lives. These questions are to be seen as a healthy sign because they represent an effort to comprehend and contextualize the experience of family violence. Through such efforts, people can regain some control over their lives in the midst of crisis.

Thus, for many individuals and families in crisis, the questions of meaning will be expressed in religious terms, and more specifically, in terms of the Jewish or Christian traditions, since the vast majority of people in the United States today grew up with some association with these traditions. Many continue as adults to be involved with a church or synagogue. In addition, Jewish and Christian values overlap with cultural values of the majority American culture, so most Americans carry a set of cultural values, consciously or unconsciously, which are primarily Jewish or Christian in nature.[1]

Religious concerns can become roadblocks or resources for those dealing with experiences of family violence because these concerns are central to many people's lives. The outcome depends on *how* they are handled.

The misinterpretation and misuse of the Jewish and Christian traditions have often had a detrimental effect on families, particularly those dealing with family violence. Misinterpretation of the traditions can contribute substantially to the guilt, self-blame, and suffering that victims experience and to the rationalizations often used by those who abuse. "But the Bible says . . ." is frequently used to explain, excuse, or justify abuse between family members. This need not be the case. Reexamining and analyzing those biblical references that have been misused can lead to reclaiming the traditions in a way that supports victims *and* those who abuse while clearly confronting and challenging abuse in the family. A careful study of both Jewish and Christian Scriptures makes it very clear that *it is not possible to use Scripture to justify abuse of persons in the family.* However, it is also clear that it *is* possible to *misuse* Scripture and other traditional religious literature for this purpose. This is a frequent practice (see below). Attempting to teach that there are very simple answers to the very complex issues that people face in their lives is another potential roadblock within contemporary teachings of some Jewish or Christian groups. Thus, religious groups have often not adequately prepared people for the traumas they will face at some point in their lives: illness, death, abuse, divorce, and so forth.

"Keep the commandments and everything will be
fine."

"Keep praying."

"Just accept Jesus Christ as your Lord and Savior
and you will be healthy, prosperous, popular, and
happy."

"Go to services each week."

"Pray harder."

While these teachings may be fundamental teachings of religious faith, alone they are inadequate to deal with the complexity
of most experiences of human suffering, such as family violence.
When offered as simple and complete answers to life's questions,
they create in the hearer an illusion of simplicity that leaves the
hearer vulnerable to becoming overwhelmed by an experience of
suffering. In addition, the teachings set up a dynamic that blames
the victims for their suffering.

"If you are a *good* Christian or a *good* Jew, God will
treat you kindly, or take care of you, or make you
prosper as a reward for your goodness."

"If you suffer, it is a sign that you *must not be* a good
Christian or a good Jew and God is displeased with
you."

If one accepts this simple formula (which makes a theological
assumption that God's love is conditional), then when one experiences any form of suffering, one feels punished or abandoned
by God. The simple answer alone cannot hold up in the face of
personal or familial suffering. When people attempt to utilize the
simple answer and it is insufficient, they feel that their faith has
failed them or that God has abandoned them. In fact, it may be
the teachings or actions of their particular congregation or

denomination that have been inadequate to their needs. Thus they may be feeling abandoned.

The religious teachings of the Jewish and Christian traditions *are* adequate to address the experiences of contemporary people when the traditions acknowledge the complexity, the paradox, and sometimes the incomprehensible nature of those experiences. The most important resource that the church or synagogue can provide is to be available to support those who are suffering, to be a sign of God's presence, and to be willing to struggle with the questions that the experiences may raise. Offering sweet words of advice to "solve" life's problems reduces the experience of the one who suffers to a mere slogan and denies the depth of the pain *and* the potential for healing and new life.

COOPERATIVE ROLES FOR SECULAR COUNSELOR AND MINISTER/RABBI

Both the secular counselor and the minister or rabbi have important roles to play in response to family violence. Families in which there is abuse need the support and expertise of both in times of crisis. Sometimes the efforts of the two will come into conflict, as illustrated by the following situation:

> We received a call at the Center from a local shelter for abused women. The shelter worker indicated that she had a badly beaten woman there whose minister had told her to go back home to her husband. The worker asked us to call the minister and "straighten him out." Ten minutes later we received a call from the minister. He said that the shelter had one of his parishioners there and the shelter worker had told her to get a divorce. He asked us to call the shelter and "straighten them out."

In the above case, both the shelter worker and the minister had the best interests of the victim in mind. Yet they were clearly at odds with each other because each did not understand the other's concerns as they related to the needs of the victim. The shelter worker did not understand the minister's concern for maintaining the family, and the minister did not understand that the woman's life was in danger. We arranged for the minister and the shelter worker to talk directly with each other, sharing their concerns in order to seek a solution in the best interests of the victim. This was accomplished successfully.

Clearly there is a need for cooperation and communication between counselors and ministers or rabbis so that the needs of parishioners, congregants, and clients are best served and so that the resources of both religious and secular helpers are utilized effectively.

Role of the Secular Counselor

In the secular setting, a social worker or mental health provider may encounter a victim or abuser who raises religious questions or concerns. When this occurs, the following guidelines are helpful:

1. Pay attention to religious questions, comments, and references.

2. Affirm these concerns as appropriate and check out their importance for the client.

3. Having identified and affirmed this area of concern, *if you are uncomfortable with it, or feel unqualified to pursue it,* refer the client to a pastor, priest, or rabbi who is trained to help and whom you know and trust.

4. If you are comfortable and would like to pursue the concern, do so, emphasizing the ways in which the client's

religious tradition can be a personal resource and pointing out that it can in no way be used to justify past abuse or to allow abuse or violence to continue in the family. (See below.)

Role of Clergy

The minister or rabbi can most effectively help family abuse victims and offenders by cooperating with secular helping professionals. Combined, these resources provide a balanced approach that can deal with specific external, physical, and emotional needs while addressing the larger religious and philosophical issues.

When approached about family violence, the minister or rabbi can use the following guidelines:

1. Be aware of the dynamics of family violence and utilize this understanding in evaluating the situation.

2. Use your expertise as a religious authority and spiritual leader to illuminate the positive value of religious traditions while clarifying the fact that they do not justify or condone family abuse. (See below.)

3. Identify the parishioner or congregant's immediate needs and *refer* the person to a secular resource (if available) to deal with the specifics of abuse, intervention, and treatment.

4. If you are comfortable pursuing the matter, provide additional pastoral support and encouragement to help families dealing with violence take full advantage of available resources.

SCRIPTURAL AND THEOLOGICAL ISSUES

Suffering

The experience of physical or psychological pain or deprivation can generally be referred to as "suffering." When a person experiences suffering, often the first question is, "Why am I suffering?" This is really two questions: "Why is there suffering?" and "Why me?" These are classical theological questions to which there are no totally satisfactory answers.

Sometimes a person will answer these questions in terms of very specific cause-and-effect relationships:

> "I am being abused by my husband as a punishment
> from God for the fact that twenty years ago, when I
> was seventeen years old, I had sexual relations with
> a guy I wasn't married to."

In this case, the victim of abuse sees her suffering as just punishment for an event that happened long ago and for which she has since felt guilty. This explanation has an almost superstitious quality. It reflects an effort on the part of the woman to make sense out of her experience of abuse by her husband. Her explanation takes the "effect" (the abuse), looks for a probable "cause" (her teenage "sin"), and directly connects the two. This conclusion is based on a set of theological assumptions that support her view: God is a stern judge who seeks retribution for her sins, and God causes suffering to be inflicted on her as punishment.

Unfortunately, the woman's explanation does not focus on the real nature of her suffering (the abuse by her husband) nor does it place responsibility for her suffering where it lies: on her abusive husband.

Sometimes people try to explain suffering by saying that it is "God's will" or "part of God's plan for my life" or "God's way of teaching me a lesson." These explanations assume God to be stern, harsh, and even cruel and arbitrary. This image of God runs counter to a biblical image of a kind, merciful, and loving God. The God of this biblical teaching does not single out anyone to suffer for the sake of suffering, because suffering is not pleasing to God.

A distinction between voluntary and involuntary suffering is useful at this point. Someone may choose to suffer abuse or indignity in order to accomplish a greater good. For example, Dr. Martin Luther King, Jr., suffered greatly in order to change what he believed to be unjust racist laws. Although the abuse he experienced was not justifiable, he chose voluntary suffering as a means to an end.

Involuntary suffering, which occurs when a person is beaten, raped, or abused, especially in a family relationship, also cannot be justified, but it is never chosen. It may, on occasion, *be endured* by a victim for a number of reasons, including a belief that such endurance will eventually "change" the person who is being abusive. However, this belief is unrealistic and generally only reinforces the abuse.

Christian tradition teaches that suffering happens to people because there is evil and sinfulness in the world. Unfortunately, when someone behaves in a hurtful way, someone else usually bears the brunt of that act and suffers as a result. Striving to live a righteous life does not guarantee that one will be protected from the sinfulness of another. A person may suffer from having made a poor decision (for example, as a result of marrying a spouse who is abusive). But this in no way means that the person either wants to suffer or deserves abuse from the spouse.

In Christian teaching, at no point does God promise that we will not suffer in this life. In Scripture, God *does* promise to be present to us when we suffer. This is especially evident in the Psalms, which give vivid testimony to people's experience of God's faithfulness in the midst of suffering (see Psalms 22 and 55).

One's fear of abandonment by God is often strong when one is experiencing suffering and abuse. This fear is usually experienced by victims of abuse, who often feel they have been abandoned by almost everyone: friends, other family members, clergy, doctors, police, lawyers, counselors. Perhaps none of these people believed the victims or were able to help. It is therefore very easy for victims to conclude that God has also abandoned them. For Christians, the promise to victims from God is that even though all others abandon them, God will be faithful. This is the message found in Romans:

> For I am convinced that neither death, nor life, nor
> angels, nor rulers, nor things present, nor things to
> come, nor powers, nor height, nor depth, nor
> anything else in all creation, will be able to separate
> us from the love of God in Christ Jesus our Lord.
> — Romans 8:38-39

Often this reassurance is very helpful to victims of violence or to those who abuse them.

Sometimes people who regard suffering as God's will for them believe that God is teaching them a lesson or that hardship builds character. Experiences of suffering can, in fact, be occasions for growth. People who suffer may realize in retrospect that they learned a great deal from the experience and grew more mature as a result. This often is the case, but only if the person who is suffering also receives support and affirmation throughout the experience. With the support of family, friends, and helpers, people who are confronted with violence in their families can end the abuse, possibly leave the situation, make major changes in their lives, and grow as mature adults. They will probably learn some difficult lessons: increased self-reliance; how to express anger; that they may survive better outside than inside abusive relationships; that someone can be a whole person without being married; that they can exercise control over their actions with others; that family relationships need not be abusive and violent.

However, this awareness of suffering as the occasion for growth *must come from those who are suffering* and at a time when they are well on their way to renewal. It is hardly appropriate when someone is feeling great pain to point out that things really are not so bad and that someday the sufferer will be glad that all of this happened. These words of "comfort and reassurance" are usually for the benefit of the minister, rabbi, or counselor, not the parishioner, congregant, or client. At a later time, it may be useful to point out the new growth that has taken place and very simply to affirm the reality that this person *has survived* an extremely difficult situation. Suffering may present an occasion for growth: whether this potential is actualized depends on how the experience of suffering is managed.

Nature of the Marriage Relationship: A Jewish Perspective

The Jewish marriage ceremony is known as "Kiddushin," or sanctification. Through it, a couple's relationship is sanctified, or set apart before God. This sanctification reminds Jews to strive to express their holiness through marriage and the home in a covenantal relationship based on mutual love and respect.

Judaism views marriage as necessary for fulfillment. Marriage is part of God's plan. The first time God speaks to Adam, God says that it is not fitting that Adam should be alone. "Shalom Bayit," peace in the home, is a major family value in Judaism. "Shalom," which is simply translated as "peace," also signifies wholeness, completeness, fulfillment. Peace in the home, domestic harmony, encompasses the good and welfare of all the home's inhabitants.

The rabbis consider domestic tranquillity as one of the most important ideals because it is the essential forerunner to peace on earth. "Peace will remain a distant vision until we do the work of peace ourselves. If peace is to be brought into the world we must bring it first to our families and communities." [2]

The concept of Shalom Bayit should not be misinterpreted as encouraging the preservation of an abusive marriage. When domestic harmony is impossible because of physical abuse, the only way for peace may be dissolution of marriage. Although marriage is viewed as permanent, divorce has always been an option according to the Jewish tradition.

In Judaism conjugal rights are obligatory upon the husband, who must be available for his wife.

> A wife may restrict her husband in his business
> journey to nearby places only so that he would not
> otherwise deprive her of her conjugal rights. Hence
> he may not set out without her permission.[3]

While the husband is responsible for his wife's sexual fulfillment, the wife, in return, is expected to have sexual relations with her husband. Maimonides[4] teaches us about the relationship between husband and wife in a Jewish marriage. He asserts that if the wife refuses sexual relations with her husband

> she should be questioned as to the reason . . . If she
> says, "I have come to loathe him, and I cannot
> willingly submit to his intercourse," he must be
> compelled to divorce her immediately for she is not
> like a captive woman who must submit to a man that
> is hateful to her.[5]

This suggests that no wife is expected to submit to sexual activity with a husband she fears or hates. The arena of sexual sharing for Jewish couples is one of mutual responsibility and choice.

Nature of the Marriage Relationship: A Christian Perspective

Christian teaching about the model of the marriage relationship has traditionally focused heavily on Paul's letters to the Ephesians, Corinthians, and Colossians. Misplaced emphasis on or misinterpretations of these texts create substantial problems for many married couples. Most commonly, directives on marriage based on Scripture are given to women, and not to men, and state that wives must "submit" to their husbands. This often is interpreted to mean that the husband and father is the absolute head of the household and that the wife and children must obey him without question. Unfortunately, this idea has also been interpreted to mean that wives and children must submit to abuse from husbands and fathers. This rationalization is used by those who abuse, as well as by counselors, clergy, and the victims of the abuse themselves.

A closer look at the actual Scriptural references reveals a different picture. For example:

> Be subject to *one another* out of reverence for Christ.
>
> — Ephesians 5:21, emphasis added

This is the first and most important verse in the Ephesians passage on marriage and also the one most often overlooked. It clearly indicates that all Christians — husbands and wives — are to be *mutually subject* to one another. The word that is translated "be subject to" can more appropriately be translated "defer to" or "accommodate to" so that v. 22 might read:

> Wives *accommodate* to your husbands as to the Lord.

This teaching implies sensitivity, flexibility, and responsiveness to the husband. In no way can this verse be taken to mean that a wife must submit to abuse from her husband.

> For the husband is the head of the wife just as Christ is the head of the church, the body of which he is the Savior. Just as the church is subject to Christ, so also wives ought to be, in everything, to their husbands.
>
> — Ephesians 5:234-24

The model suggested here of husband-wife relationship is based on the Christ-church relationship. It is clear from Jesus's teaching and ministry that his relationship to his followers was not one of dominance or authoritarianism, but rather one of servanthood. For example, Jesus washed the feet of his disciples in an act of serving. He taught them that those who would be first must, in fact, be last. Therefore, a good husband will not dominate or control his wife but will serve and care for her, according to Ephesians.

> In the same way, husbands should love their wives as they do their own bodies. He who loves his wife loves himself. For no one ever hates his own body, but he nourishes and tenderly cares for it, just as Christ does for the church.
>
> — Ephesians 5:28-29

This instruction to husbands is very clear and concrete. A husband is to nourish and cherish his own body *and* that of his wife. Physical battering that occurs between spouses is probably the most blatant violation of this teaching and a clear reflection of the self-hatred in the one who is abusive.

It is interesting that the passages quoted above from Ephesians (5:21-29), which are commonly used as instruction for marriage, are instructions primarily for husbands. Nine of the verses (5:25-33) are directed toward the husband's responsibilities in marriage; only three of the verses (5:22-24) refer to wives' responsibilities, and one verse (5:21) refers to both. Yet contemporary interpretation often focuses only on the wives and often misuses those passages to justify the abuse of the wives by their husbands. While spouse abuse may be a common pattern in marriage, it certainly cannot be legitimated by Scripture.

In terms of sexuality in marriage, again this passage from Ephesians (see also Colossians 3:18-21) has been used to establish a relationship in which the husband has conjugal *rights* and the wife has conjugal *duties*. In fact, other Scriptural passages are explicit on this issue:

> The husband should give to his wife her conjugal
> rights, and likewise the wife to her husband. For the
> wife does not have authority over her own body, but
> the husband does; likewise the husband does not
> have authority over his own body, but the wife does.
> — 1 Corinthians 7:3-4

The rights and expectations between husband and wife in regard to sexual matters are explicitly equal and parallel and include the right to refuse sexual contact. The expectation of equality of conjugal rights and sexual access and the need for mutual consideration in sexual activity is clear. The suggestion that both wife and husband have authority over the other's body and not their own refers to the need for joint, mutual decisions about sexual activity rather than arbitrary, independent decisions. A husband does not have the right to act out of his own sexual needs without agreement from the wife; this applies to the wife also. This particular passage directly challenges the incidents of sexual abuse (rape) in marriage that are frequently reported by physically abused wives.

The Marriage Covenant and Divorce

A strong belief in the permanency of the marriage vows may prevent an abused spouse from considering separation or divorce as options for dealing with family violence. For the Christian, the promise of faithfulness "for better or for worse . . . until death do us part" is commonly taken to mean "stay in the marriage no matter what," even though death of one or more family members is a real possibility in abusive families. Jews view marriage as permanent, but "until death do us part" is not part of the ceremony. The Jewish attitude embodies a very delicate balance. Marriage is taken very seriously. It is a primary religious obligation and should not be entered into or discarded flippantly. Nevertheless, since the days of Deuteronomy, Jewish tradition has recognized the unfortunate reality that some couples are hope-lessly incompatible and divorce may be a necessary option.

For some Christians, their denomination's strong doctrinal position against divorce may inhibit them from exercising this means of dealing with violence in the family. For others, a posi-tion against divorce is a personal belief, often supported by their family and church. In either case, there is a common assumption that any marriage is better than no marriage at all and, there-fore, that a marriage should be maintained at any cost. This as-sumption arises from a superficial view of marriage, a view concerned only with appearances and not with substances. In other words, as long as marriage and family relationships main-tain a facade of normalcy, there is a refusal by church and com-munity to look any closer for fear of seeing abuse or violence in the home. The covenant of Christian marriage is a lifelong, sa-cred commitment made between two persons and witnessed by other persons and by God. Jews also regard marriage as sacred and intend that it be permanent. A marriage covenant has the following elements:

1. It is made in full knowledge of the relationship.

2. It involves a mutual giving of self to the other.

3. It is assumed to be lasting.

4. It values mutuality, respect, and equality between persons.

A marriage covenant can be violated by one or both part-ners. It is common thinking in both Jewish and Christian tradi-tions that adultery violates the marriage covenant and results in brokenness in the relationship. Likewise, violence or abuse in a marriage violates the covenant and fractures a relationship. In both cases, the trust that was assumed between partners is shat-tered. Neither partner should be expected to remain in an abu-sive situation. Often one marriage partner feels a heavy obligation to remain in the relationship and do everything possible to make it work. This is most often true for women. A covenant relationship only works if both partners are able and willing to work on it. In both Christian and Jewish traditions, it is clear that God does not expect anyone to stay in a situation that is abusive (that is, to become a doormat). In the Christian tradition, just as Jesus did not expect his disciples to remain in a village that did not respect and care for them (Luke 9:1-6), neither does he expect persons to remain in a family relationship where they are abused and violated. In Jewish literature, the expectation is also clear:

> If a man was found to be a wife-beater, he had
> to pay damages and provide her with separate
> maintenance. Failing that, the wife had valid
> grounds for compelling a divorce.[6]

If there is a genuine effort to change on the part of the one who is abusive, it is possible to renew the marriage covenant, including in it a clear commitment to nonviolence in the relationship. With treatment for the family members, it *may* be possible to salvage the relationship. If the one who is being abusive is not willing or able to change in the relationship, then the question of divorce arises. At this point in the marriage, divorce is really a matter of *public* statement: "Shall we make public the fact that our relationship has been broken by abuse?" The other option, of course, is to continue to *pretend* that the marriage is intact. (A woman reported that she divorced only a month ago but that her marriage ended ten years ago when the abuse began.)

In violent homes, divorce is not breaking up families. Violence and abuse are breaking up families. Divorce is often the painful, public acknowledgment of an already accomplished fact. While divorce is never easy, it is, in the case of family violence, the lesser evil. In many cases, divorce may be a necessary intervention to generate healing and new life from a devastating and deadly situation.

Parents and Children

"Honor your father and your mother" is one of the Ten Commandments taught to all Jewish and Christian children. Unfortunately, some parents misuse this teaching in order to demand unquestioning obedience from their children. In a hierarchical, authoritarian household, a father may misuse his parental authority to coerce a child into abusive sexual activity (incest). Parents may use this commandment to rationalize their physical abuse of a child in retaliation for a child's lack of obedience.

For Christians, the meaning of the Third Commandment is made very clear in Ephesians:

> Children, obey your parents *in the Lord,* for this is
> right. "Honor your father and mother" — this is the
> first commandment with a promise: "so that it may
> be well with you and you may live long on the earth."
> And, fathers, do not provoke your children to anger,
> but bring them up *in the discipline and instruction
> of the Lord.*
>
> — Ephesians 6:1-4, emphasis added

Children's obedience to their parents is to be "in the Lord"; it is not to be blind and unquestioning. In addition to instructions to children, instructions are also given to parents to guide and instruct their children in Christian values, that is, love, mercy, compassion, and justice. Any discipline of a child must be for the child's best interest. The caution to the father not to provoke the child to anger is most appropriate. If there is anything that will certainly provoke a child to anger, it is physical or sexual abuse by a parent.

Jewish tradition deals with the same concern, making a distinction between children based on maturity.

> One is forbidden to beat his grownup son; the word
> "grownup," in this regard, refers not to age but to
> his maturity. If there is reason to believe that the son
> will rebel, and express that resentment by word or

> deed, even though he has not yet reached the age of
> Bar Mitzvah (13), it is forbidden to beat him.
> Instead he should reason with him. Anyone who
> beats his grownup children is to be excommunicated,
> because he transgresses the Divine Command (Lev.
> 19:14) "Thou shalt not put a stumbling block before
> the blind" (for they are apt to bring sin and
> punishment upon their children).[7]

Even though Jewish law gives great authority to the father in relationship to the children, the requirement for restraint is clearly indicated. Again, the priority is on the welfare of the child. The other Scriptural injunction that is commonly used to justify abusive discipline of children is the adage, "Spare the rod and spoil the child." This adage, a quotation from Samuel Butler's *Hudibras,* is based on Proverbs 13:24, "Those who spare the rod hate their children . . ." It is commonly interpreted to mean that if a parent does not use corporal punishment on a child, the child will become a spoiled brat. This is a good example of a misinterpretation based on a contemporary understanding. In fact, the image referred to in Proverbs 13:24 is probably that of a shepherd and the rod is the shepherd's staff (see Psalm 23:4: "your rod and your staff — they comfort me"). A shepherd uses his staff to guide the sheep where they should go. The staff is not used as a cudgel.

With this image of the shepherd guiding the sheep in mind, it is certainly clear that children need guidance and discipline from parents and other caring adults in order to grow to maturity. Children do not need to be physically beaten to receive guidance or discipline. Beating children as discipline teaches them very early that it is all right to hit those you love "for their own good." This kind of lesson fosters early training for persons who grow up and subsequently physically abuse their spouses and children.

Confession and Forgiveness

The need of an abusive family member to admit wrongdoing is a healthy sign that the offender is no longer denying the problem but is ready and willing to face it. The offender may seek out a minister or rabbi for the purpose of confessing.

Sometimes, however, an abusive father confesses, asks forgiveness, and promises never to sexually approach his daughter again, or a mother swears never to hit her child in anger again. The minister or rabbi is then put in a position of assuring forgiveness *and* evaluating the strength of the person's promise not to abuse again. Even an abuser who is genuinely contrite is seldom able to end the abuse without assistance and treatment.

The minister or rabbi needs to assure the person of God's forgiveness *and* must confront the person with the fact that he or she needs additional help in order to stop the abuse. For some people, a strong word from a minister or rabbi at this point is an effective deterrent: "The abuse *must* stop now." Sometimes this strong directive can provide an external framework for beginning to change the abusive behavior.

For the Jew, the Hebrew term "teshuvah" is the word for repentance. "Teshuvah" literally means "return," clearly denoting a return to God after sin. In Judaism there is a distinction between sins against God and sins against people. For the former, only regret or confession is necessary. For sins against people, "teshuvah" requires three steps: first, admission of wrongdoing; second, asking for forgiveness of the person wronged (here, the person abused); third, reconciliation, which can be accomplished only by a change in behavior.

The issue of forgiveness also arises for victims of abuse. A friend or family member may pressure the victim: "You should forgive him. He said he was sorry." Or it may arise internally: "I wish I could forgive him. . . ." In either case, the victim feels guilty for not being able to forgive the abuser. In these cases, often forgiveness is interpreted to mean forgetting, or pretending that the abuse never happened. Neither is possible. The abuse will never be forgotten — it becomes a part of the victim's history. Forgiveness is a matter of victims' being able to say that they will no longer allow the experience to dominate their lives — and will let go of it and move on. This is usually possible if there is some sense of justice in the situation, either officially (through the legal system) or unofficially. Forgiveness by the victim is possible when there is repentance on the part of the abuser, and real repentance means a change in the abuser's behavior.

Another issue is timing. Too often the minister or rabbi or counselor's need for the victim to finish and resolve the abusive experience leads the helping professional to push a victim to forgive the abuser. Forgiveness in this case is seen as a means to hurry the victim's healing process along. Victims will move to forgive at their own pace and cannot be pushed by others' expectations of them. It may take years before they are ready to forgive; their timing needs to be respected. They will forgive when they are ready. Then the forgiveness becomes the final stage of letting go and enables them to move on with their lives.

CONCLUSION

This commentary addresses some of the common religious concerns raised by people dealing with family violence. It is an attempt to help the reader begin to see ways of converting potential roadblocks into valuable resources for those dealing with violence in their families.

Personal faith for a religious person can provide much-needed strength and courage to face a very painful situation and make changes in it. Churches and synagogues can provide a much-needed network of community support for victims, abusers, and their children.

It is clearly necessary for those involved in Jewish and Christian congregations and institutions to begin to address these concerns directly. In ignorance and oversight, we do much harm. In awareness and action, we can contribute a critical element to the efforts to respond to family violence in our communities.

NOTES

1. The discussion of religious issues included here reflects a Jewish and Christian perspective owing to the background and experience of the authors and contributors. Although there are other religious traditions present in the pluralistic American culture, the focus of this discussion is limited by the authors' perspectives and experiences.

2. *Gates of Repentance* (High Holy Days Prayer Book). Central Conference of American Rabbis. 1978. 67.

3. Yad. Ishut. XIV-2. Yale Judaica Series. 87.

4. Maimonides was a Jewish philosopher (1135-1204) whose *Mishneh Torah* became a standard work of Jewish law and a major source for all subsequent codification of Jewish law.

5. Yad. Ishut. XIV-8. 89.

6. Maurice Lamm, *Jewish Way in Love and Marriage*. 157.

7. Kizzur Shulhan Arukh

Substantial contributions were made by Judith Hertz from the National Federation of Temple Sisterhoods.

Reprinted with permission from *Violence in the Family: A Workshop for Clergy and Other Helpers* by Marie M. Fortune (Cleveland: Pilgrim Press, 1991).

The Transformation of Suffering: A Biblical and Theological Perspective

Marie M. Fortune

A religious person who is victimized by rape, battering, or child sexual abuse frequently faces the questions, Why do I suffer in this way? and, Where is God in my suffering? These profound theological questions cannot be answered simply with platitudes and then dismissed. The question of why there is suffering at all is one of classic theological debate, that is, the question of theodicy, to which there is no completely satisfactory answer. Human suffering in the midst of a world created by a compassionate and loving God is a dimension of human experience which is most disturbing and disquieting. The particular experience of suffering that accompanies victimization by sexual and domestic violence raises particular issues in regard to theodicy.

WHY SUFFERING?

People struggle with two fundamental aspects of the experience of suffering when they ask, Why do I suffer? First is the question of cause, that is, the source of the suffering. The second aspect involves the meaning or purpose of suffering.

Why is there suffering? It suffices to say that some suffering results from arbitrary, accidental sources such as natural disasters. However, much suffering is caused by human sinfulness: sinful acts by some bring suffering to others. These acts can generally be understood as acts of injustice. God allows such sinfulness because God has given persons free will and does not intervene when they choose to engage in unrighteous, unjust acts. Other people suffer from the consequences of these acts. This explanation may be adequate for situations clearly caused by human negligence or meanness, intended or not: for example, a fatal car accident caused by a drunk driver, chronic brown lung disease in textile workers who are denied protection from occupational hazards, birth defects in families living near toxic waste dumps, or incestuous abuse inflicted by a father upon his children. Yet it is still not a wholly satisfactory explanation. Those who suffer search further for answers, or at least for someone to blame.

Victims of sexual or domestic violence have a strong tendency to hold God or themselves responsible for the abuse even though there is clearly a perpetrator whose actions resulted in the victim's suffering. While his/her sinful acts may be understood as a consequence of his/her own brokenness and alienation (sometimes rooted in his/her own victimization), he/she is nonetheless responsible for actions that bring suffering to others. Self-blame or God-blame for one's experience of victimization simply avoids acknowledging that a particular person is responsible for the abusive acts.

Another explanation that is frequently utilized by victims is really old-fashioned superstition. It seeks to explain a current experience of suffering in terms of a previous "sinful" act on the part of the victim: the current suffering is God's punishment for the preceding "sin" which God has judged. Hence a battered woman now being abused by her husband can "explain" why this is happening by remembering that, when she was sixteen, she had sexual intercourse once with her boyfriend. She knows this was a "sin" and that God was displeased with her, so God must now be punishing her teenage indiscretion. Or she may have been "disobedient" and not submitted to her husband. She understands the situation to reflect God's acting to bring about her suffering for a justifiable reason; she blames herself and accepts her battering as God's will for her. At least she can "explain" why this happened to her; unfortunately, her explanation leaves no room for questioning her suffering or for confronting her abuser with his responsibility for it.

If God is to blame for the misfortune, one can direct anger at God for causing the suffering. For whatever reason, it is argued, God has singled out the victim of sexual or domestic violence to suffer. Two things result. First she/he is driven away from God by the pain and anger; second, no one is held accountable for what he/she has done to the victims. The suffering of the victim is exacerbated by the feeling that God has sent this affliction to her/him personally and has abandoned her/him in the midst of it. Harold Kushner offers a valuable reframing of this assumption:

> We can maintain our own self-respect and sense of goodness without having to feel that God has judged us and condemned us. We can be angry at what has happened to us, without feeling that we are angry at God. More than that, we can recognize our anger at life's unfairness, our instinctive compassion at seeing people suffer, as coming from God who teaches us to be angry at injustice and to feel compassion for the afflicted. Instead of feeling that we are opposed to God, we can feel that our indignation is God's anger at unfairness working through us, that when we cry out, we are still on God's side, and He [sic] is still on ours.[1]

God is not only *not* the cause of injustice and suffering but is instead the source of our righteous anger at the persons or circumstances that do cause suffering as well as our source of compassion for those who suffer.

The second aspect of the experience of suffering involves the attribution of meaning or purpose. What meaning does this experience of suffering hold for the victim? People have great difficulty accepting the irrational and often arbitrary nature of sexual and domestic violence. Instead of realizing that these things happen for no good reason, they attempt to manufacture a good reason or seek a greater good; for example, suffering "builds character" or is "a test of one's faith." The purpose of suffering is then the lesson it teaches, and the result should be a stronger faith in God. Purposefulness somehow softens the pain of the suffering. If some greater good is salvaged, then perhaps the suffering was worth it.

An understanding of the meaning of one's suffering begins with the differentiation between voluntary and involuntary suffering. Voluntary suffering is a painful experience which a person chooses in order to accomplish a greater good. It is optional and is a part of a particular strategy toward a particular end. For example, the acts of civil disobedience by civil rights workers in the United States in the 1960s resulted in police brutality, imprisonment, and sometimes death for these activists. These consequences were unjustifiable but not unexpected. Yet people knowingly chose to endure this suffering in order to change the circumstances of racism, which caused even greater daily suffering for many. Jesus' crucifixion was an act of unjustifiable yet voluntary suffering; in 1 Peter it is viewed as an example:

> For to this you have been called, because Christ also suffered for you, leaving you an example, so that you should follow in his steps. "He committed no sin, and no deceit was found in his mouth." When he was abused, he did not return abuse; when he suffered, he did not threaten; but he entrusted himself to the one who judges justly.
>
> — 1 Peter 2:21-23

But it is an example not of simply being a sacrificial doormat but of choosing, in the face of the violence of oppressive authority which threatened him, to suffer the consequences of his commitment. It was a witness to his love, not his suffering. Beverly Wildung Harrison further reframes Jesus' suffering on the cross:

> But those who love justice, and have their passion
> lovingly shaped toward right relation act not because
> they are enamored of sacrifice. Rather, they are
> moved by a love strong enough to sustain their action
> for right relation, even unto death. . . . Jesus's
> paradigmatic role in the story of our salvation rests
> not in his willingness to sacrifice himself, but in his
> passionate love of right relations and his refusal to
> cease to embody the power-of-relation in the face of
> that which would thwart it. It was his refusal to
> desist from radical love, not a preoccupation with
> sacrifice, which makes his work irreplaceable.[2]

Jesus' crucifixion was the tragic consequence of his faithfulness and refusal to give up his commitment in the face of Roman oppression. He voluntarily accepted the consequence, just as did civil rights workers, in order to bring about a greater good.

Like voluntary suffering, involuntary suffering is unjustifiable under any circumstance. However, unlike voluntary suffering, involuntary suffering is not chosen and never serves a greater good; it is inflicted by a person(s) upon another against their will and results only in pain and destruction. Sexual and domestic violence are forms of involuntary suffering. Neither serves any useful purpose; neither is chosen by the victim; neither is ever justified. Yet both cause great suffering for large numbers of people.

Many victims of involuntary suffering respond with the question: Why did God send *me* this affliction? In the face of the personal crisis of violence, one's deepest need is to somehow explain this experience, to give it specific meaning in one's particular life. By doing this, victims begin to regain some control over the situation and the crisis. If one can point accurately to the cause, perhaps she/he can avoid that circumstance in the future; if one can ascribe meaning, then she/he can give it purpose, can incorporate the experience more quickly and not feel so overwhelmed by it.

Neither superstition nor the search for a greater meaning necessarily encourages the victim of violence to deal with the actual source, that is, the abuser's behavior. Neither encourages the victim to question the abuse she/he is experiencing. Neither motivates the victim to act in seeking justice. Neither is theologically adequate for the person who is struggling to comprehend his/her experience of abuse in light of faith.

In Jesus' encounter with the man born blind (John 9:1-12), he is confronted with the question about the cause of suffering.[3] "His disciples asked him, 'Rabbi, who sinned, this man or his parents, that he was born blind?'" (v. 2). Jesus answers their question in terms of the meaning rather than the cause of his suffering: "Neither this man nor his parents sinned; he was born blind so that God's works might be revealed in him. We must work the works of him who sent me while it is day; night is coming when no one can work." (vv. 3-4).

Jesus proceeds to make a medicine and heal the man's blindness. He dismisses the request for a superstitious cause and restates the search for meaning. The blind man's suffering is a fact. Where is God in this suffering; what can God do in this situation; and what are we called to do? Jesus acts to relieve suffering rather than discuss its cause. He is teaching that the responsibility belongs to us to act regardless.[4] The question for us is not who sinned (in cosmic terms) or how can God allow women to be beaten and raped, but how can *we* allow this to go unchallenged? In challenging this victimization, the question is, Who is accountable for this suffering and how can justice be wrought here?

What Jesus does not address in this parable is the situation in which there is clear responsibility for the suffering of another. A more current reading of this story might include the information that the man's father beat his mother during her pregnancy with him, and the child's blindness resulted. In this case, when asked the question who sinned, Jesus might have said, "The one who beat his mother is accountable for his acts. Rebuke him. If he repents, forgive him. [See Luke 17: 1-4.] Here we must work the works of the one who sent me." Part of that work, which is clearly expected in the prophetic tradition of Hebrew and Christian theology, is that of calling to repentance and accountability and making justice in order to accomplish forgiveness, healing, and reconciliation. These responses to experiences of suffering at the hands of another are requisite if the suffering is to be more than simply endured.

ENDURANCE

In both the explanation of superstition and the attribution of greater meaning, God is held responsible for the suffering itself. This presupposes a belief in God as omnipotent and omniscient. If God is in control and choosing to exercise that control by bringing suffering upon the afflicted as punishment or in order to teach them something, then both cause and meaning are clearly determined to be in God's hands.

In the face of this interpretive framework, most victims accept endurance as the means of dealing with this suffering. Deciding that being battered or molested is justifiable punishment, one's lot in life, cross to bear, or God's will, sets in motion a pattern of endurance that accepts victimization and seeks ways to coexist with it. Victims are encouraged to endure when support and advocacy to get away from the violence are not provided, when they are told to go home and keep praying, and when they are expected to keep the family together even though the violence continues and they are in danger. This "doormat theology" teaches that it is God's will that people suffer and the only option is to endure it. There is no space to question or challenge the suffering that comes from this injustice, to feel anger, or to act to change one's circumstance. The result of this theology is that a victim remains powerless and victimized and her/his physical, psychological, and spiritual survival are jeopardized. This understanding of the meaning of suffering comforts the comfortable and afflicts the afflicted but ignores the demands of a God who seeks justice and promises abundance of life.

There is no virtue in enduring suffering if no greater good is at stake. Certainly, being battered or sexually abused is such a situation. There *is no greater good* for anyone — certainly not for the victim and children and others who witness the violence but also not for the abuser. Endurance that merely accepts the violence ignores the abuser's sinfulness and denies him a chance for repentance and redemption which may come from holding him accountable for his acts. Endurance in order to "keep the family together" is a sham because the family is already broken apart by the abuse. There is no virtue to be gained in these situations where everyone loses; there is no virtue in encouraging a victim of abuse to accept and endure it.

TRANSFORMATION

For the Christian, the theology of the cross and the resurrection provides insight into the meaning of suffering and transformation. God did not send Jesus to the cross as a test of his faith, as punishment for his sin, or to build his character. The Romans crucified Jesus and made him a victim of overt and deadly anti-Semitic violence. It was a devastating experience for Jesus' followers who watched him murdered. They were overwhelmed by fear, despair, and meaninglessness. They left the scene of the crucifixion feeling abandoned and betrayed by God. The resurrection and subsequent events were the surprising realization that in the midst of profound suffering, God is present and new life is possible.

This retrospective realization in no way justified the suffering; it transformed it. It presented the possibility of new life coming forth from the pain of suffering. Sometimes Jesus' crucifixion is misinterpreted as being the model for suffering: since Jesus went to the cross, persons should bear their own crosses of irrational violence (for example, rape) without complaint. But Jesus' crucifixion does not sanctify suffering. It remains a witness to the horror of violence done to another and an identification with the suffering that people experience. It is not a model of how suffering should be borne but a witness to God's desire that no one should have to suffer such violence again. The resurrection, the realization that Christ was present to the disciples and is present to us, transformed but never justified the suffering and death experience. The people were set free from the pain of that experience to realize the newness of life among them in spite of suffering.

Personal violence presents a victim with two options: endurance and acceptance of continued suffering, or an occasion for transformation. Endurance means remaining a victim; transformation means becoming a survivor.

In order to become a survivor and transform one's suffering, persons must use their strength and all available resources within themselves and from others to move away from a situation in which violence continues unabated. God is present in this movement as a means to transform. A young woman, raped at age eighteen, reflected on her rape experience in light of her faith. As she recovered, she observed that her prayer life had shifted dramatically after the assault. Prior to the rape, she recalled that her prayers most often took the form of "Dear God, please take care of me." As she recovered from the rape, she realized that now her prayers began, "Dear God, please help me to remember what I have learned." She moved from a passive, powerless position of victim in which she expected God to protect her to a more mature and confident position of survivor in which she recognized her own strength and responsibility to care for herself with God's help. In addition, her compassion and empathy for others increased and she was empowered to act to change things that cause violence and suffering. She was able to transform her experience and mature in her faith as she recovered from the assault with the support of family and friends.

One of the most profound fears experienced by one who suffers is that God is literally abandoning her/him. The experience of suffering and the resulting righteous anger in the face of that suffering need not separate us from God. Paul gives witness to this in Romans.

> For I am convinced that neither death, nor life, nor
> angels, nor rulers, nor things present, nor things to
> come, nor powers, nor height, nor depth, nor
> anything else in all creation, will be able to separate
> us from the love of God in Christ Jesus our Lord.
>
> — Romans 8:38

God is not responsible for suffering; God is not pleased by people's suffering; God suffers with us and is present to us in the midst of the pain of sexual and domestic violence; God does not abandon us even though everyone else may. This is the promise of the Hebrew and Christian texts — that God is present in the midst of suffering and that God gives us the strength and courage to resist injustice and to transform suffering.

Just as God does not will people to suffer, God does not send suffering in order that people have an occasion for transformation. It is a fact of life that people do suffer. The real question is not, Why? but, What do people do with that suffering? Transformation is the alternative to endurance and passivity. It is grounded in the conviction of hope and empowered by a passion for justice in the face of injustice. It is the faith that the way things are is not the way things have to be. It is a trust in righteous anger in the face of evil which pushes people to action. Transformation is the means by which, refusing to accept injustice and refusing to assist its victims to endure suffering any longer, people act. We celebrate small victories, we chip away at oppressive attitudes cast in concrete, we say no in unexpected places, we speak boldly of things deemed secret and unmentionable, we stand with those who are trapped in victimization to support their journeys to safety and healing, and we break the cycle of violence we may have known in our own lives. By refusing to endure evil and by seeking to transform suffering, we are about God's work of making justice and healing brokenness.

NOTES

1. Harold S. Kushner, *When Bad Things Happen to Good People* (New York: Schocken Books, 1981), 45.

2. Beverly Wildung Harrison, *Making the Connections* (Boston: Beacon Press, 1985), 18-19.

3. "It is assumed that sin, by whomsoever committed, was the cause of the blindness. This was the common belief in Judaism; see e.g., Shabbath 55a: There is no death without sin (proved by Ezek. 18:20) and no punishment (i.e., sufferings) without guilt (proved by Ps. 89:33). When a man has been blind from birth, the sin must be sought either in the man's parents, or in his own ante-natal existence" (C. K. Barrett, *The Gospel According to St. John* [London: SPCK, 1955], 294).

4. In light of the Holocaust some have asked, Where was God? and many Jews have reframed the question to, Where were the people who could have stopped this?

Reprinted with permission from *Violence in the Family: A Workshop for Clergy and Other Helpers* by Marie M. Fortune (Cleveland: Pilgrim Press, 1991).

The Story of One Family's Struggle to Say No to Abuse

EPILOGUE

According to statistics, our family won't make it. The chance of lasting change in abusive situations that have been going on for as long as ours is practically zero. Freedom from violence for our family cannot be guaranteed. It can only be sought after with dedicated determination. Our struggle isn't over just because we have completed two years of therapy. Like everyone else, we still have challenges with our children, struggles with health problems, bills to pay, decisions to make. What therapy did was to give us the tools for these challenges. But like athletes training for a race, we must continually exercise and practice to guard against the old behavior patterns that try to creep back into our lives. So in order to help keep alert, we have become involved in helping others who suffer from and with abuse.

Chuck works as a volunteer facilitator in charge of a men's self-help group that meets once a week. I'm working in a similar fashion with a battered women's group. Another way we remind ourselves of all we've been taught is by sharing our story as public speakers.

This is our maintenance program. It benefits us as much as it helps others.

Yet there is another reason we are willing to expose ourselves and to share our story. We want to take part in eradicating the disease. Countless others have paved the way. They have labored without reward or recognition to get laws changed, and to establish shelters and safe houses. Many have studied and researched, gathering information and statistics. Workshops to train and educate police and judges are being held. Because of these efforts, we have been helped. We want to join the ranks of those who are working to stop domestic violence.

I would like to be able to end this narration with "and they lived happily ever after." But that would not be accurate or realistic in the face of the daily conflicts of life. Our problem is not extinct. Like a dormant volcano, it could erupt unanticipated. If that happens, does it mean we have failed? We don't think so. Failure takes place when we quit, when we give up, when we walk away. We have a responsibility to ourselves and to each other to continue to participate in those things that stimulate us in the direction of our goal. Should there ever be a moment of violence again in our marriage, it will serve as a warning, not that we've failed, but that we've become complacent and indifferent, or overconfident and high-minded. We'll need the humility of spirit to examine ourselves and the determination of heart to get up and try again. May God grant us patience with each other as we grow and as we fail. May we have humility to remember where we've been, how we got to where we are now, and how much further we still need to go. And most of all, grace to forgive those who have failed us, and love to forgive ourselves.

LEARNING TO LIVE WITHOUT VIOLENCE: A Handbook for Men by Sonkin & Durphy

There are over 200,000 copies in print of this unique workbook, developed over years of counseling men who batter. It explains how to effectively control and channel anger, discusses issues of drug and alcohol abuse, alienation, jealousy, and how to "let go" of a relationship, if necessary. Contains bibliography, appendices, weekly exercises, anger journals, and a detailed description of how men can start their own support group.

LEARNING TO LIVE WITHOUT VIOLENCE: a Worktape for Men, adapted to audio cassette tapes, is an excellent adjunct to the handbook, and can be used separately as well. It has been observed that men who batter frequently have other problems, including that of illiteracy and/or discomfort with the written word. The Worktape can be listened to while driving to and from work, or in other informal free time.

THE COUNSELOR'S GUIDE TO LEARNING TO LIVE WITHOUT VIOLENCE by Daniel Sonkin, co-author of the above-mentioned handbook, is designed for clinicians, and yet can be highly informative for the concerned lay reader as well.

Dr. Sonkin describes the evolution of treatment programs, their theoretical perspectives, the current controversies, and the political context of different modes of treatment. He advocates flexibility in assessing offenders and victims to determine the best approach, depending on situation, level of violence, and dangerousness.

Dr. Robert Geffner, the president of the Family Violence and Sexual Assault Institute, says "... remains open-minded to the various approaches that can be used in treating domestic violence, since there is a lack of adequate research data to evaluate outcomes at the present time ... this flexibility is often overlooked in many books due to the particular bias or orientation of the author."

SOURCEBOOK FOR WORKING WITH BATTERED WOMEN
and
EVERY EIGHTEEN SECONDS: A JOURNEY THROUGH DOMESTIC VIOLENCE

Both books are by a former battered wife, Nancy Kilgore, who was able to transcend her experiences and offer help to other women and to all men and women who want to better understand the phenomena of domestic violence.

The **SOURCEBOOK FOR WORKING WITH BATTERED WOMEN** is a unique, valuable resource to help counselors, therapists, ministers and group leaders give battered women a sense of involvement in their own recovery, as well as information, ideas, and hope. It contains lesson plans that are adaptable to the individual or group setting, and handouts for the counselor. (See excerpt from the Sourcebook starting on page 147.)

In **EVERY EIGHTEEN SECONDS** (current statistics tell us this should be "Every Nine Seconds"), Nancy Kilgore writes letters to her young son, describing the events and circumstances of her relationship with his father. This book is powerful and revealing—this is what abuse looks and feels like.

BATTERED WIVES by Del Martin is the first book on the subject published in the United States in 1976, and updated in 1981. It includes excellent critical summaries of the legal and political status of battered wives, and the extent to which their predicament must be understood. The National Clearinghouse on Domestic Violence considers it "... the first and still the best general introduction to the problem of abuse." (See *Letter from a Battered Wife* starting on page 5.)

CONSPIRACY OF SILENCE: THE TRAUMA OF INCEST by Sandra Butler tells us that incest victims are white, black, Latin and Asian. They are five, seven and twelve years old. They are fat, skinny, ugly, beautiful, poor, wealthy and middle class. Incest is relentlessly democratic.

After years of what had been unspeakable and unspoken, **CONSPIRACY** has become the classic reference and guide to the complex issues of child sexual assault.

THE PHYSICIAN'S GUIDE TO DOMESTIC VIOLENCE: How to ask the right questions and recognize abuse by Patricia R. Salber, M.D. and Ellen Taliaferro, M.D.

The authors have been practicing emergency physicians for many years, and have served with distinction on professional boards in their field.

Dr. Taliaferro has received the James D. Mills Award for outstanding contribution to the field of emergency medicine.

Together, they created a "how to" manual that every busy practitioner and health care provider should have.

The president of the American Medical Association, Robert E. McAfee, M.D., says "If every physician in this country could have access to this publication, we could indeed make a difference in breaking the cycle of violence."

Order Form

____ **The Counselor's Guide to Learning to Live Without Violence** $29.95
by Daniel Jay Sonkin, Ph.D., hardcover

____ **Learning to Live Without Violence:** *A Handbook for Men* $14.95
by Daniel Jay Sonkin, Ph.D. and Michael Durphy, M.D.

____ **Learning to Live Without Violence:** *Worktape* $15.95
(2 C-60 cassettes)

____ **Family Violence and Religion: An Interfaith Resource Guide** $29.95
Compiled by the Staff of Volcano Press, hardcover

____ **The Physician's Guide to Domestic Violence:** *How to ask* $10.95
the right questions and recognize abuse . . . another way to save a life
by Patricia R. Salber, M.D. and Ellen Taliaferro, M.D.

____ **Sourcebook for Working with Battered Women** $17.95
by Nancy Kilgore

____ **Every Eighteen Seconds:** *A Journey Through Domestic Violence* $8.95
by Nancy Kilgore

____ **Battered Wives** by Del Martin $12.95

____ **Conspiracy of Silence:** *The Trauma of Incest* $12.95
by Sandra Butler

____ **Menopause, Naturally:** *Preparing for the Second Half of Life,* $14.95
Updated, by Sadja Greenwood, M.D., M.P.H.

____ **Menopausia Sin Ansiedad.** Spanish edition of $14.95
Menopause, Naturally

____ **Period.** by JoAnn Gardner-Loulan, Bonnie Lopez and $9.95
Marcia Quackenbush

____ **La Menstruacion.** Spanish edition of *Period.* $9.95

____ **Lesbian/Woman** by Del Martin and Phyllis Lyon, hardcover $25.00

(continued on next page)

Youth and other titles from Volcano Press

____ **It's the Law!** *A Young Person's Guide to Our Legal System* $12.95
by Annette Carrel

____ **Facilitator's Guide to It's the Law!** by Annette Carrel $16.95

____ **African Animal Tales** by Rogério Andrade Barbosa, full $17.95
color, hardcover, illustrated by Ciça Fittipaldi,
translated by Feliz Guthrie

____ **Save My Rainforest** by Monica Zak, full color, hardcover, $14.95
illustrated by Bengt-Arne Runnerström

____ **Berchick** by Esther Silverstein Blanc, hardcover, illustrated by $14.95
Tennessee Dixon

____ **Mother Gave a Shout,** *Poems by Women and Girls* edited $14.95
by Susanna Steele and Morag Styles, hardcover,
illustrated by Jane Ray

____ **Mighty Mountain and the Three Strong Women,** full color, $14.95
hardcover, written and illustrated by Irene Hedlund

____ **Random Kindness & Senseless Acts of Beauty** by $14.95
Anne Herbert and Margaret Pavel with art by Mayumi Oda,
hardcover, accordion-fold

____ **People of the Noatak** by author/artist Claire Fejes $15.95

____ **Coit Tower:** *Its History & Art* by Masha Zakheim Jewett $10.00

____ **Goddesses** by Mayumi Oda, full color $14.95

To order directly, please send check or money order for the price of the book(s) plus
$4.50 shipping and handling for the first book, and $1.00 for each additional book to
Volcano Press, P.O. Box 270 FVR, Volcano, CA 95689. Order by phone with a VISA
or MasterCard by calling toll-free, 1-800-VPWYMEN (1-800-879-9636).

California residents please add appropriate sales tax.

Volcano Press books are available at quantity discounts for bulk purchases,
professional counseling, educational, fund-raising or premium use. Please call or
write for details.

☐   Please send Volcano Press catalogs to:

Name: _____

Address: _____

City, State, Zip: _____